SOME LIKE IT HOTTER

The Official Cookbook Of The Galvanized Gullet

Geraldine Duncann

101 PRODUCTIONS
San Francisco

To my father, Gerald Duncann Wenker,
who laid the solid foundations for my love
of hot foods, good beer, and people.

ACKNOWLEDGMENTS: I would like to give thanks to the following people and organizations, without whose help I might not have been able to complete this project: to the patient staff at the Bancroft Library, University of California, Berkeley; to numerous people at the University of California at Davis; to Graham Proud, barman extraordinaire, for sharing his knowledge about the great brews of Britain; to the helpful staff of The Turf Tavern, Oxford, England; to Fritz Maytag, Anchor Brewing Company, San Francisco; to the staff of the Mexican Tourist Board. And a most special thanks to the ground and flight crews of British Airways, who on numerous flights have gone out of their way to accommodate me and my research materials.

ILLUSTRATIONS: Geraldine Duncann

COLOR PHOTOGRAPHS: Rik Olson

DESIGN: Lynne O'Neil

Published by 101 Productions
834 Mission Street, San Francisco, California 94103
Distributed to the book trade in the United States
by The Scribner Book Companies, New York.

Library of Congress Cataloging in Publication Data

Duncann, Geraldine.
    Some like it hotter.

    Includes index.
    1. Cookery, International.   2. Condiments.
3. Spices.
TX725.A1D85   1985   641.6'384   85-334
ISBN 0-89286-245-9

CONTENTS

FOREWORD

Out of this world is out of this world, whether in the creative kitchen or on the printed page. There is an affinity between having a *jalapeño*-Vesuvius erupt on your tongue and having an explosive idea erupt in your consciousness. Each can be a startling and, in reflective savoring, a very great pleasure.

Some Like It Hotter says it for me. Every recipe I've sampled from this marvelous collection is a delight. But then I suffer withdrawal symptoms if you keep me too long away from capsicum. Not to mention horseradish, mustard, and ginger—all of which I keep in my garden whenever possible, because the fresher the hotter the better.

My exploratory ventures into chili seasoning started while I was living in a mountain village called Tlalpujahua deep in the heart of Mexico. This is where I began research into the early history of the spice trade, an essential background for building the worlds of Dune. At the time, Mexico was a haven for the poor writer, a guarantee that even if you had little money you would not starve in a garret.

Market day in this tiny Michoacan village was Wednesday, and the array of different chilies was an invitation to experiment.

Geraldine once counted thirty-seven different varieties of chili in a Mexican market. Not to play one-upmanship with her, but I have counted more than forty varieties in the Toluca market, and the number was even greater if you counted fresh and dried as separate, which you should do because the flavor definitely is different.

Mexican friends say the variations are much greater if you factor in the time of harvesting. Some chilies are considered best if picked immature, others (they say) must be allowed to ripen on the vine.

Those of us with galvanized gullets owe a great deal to the evolution of food preferences in that band around the globe about ten degrees north and south of the equator, a cumberbund of human development that I refer to as "the capsicum belt." The spiced foods of this region, *picante* as hell, often will make you sweat—which is what they are supposed to do because that's an essential hot-climate air-conditioning for the body. Chili-spiced foods also are very high in Vitamin C and, if grown in the proper soils, contain essential minerals.

The general rule is, "If it doesn't clear your sinuses, it's not hot enough."

It's not difficult to acquire an addictive taste for these foods. If they are new to you, start slowly. Turn to page 136, where Geraldine has placed my recipe for "Pre-Dune Fried Rice." Go easy on the ginger at first. Later, you will want to increase it and, just perhaps, add more freshly chopped green onions, a bit more chili, more garlic, and hot mustard on the side. (That hot mustard you get in Chinese restaurants is best made with stale beer, a trade secret from San Francisco's Chinatown.)

After reviewing all of the recipes in this collection and finding many old friends here, I can recommend this without reservation as a wonderful introduction to the world of the galvanized gullet. And when you go into the kitchen to prepare these delicious foods, remember how to greet all intruders who would have you soften the blow: "If you're not here for the heat, get out of my kitchen."

Frank Herbert
Somewhere in Space
(where we all are)

SOME LIKE IT HOTTER

THE GALVANIZED GULLET This book was born about eight years ago in Berkeley at the home of an Anglican priest. Father Green and his family hosted "Sunday Supper" every week for years. It was a potluck communion of friendship for Christian and non-Christian alike. One Sunday, Father Green's contribution was a dish that was most definitely above and beyond the call of duty as far as most people's capsicum tolerance was concerned. To his great joy and delight, there were about six of us who came back for bowl after fiery bowl of the delightful pottage, bypassing the other more traditional potluck contributions of lasagna, tuna and cream of mushroom soup casserole, macaroni salad, and pineapple upside-down cake.

Through Father Green's creativity, those of us sharing a love of things robust found each other. We decided to make a pilgrimage to the, at that time, almost unknown Hunan Restaurant in San Francisco. That proved so successful that we arranged to get together for a potluck of nothing but hot, *hot,* foods. Twelve people participated in that first extravaganza. The contributions ranged from chili to *ceviche.* Jars of *kim chee* and *jalapeño* pepper jelly were present as just a little something extra to nibble on.

My ex-husband, who can't even tolerate a little black pepper on his morning eggs, bit into a slice of chili-cheddar cornbread and, with tears in his eyes, exclaimed, "You guys must have galvanized gullets to be able to eat this!" An organization was born.

The Galvanized Gullet meets about once a year. The last time the dishes ranged from *couscous* and *wat* with *injera* to curries, Szechwanese stir-fry, a Thai rice and shrimp concoction that was pure ecstasy, and, of course, a reputable selection of the world's fine brews.

Who are these strange few who are imbued with such a unique perversion? David and Ernie are priests; Gail is an insurance adjuster, Ardis is a jeweler, Michael is a football coach, Pete is head of the mathematics department of his high school, Ellen sings in the San Francisco Opera Chorus, and another David is an attorney. The list includes computer programmers, musicians, dancers, a psychologist, a wine maker, an electrical engineer, a union negotiator, a probation officer, a policewoman, a trucker, a lab technician, two business executives, a restaurateur, a rock concert producer, a falconer, a classical-music radio announcer, two science-fiction authors, an ex-Mousketeer, and me.

If the concept of the Galvanized Gullet tantalizes you, why not found a branch? The rules are simple. Get together with friends to eat fine hot and zesty foods, drink good beer, and engage in brilliant conversation.

WHY HOT? Those of us who revel in the tingling delights of the capsicum, the lusty joy of ginger, and the warm pleasures of horseradish are a sorely misunderstood lot indeed. More timid souls, possessed of paltry palates, can never fathom the ecstasies we share. They are confirmed in the mistaken belief that we exemplify some unique cult of S and M— that we are displaying undue bravado, indulging in *machismo* to the maximum. It is their true belief that we are into it for the pain alone.

I attempt to explain to them that in dishes designed to be hot, the heat-producing elements only enhance the total sensation of the combined flavors. The answer is always the same. "Don't talk to me about flavor. When you've burned out all your taste buds with chilies and horseradish, there isn't any way you can taste anything at all."

My favorite answer to this is that one of the few people I have ever met who had a tolerance for hot foods that equalled my own is the wine maker at one of California's most prestigious premium wineries. Now *that* is a job that requires a sensitive palate.

Over the centuries many cultures have developed hot cuisines. What almost certainly began as a culinary necessity has gradually been refined into some of the most sophisticated dishes in the world. You can hardly say that one eats fine Hunan, Szechwanese, Ethiopian, Thai or Ceylonese food just for the pain. Like any distinctive gastronomic experience, these exciting cuisines are based on a careful blending of elements, and have been developed over generations, and sometimes centuries.

It is probably true that those cultures that originally developed hot foods did so out of necessity. Usually these cultures were in hot climates and, in the time before mechanical refrigeration, food tended to spoil quickly. There is some evidence that the heavy seasoning of foods will retard spoilage. In the early Middle Ages it was discovered that adding a lot of black pepper to sausages made them into good travelers. Black pepper is still a major ingredient in sausages that are designed to keep.

Despite the fact that heavy seasoning was of some aid in the retardation of spoilage, its contribution in that respect was relatively minor. Its greater use was to cover up the fact that the food had already spoiled, or at least gone off a bit. It is quite possible to kill most toxins that attack elderly victuals by recooking them for a prescribed length of time. However, it is not possible, no matter how long you boil that stew, to cover up the repugnant flavor that results from decomposition. It probably won't make you sick, but it isn't much fun to eat. With the addition of heavy and pungent seasonings, the unsavory aspects of food too long kept could be masked. Pepper, mustards, clove, anise, fenugreek, cinnamon, and turmeric were well known for their powers of camouflage in Eastern cultures. After the West began significant intercourse with the East, usually attributed to the Crusades, Western societies discovered that they no longer had to endure the flavors of tainted foods. So the race to discover safer and more economical routes to the spice-producing lands was on.

For those living in a hot climate, there is another benefit to consuming zestily seasoned foods. Hot foods make you sweat, and in hot weather, sweating is beneficial. Sweating causes garments and skin to become moist, and, through the radiator effect of evaporation, a degree of air conditioning occurs.

WHAT IS HOT?

We are told by the world of science that the human tongue is only capable of distinguishing four sensations: sweet, sour, bitter, and salt. If that is true, why are we capable of distinguishing the difference between a 1979 Hacienda Chenin Blanc and a 1980 Stevenot Chardonnay? How could we tell the difference between crab and lobster, or, for that matter, between fat and succulent Pacific oysters, delicate, firm oysters from the coast of Louisiana, and *belons* captured off the western coast of France?

The foods that are most often used to produce the sensation of heat are garlic, onion, ginger, mustard, horseradish, pepper, and chilies. "You forget chili powder and curry powder," you say. Remember, they don't grow—they were invented. Chili powder and curry powder are what happens when you invite garlic, dried ground chilies (i.e., cayenne), ginger, pepper, and a bunch of other spices to jump into the same little can. "Chili powder" was invented in the Southwestern United States. Curry is a blending of spices and other flavoring agents ranging from as few as five to as many as thirty.

HOT STUFF

ONIONS AND GARLIC

Some people consider onions and garlic to be hot. They possess an acid which, when the vegetables are eaten raw, produces a harshness some find unpleasant. For those of you who love these flavors but do with they weren't quite so pushy, despair not. Help is on the way. The longer either vegetable is cooked the more the acid breaks down and the harshness is dissipated. Therefore, when preparing a dish that requires long cooking— a stew, roast, or casserole, perhaps— you can put in as much garlic as you like. The harshness will all get up and move to a better neighborhood, leaving you with the delightful flavor alone. I have a recipe for a lamb shank stew from Turkey that uses thirty or forty teeth of garlic. The meat, vegetables, and garlic are slowly cooked in the oven for five hours. The result is a rich and delightful concoction, strong in personality but easy to get along with.

For dishes that require little or no cooking the problem of lots of garlic is somewhat more difficult, but definitely not insurmountable. In dishes such as a delicate omelet, or *piperade,* quiche, and the like, where you want a lot of lovely garlic flavor but the essence of the dish would be destroyed by its harshness, you can cook the garlic first. I often mince my garlic and then slowly simmer it in just enough water to almost cover, or I gently sauté it in butter, or a mixture of butter and white wine. This will civilize your garlic and make it ready to introduce into polite society.

MUSTARD

The seeds of the mustard plant are hot. Prepared mustards run the gamut of culinary needs from the yellow goo we spread on hot dogs at the ballpark, through many delightful and varying cultural adaptations ranging from the fire-hot Chinese mustard to the subtle and multiflavored concoction known as Dijon mustard.

Mustard is common in wine-producing regions since it is often used as a regenerative cover crop between the rows of vines. In the Côte d'Or, as in the Napa and Sonoma valleys, winter and spring are made even more glorious by the brilliant yellow of the flowering mustard plants stretching away through acre after acre of noble vines.

HORSERADISH

Hot, heady, eye-crossing, and sinus-clearing. Freshly grated from your own garden, horseradish can bring the most robust member of a Galvanized Gullet to his or her knees. Bottled products that have just "horseradish" on the label are usually quite hot; however, to my tastes, those products labeled "horseradish sauce" are a little on the wimpy side.

GINGER

Ginger is delightfully hot and has the unique characteristic of being able to live comfortably with both sweet and savory foods. I use it in all its forms: fresh; ground; Oriental pickled and preserved; salty and sweet pickled; sweet and sour dried strips; sweet and preserved in jars; and, of course, candied. Go into an Oriental food store sometime and discover the great variety of ginger products available. Ginger is one of the foods that Orientals consider to be essential in the cleansing of both the body and the soul.

PEPPER

Black, white, fine, or coarse, pepper is hot and more. Pepper imparts a flavor all its own that cannot be reproduced. There is no substitute for fresh-ground pepper. Now, if I may, I would like to shatter a myth; how many recipes have you seen that call for several whole peppercorns to be added to a soup or stew? James Beard once did an experiment: he put a handful of whole peppercorns in a kettle of water and boiled them for an hour. The result was nothing. There was no measurable change in the flavor of the water. Pepper will not release its flavor unless it's ground or cracked.

Even when I am not particularly into something hot, I use black pepper. I can't imagine my kitchen being without it. I seldom add salt at table, but I always find I want more pepper and feel sorely put upon when the headwaiter of a prestigious restaurant comes to my table with his gigantic pepper-mill and, with a great flourish, allots me a penurious twist or two.

Pepper is not only one of the elements in any hot cuisine, it has been a pretty hot item throughout history. Among the wealthiest men of medieval Europe were the spice merchants: a pound of ginger bought a sheep; a pound of cloves was worth three cows in milk with their calves, or the finest well-trained stud horse; an ounce of peppercorns was worth a man's life. Kings gave gifts of pepper to the pope. Taxes and debts could be paid with peppercorns.

It was the quest for spices, not the lust for gold, that sent those first cumbersome wooden vessels across thousands of miles of turbulent and uncharted seas. Their newly discovered continent never was to fill the Old World coffers with the sought-after cinnamon, nutmegs, ginger, and cloves. However, the Old World would benefit by the introduction of tomatoes, potatoes, chilies, and an expansion of thought that was to alter the world forever.

When Captain Francis Drake, the greatest adventurer to ever swash a buckle, sailed up the western coast of the New World in 1579, he replaced all the bags of Devon sand, which had been placed in the hold of the *Golden Hind* for ballast, with gold and silver bullion pillaged, or liberated, depending on your point of view, from Spanish strongholds. Yet the pepper and cloves he added to his treasure trove as he continued on to circumnavigate the globe were considered to be the greatest part of his bounty.

CHILIES

We know that it was in quest of spices that Western man first set out across the seas. For centuries the spice trade had been monopolized by the Eastern cultures. When those first enlightened few perceived that the world was round and you really wouldn't fall off the edge, they conceived the idea that if they sailed west, instead of jogging east on camelback and perhaps falling prey to bands of robbers and the torments of the deserts, they would reach with relative ease the lands where the coveted spices grew. What they hadn't reckoned with was having a very large continent plopped down in the middle of their path. So, when they put in on the coast of the Americas, thinking that they had reached their destination, they naturally shouted, "Where's the pepper?"

Upon being served dishes containing chilies, and experiencing the "bite" that they produce, these visiting merchant-adventurers decided it was almost as good as pepper, and that they could make their fortunes back home by selling it as such. The name stuck, just

like the name "Indian" stuck to the Native American, and so chilies, or capsicums if you are scientifically inclined, became known interchangeably as peppers. But not in this book. To avoid confusion, I shall always refer to black and white pepper as pepper and chilies as chilies or capsicums—with the one exception of the chili known as *bell pepper*.

And just in case you happened to be interested in such things, it is only a one-gene variation that determines whether a member of the genus *Capsicum* is hot or sweet.

A CHILI IS A CHILI IS A CHILI (Or Is It?)
Since I do not specifically name the varieties of chilies used in any of the recipes, you may be left in some confusion as to just which ones to use. First, should you use fresh or dry? This I almost always state. Dried chilies can be used in place of fresh, but the flavor is slightly different. They can produce the same level of heat but not the same complexity of flavor. Now, when I say "fresh chilies" just what do I mean?

There are dozens of varieties of chilies. In one marketplace in Mexico I counted thirty-seven varieties at one stall. In the markets where I shop in the pan-ethnic San Francisco Bay area, I can, during most of the year, get about four varieties, plus bell peppers. I'm sure that the variety is less in communities that have a less-diversified population. Although the varieties have their individual names, I have not used them in this book. First, in my experience, the same pepper is often marketed under a variety of names, and, likewise, one name may be given to a number of chilies.

So how do we know how hot a chili is? Well, that's a loaded question. Lots of elements determine this. The variety, of course, determines the hotness most of the time, but things can alter a lot even within a particular variety. The type of soil a chili was grown in has a lot to do with the intensity of the heat. How much water did it get during its growing period? That has a lot to do with it, too. Accidental cross-pollination can get in there and really muck things up as well. So even if in your previous experience the light-yellow ones are not quite as hot as the bright-red ones, don't always count on it.

In my experience, bell peppers, green, red, or golden, are always sweet and mild, as are fresh pimientos. The long (5 or 6 inches) light-green and often sort of twisted chilies are mild, quite similar to the green bell pepper, but don't count on it. For years I've been buying them and they have always been mild but a little more flavorful than standard bell peppers, but last week one of them went for the kill.

The very dark-green, sort of heart-shaped chilies, about 4 inches long, I find usually to be lightly hot and very flavorful. Remove the seeds and they are quite mild indeed, most of the time. Next we have the little chilies that are about the size of your thumb. In general, the dark-green ones range from hot to quite hot. Remove the seeds and they should be tolerable even for a beginning Galvanized Gullet. The yellow "wax" chilies can be hotter, some of the time. Remove the seeds and the flesh is usually tolerable to most people. The bright blood-red ones are from quite hot to hand me a beer *QUICK!* Taking out the seeds doesn't do a blasted thing.

The hottest chilies I have ever experienced were about the same length as the last three mentioned above, but only about half as thick and tapering to a very slim point. They ranged from dark forest green to bright red, with a few mottled ones. I bought them in Southall and one, I repeat one, was enough to make a bowl of guacamole made from six avocados hotter than I normally make it. I have seen them in Oakland's Chinatown.

Another example of things varying in description are the little brown speckled chilies usually called Szechwanese chilies. In the Time-Life book *Foods of China* they are described as being distinctively flavorful and mildly hot. Now my heat tolerance is pretty high, but the first time I had them they brought me to my knees begging for mercy. The next time they were only moderately hot. So, all of this is to explain why I do not use names for the species of chilies in this book. I'm sorry. There is only one sure-fire way to determine the heat and that's to bring one of each kind of chili home and do a taste test. Also bring home a carton of cottage cheese and a couple of quarts of lager beer. (I have included a general guide to chilies at the end of this section for those of you who insist on the principle of naming and ordering the confusing world of the capsicums.)

I have found the best way to do comparative chili taste testing is to put 3 tablespoons of cottage cheese in each of several small bowls. Then mince the chilies and put 1 teaspoon into each bowl of cottage cheese and mix. Let them sit for about 5 minutes. Better label the bowls so that you can keep the chilies straight. Then, beer in hand, start tasting down the line and make your own designations as to degrees of hotness. You might, incidentally, want to do this with all of the hot ingredients used in this book. Try the fresh chilies seeded and with seeds, dry crushed chilies, powdered cayenne, Tabasco, etc., and then on to the various mustard products, i.e. horseradish, dry Chinese, English, German, and Japanese *wasabi*. By doing this you can define your own perimeters.

When I say fresh chilies in a recipe, I mean that fresh are better. They add a dimension of flavor that will be missing if you use dried chilies or cayenne. However, if you live in an area where fresh chilies are just not available, for gods' sake, don't go without any of the dishes that call for them. Use one of the other products, adding it gradually until it suits your taste. You can substitute about 1 tablespoon of chopped or minced fresh bell pepper (available almost every place) for each chili called for. This will give you the

flavor of a fresh chili, and you can add the heat with crushed dried chilies or cayenne. Tabasco is a condiment and has a flavor all its own, which often is desirable, but it is not interchangeable with fresh chilies.

WARNING: You should always wear rubber gloves when dealing with chilies—not even soap and water will remove the heat from your skin. Be careful not to touch your eyes or mouth with your fingers after you have touched chilies.

A CHILI GLOSSARY

Most of the dried chilies used in this book are small whole dried red chilies, usually called just that; the same chilies in their crushed form; and ground cayenne. All the other chilies are fresh (except for canned peeled green chilies and a pickled *jalapeño* or two). Following is a glossary of chilies to be used as a general guide; you will find that the names of chilies are far from being standardized in the market, and, as I explained earlier, you can't count on any given type or variety to maintain its degree of hotness from individual chili to individual chili.

ANAHEIM About 6 inches long, light green, 1 to 2 inches wide. Medium hot to hot.

BELL PEPPERS Red, green, and yellow. Sweet, mild, 4 to 5 inches long, often almost as wide.

CREOLE or LOUISIANA Small, slender, bright green or red, 1-1/2 to 2 inches long. Hot.

FRYING CHILIES Bright green or red, smooth-skinned, 6 to 7 inches long, tapering and slightly twisted. Usually mild in heat but with a little more flavor than the standard bell pepper.

GUERO Sometimes called *California* or *New Mexican* chilies. Pale smooth yellow to yellowish green, 3 to 4 inches long, 2 to 2-1/2 inches in diameter. Slightly curved and tapering. Usually mild, but not always.

ITALIAN CHILIES 4 to 5 inches long, heart shaped, deep forest green. The flesh is somewhat bitter and a bit on the tough side. Usually medium hot, but don't count on it. This is the only chili I have experienced whose flesh is just as hot as its seeds.

JALAPENO The quintessential chili. Two inches long, yellowish through grass green, smooth skinned. Hot.

PAPRIKA Dark red, heart shaped. Smaller and sweeter than red bell peppers.

PASILLA Very similar in appearance and taste to the *poblano*.

PEQUIN Tiny, bright red or green, usually no more than 1/2 inch long. *Very* hot.

PIMIENTO Very similar in appearance and taste to the paprika chili.

POBLANO Dark green, similar to Italian chilies, medium hot to hot. Will change from green to red in several weeks off the vine. Sometimes called *ancho*.

SERRANO A tapering bright-green smooth chili, 2 to 3 inches long, hot and flavorful.

SZECHWAN CHILIES Small brown-speckled uniquely flavored round chilies. Medium hot to hot.

THAI Very narrow, green or red, 2 or 3 inches long. *Very* hot.

WAX CHILIES Whitish yellow, turning somewhat red after picking, these are almost translucent, smooth-skinned chilies, about the size and shape of your thumb. Hot.

OTHER INGREDIENTS

BROTH

Wherever you see this ingredient you have several options open to you. You may use commercial canned beef or chicken broth, which is a perfectly adequate product. I never use it because it is expensive. I resent paying a lot of money for a product whose main ingredient is water.

If you have the time, of course the ideal thing to do is to make your own stock, which is not nearly as difficult as people seem to think. To produce stock you may use any of a variety of products: used bones and meat scraps, i.e., the bones from cooked steaks and roasts, the remains of a roast chicken or turkey, etc., or you may use raw bones and trimmings. When chickens are on sale, I buy a dozen at a time, remove the breasts and freeze them in one package to use for Chinese stir-fry or stuffed chicken breasts; the wings, legs, and thighs are packaged for frying, roasting, or teriyaki, the livers and giblets go into another package, and the necks and backs go into the stock pot.

There is no particular recipe for stock. I put the bones and or trimmings into a heavy pot and cover them with enough water to make sure that they are totally submerged. Into this I toss an onion cut in half, a bulb or two of garlic cut in half crosswise, and either a bouquet of fresh herbs or some mixed dried herbs. Whenever making stock soups or stews I put my dried herbs into a tea ball and then toss the tea ball into the pot. Another excellent flavoring agent for soups, stews, or stock is a teaspoon or so of mixed pickling spices put into a tea ball and boiled with the bones. Bring the pot to the boil, then reduce the heat, cover, and cook at a rapid simmer for at least 2 hours. If the level of the liquid should drop below the level of the bones and scraps, add enough boiling water from a tea kettle to cover the bones again. When finished, strain through a colander, then through a fine sieve or piece of soft muslin, defat and store.

I find that the perfect method for storing is to pour the stock into ice-cube trays, freeze, then pop out the frozen cubes and store in plastic bags in your freezer. This way you have stock in an easy-to-use form ready at all times.

A third alternative is, dare I say it, powdered bouillon. It doesn't have to be icky. I find that powdered is less salty than the cubes and I am able to make a perfectly reasonable product by mixing the powder about 20 percent weaker than the manufacturer's instructions. For each quart of bouillon I add half an onion, 5 or 6 teeth of garlic, a *bouquet garni* made of fresh parsley, some leaves from the center of a head of celery, a small bay leaf, and fresh dill if available. If you do not have fresh herbs, add 1/2 teaspoon mixed dried herbs. I also add 1/4 cup of cream sherry and a tablespoon of butter. Simmer this for half an hour, strain, and use like any other stock.

CILANTRO

When I say cilantro, I mean cilantro. Parsley and cilantro are not interchangeable. White wine can be used in place of red or Swiss in place of Cheddar more readily than parsley can be used in place of cilantro. However, if you can't get it, make the dish anyway. It just won't have quite the depth. My younger son hates cilantro with a passion, so I always dish up his *gazpacho* before I add the cilantro.

CLAMS AND MUSSELS

Clams and mussels are bivalves. The typical cookbook warning is to look out for the red tide, which occurs occasionally, and during which bivalves can make you sick.

That may be true on the East Coast but on the West Coast it's *every year,* and they don't make you sick, *they make you dead!* I shan't take the time to go into the scientific explanation of this West Coast phenomenon, but it happens every year and it is exceedingly dangerous. You may have heard the myth about not gathering clams and mussels when there were, or perhaps it was when there weren't, r's in the month. Well, I always figure clams and Pacific Coast blue mussels can't read very well, so they don't know where the r's are or aren't. There is only one sure-fire method for telling when a bivalve is safe to eat in California. Call the California State Department of Health or the Department of Fish and Game and ask if the quarantine is on or off.

This, incidentally, is not a new phenomenon. Before Captain Francis Drake landed in California, the coastal Indian nations would set up sentries along the trails to the beaches during the period of quarantine to warn Indians from inland regions.

COCONUT MILK

To make coconut milk you must first open the coconut. Now this can present a problem. There are three vulnerable points of entry in any coconut, called the eyes. Armed with a very large nail or a screwdriver, pound the sharp implement into two of the eyes, thus making holes. Let the liquid drain out through the holes. Reserve the liquid if the recipe calls for it. When the liquid is all out you must attempt to crack the nut. If this isn't where the term "a hard nut to crack" came from, it should have been. After years of maiming myself with saws, pry-bars, and sledgehammers, I have one safe and workable method of cracking a coconut. Stand on the top stair of your front porch and slam the sucker down on the concrete walkway with all your might. With luck it will crack. Use the screwdriver to pry out the meat. Use a knife and you are begging for a trip to the emergency ward of your local hospital. The meat comes away from the shell easily if you freeze the thing. Once you have convinced the flesh of the coconut to leave its shell, shred it on the large holes of a grater. It's not necessary to remove the brown skin.

Put the shredded coconut into a bowl and pour the boiling water over it. Let sit until cool. Then place a clean cloth over another bowl and pour the coconut mixture into it. Lift up the cloth and squeeze until no more liquid will come. Save the resulting milk. You can toast the pulp and use it for cakes and cookies.

CRABS

Getting on intimate terms with these tasty crustaceans is an exceedingly personal matter, and everyone has his or her own ideas as to how it should be done.

All the instructions given below are for crabs that are already dead or cooked, whether you buy them that way or do it yourself. Why do I prefer to work with already cooked crabs? Because I am a sentimental sap, and, although I am a flesh eater, I rest a little easier if I know that the critter that is providing my sustenance met his maker with as little discomfort as possible. The only way that crustaceans die instantly is by being plunged into a large pot of rapidly boiling water. If you put them live into a sauce or stew, it isn't quite hot enough to do the job instantly, and I am just too squeamish to wrench apart live crabs.

The easiest and most commonly used method of cleaning crabs in mainstream American society is to say to your fishmonger, "Two large crabs, please. And, oh yes. Clean them. Thank you very much." For this service you will most likely pay an additional ten to fifty cents per pound, which seems a shame to me since the guy is going to chuck out some of the best part—the crab butter.

Now, if you really want to get to know your crab and save a bit of change at the same time, buy one whole and take it home. Set it in a clean sink and scrub thoroughly under cold running water with a vegetable brush. Now, pick up the crab and check him out to determine which is his front and which is his back. The big claws and the little things that might just be eyes are at the front, and that's not the part we are concerned about at this point. Turn him around and, holding him firmly, put your thumbs in the center of the back of the critter, one thumb on the top shell and one thumb on the bottom part. Then pull, and with any luck at all the top shell will come off, leaving the now-naked body with legs attached.

Set the top shell aside. You will see when you look at the crab that there are sort of white fibrous things in a row down each side of the body. Those are the lungs and the only part besides the shell that is absolutely inedible. They won't make you sick, but I don't think you would enjoy eating them. The next part that I always throw away is the thing that looks suspiciously like an intestinal tract. Again, it won't hurt you, but I am a little squeamish.

Now, from here on it's a matter of choice and of recipe. You will see that in a layer over the body and in the corners of the top shell there is a creamy, buttery substance ranging in color from creamy white to ochre yellow and in texture from quite liquid to fairly solid. This is the butter, and it is delicious. The light-colored solid part is to my taste nicer than the darker liquid. I save the liquid if I am making a soup, stew, or chowder, otherwise I pour it out. For those types of dishes I also save all of the solid butter. For things like cracked crab or crab salad, I do not use any of the butter, but I will remove the solid part of it and freeze it until I have enough to use in dips and the like. It's delicious mixed with sour cream.

Now, after removing the butter, rinse the body of the crab under cold running water and set upside down to drain. Also wash the top shells and drain if you are going to make stuffed crabs or use them for decoration. (When I serve whole crab I clean and wash the body, leaving the legs and claws attached, and serve it on a large platter with the top shell sitting in its proper place.)

Shelling the crabs is done in two phases. First the legs and claws. This is easy. I use a nutcracker and gently crack the shell, then remove the meat, usually in one piece. Now, the body is another matter, for you will find that the delicious, sweet, and delicate body meat is ingeniously enclosed in a little honeycomb chambers made of a substance similar to celluloid. It isn't difficult to get at, just tedious and time-consuming. I break the body into halves and then proceed to disassemble each half, chamber by chamber, removing the white meat as I go. This can then be shredded or left whole for use in soups, salads, sandwiches, quiches, omelets, soufflés—need I go on?

GARLIC

You will notice that I use the term tooth or teeth of garlic. That is because I have heard one little section referred to both as a clove and a bud. A bud may be confused with a bulb, which refers to the whole thing. Since the individual segments look like teeth, I figure that is pretty unmistakable.

GREEN ONIONS

I always say green onions instead of scallions. In England they are called spring onions. They are all the same critter.

MIXED DRIED HERBS

This is a product I use a lot. It is a good basic blend of savory herbs: thyme, rosemary, sage, savory, etc. Mixed herbs and Italian seasoning are basically the same thing and are marketed by a variety of distributors including Spice Island and Schilling, and some house brands and generics. It is a good blend, and I find it much more convenient to use 1/2 teaspoon of mixed dried herbs than 1/8 teaspoon of each single herb.

OIL

Unless otherwise stated, any light-flavored vegetable oil will do. Use a brand you are comfortable with and can afford. Generics are fine. However, if I say olive oil, peanut oil, or sesame oil, I mean just that. Their flavor is essential to the flavor of the dish. For frying, in particular deep-frying, I use the cheapest oil I can get because I change my oil very often. Now, if you must have special oils for special dietary reasons, that's another matter. Do what you must.

In recipes where you find instructions to use half olive oil and half light-flavored oil, or half butter and half oil, that is because you need the flavor of the olive oil or the butter, but since both of them tend to burn easily, you add plain vegetable oil to decrease that possibility.

SALSA

Salsa is something our house couldn't live without. In the amounts we use it, it could become a significant drain on our finances. That's why we put up our own each year. Salsa is a convenience food for us. If there is cheese, tortillas, lettuce and salsa in the house, no one ever feels like the larger is bare. Salsa and cottage cheese is a favorite snack food for my crew. You can put salsa and cheese inside an omelet when you haven't time to sauté vegetables. Salsa and mayonnaise can make an adequate quick dip, and there's nothing wrong with just plain salsa as a dip. It can be used also as dressing or sauce.

SALT

I almost never give a specific amount of salt, stating instead, salt to taste. Remember, there is no substitute for salt. If you are on a salt-free diet, then don't add salt, but please, don't add a salt substitute. Salt, let me tell you, is way up there on the public enemy list with drugs, alcohol, tobacco, and caffeine. Like all of its partners in crime, one of the most dangerous things it does is remove elasticity from living tissue. This is a major cause of heart, circulatory, respiratory, kidney, and brain diseases, all organs whose functioning is dependent on their being elastic. The other disastrous effect is that when your skin and muscles loose their elasticity, gravity can do its thing to your face a lot faster than it might do otherwise. I do use salt, but I try to use it sparingly, and I try not to push it.

SUGAR

You will notice that I often use sugar in my cooking. Usually the amount is not enough to actually make the dish sweet, it just lets all of the other ingredients get chummy and strike up a friendship. It does the same that adding Accent or M.S.G. does and isn't nearly as harmful. I find the addition of a bit of sugar takes a dish with the personality of a street urchin and makes it behave as if it had gone to finishing school.

ABOUT THE RECIPES

You will notice that I have not included recipes for standard Indian curries or the Mexican foods that in the past two decades have become thoroughly incorporated into the American cuisine. There are no recipes for tacos, quesadillas, and the like. These are things that in this day and age almost everyone slings together for a quick and easy snack. I have tried instead to focus on excellent dishes that are probably less standard fare, things not in your culinary repertoire.

You will also notice that there is no recipe for chili. Everyone in America has ten already. Even my friends in England have chili recipes.

PARTY NIBBLES

Although the consumption of foods boasting an acquaintance with garlic, mustards, and capsicum will produce a significant thirst, I would never consider serving alcohol in any form without a bountiful accompaniment of zesty dishes. The threat of inebriation is definitely lessened by an ample supply of munchies, and, somehow, foods that are highly seasoned, starchy, and oily seem to retard the total disintegration of the frontal lobe.

The hors d'oeuvre, or party munchy, is one of my favorite classifications of foods. The possibilities are virtually without end, the only limitation being your own creativity. The only problem I have had with this section of the book has been in deciding which of my favorite recipes to leave out. Having a repertoire of several hundred and being able to use only a handful has kept me in agonies of indecision.

You will notice that some of the recipes in this section list the amount made rather than the number of servings. There is no way you can determine how far a dish will go at a party. Unlike a dinner, where everyone has come for a meal, at a party food isn't needed to provide nourishment. The foods served at a party are intended to enhance the total experience. Party foods are as much entertainment as they are sustenance. Not everyone will eat some of everything, and, most important, you have no responsibility to see that every guest has eaten a full meal. If you run out, who's to worry? A party is for enjoyment, yours as well as everyone else's. Just serve forth a variety of delightful things you feel like preparing, and have a good time.

DIPS

Dips, with a few exceptions, appear to be an American phenomenon. Food tastes are, however, rapidly expanding throughout the world. Ten years ago when I made guacamole from two precious avocados smuggled through customs at Heathrow, my English friends insisted on putting a handful of crisps (potato chips) on their plates, spooning the guac over them and eating the mess with a knife and fork. This spring, however, at a party I gave in Oxford, the guests eagerly scooped up a bowl of guacamole with chips I had made from Indian *pappadams,* tortillas not being available.

In France, my friends have always been willing to scoop my dips up with the thin slices of toasted French bread I prepare, but they refuse to do it casually before dinner while having drinks and indulging in chitchat. Instead, the bowl of dips and basket of bread are placed in the middle of the table, and we all sit about diligently dipping and eating until the next course is served.

Dips, in my opinion, are a godsend to the host or hostess, having that glorious quality of being able to be made well in advance, leaving you free to enjoy your party and your guests.

ONE-STEP-BEYOND GUACAMOLE
California-Mexican Cuisine

Guacamole is, in my book, the dip supreme, king of dips, a dip worthy of beatification, if not canonization. Now I realize that to a lot of you guacamole is only mushed-up avocados with a little lemon juice and pepper chucked in. I happen to think that a good guacamole should have a lot more going for it than that. However, if you want to continue to live with mushed-up avocados and a squirt from a plastic lemon, be my guest, but be warned! The ghost of Montezuma may smash all your pre-Columbian artifacts and a feathered serpent may swoop down and curdle your Margaritas. So for those of you who are rather fond of your pre-Columbian artifacts and like a good Margarita, here is a delightful alternative.

Makes about 2 cups
3 very ripe avocados
Juice of 2 to 4 lemons
1 large tomato, cut into small dice
1 large yellow onion, minced
1 celery stalk, minced
4 green onions, minced
1 bell pepper, seeded and minced
4 to 6 teeth of garlic, finely minced
3 or 4 small fresh hot chilies, seeded and finely minced
1/4 cup minced fresh parsley
1 teaspoon finely minced fresh cilantro
1 teaspoon sugar
1/8 teaspoon ground cumin
1/4 teaspoon coarsely ground black pepper
1/3 cup vegetable oil
Salt and additional heat in the form of cayenne or Tabasco, to taste

Scoop the avocados into a bowl and mash thoroughly with a fork. Add the lemon juice a bit at a time, tasting after each addition, and stir well. Add all the remaining ingredients and mix.

As a dip, serve with potato chips, tortilla chips, thin slices of

French baguette, or fresh vegetables. A dollop is nice served alongside a tossed salad. Spoon it inside crisp tacos. A spoonful on top of an omelet or a burrito is a very welcome addition. Try serving a platter of alternate slices of avocado, tomato, and cucumber on a bed of romaine lettuce with guacamole spooned over the top and the whole sprinkled with pitted black olives. *Olé!*

GOBBA GHANNOUJ
Leyla
Turkish Guacamole

No, the typesetter didnt' make a mistake on this one. *Baba ghannouj,* as described in most cookbooks, is a rather nondescript purée, like a lot of guacamole, just a mush with a little lemon, salt, and pepper. Leyla, my culinary guru, taught me to make this delightful concoction, which will never be accused of being a bore at a party. It contains chunks and gobs of many delightful things and therefore my sons christened it Gobba Ghannouj.

Makes about 3 cups
1 large eggplant
1 large tomato, minced
2 celery stalks, minced
1 large yellow onion, minced

3 or 4 green onions, including tops, minced
1 green bell pepper, seeded and minced
1 red bell pepper, seeded and minced
3 or small fresh hot chilies, seeded and minced
8 to 10 teeth of garlic, minced
1/4 cup minced fresh parsley
1/3 cup fresh lemon juice
1/2 tablespoon sugar (optional)
1/2 teaspoon coarsely ground black pepper
2/3 cup olive oil (trust me)
Salt, sugar, and cayenne to taste

Using a barbecue fork, hold the eggplant over hot coals or a gas flame and turn slowly until the skin is blistered and singed in places. With a cloth, rub off what is loose. This will leave just a bit of the burned skin, which is necessary for the unique flavor of this dish. Now put the eggplant into the oven and bake at 350° until it is soft, 30 to 45 minutes. Remove it from the oven and cool until it

---

Garlic was held in such high esteem in Egypt that vows were sworn on it.

---

can be handled. Remove the stem and, with your hands, thoroughly mush the flesh up in a bowl. Continue kneading with your hand until all the lumps are gone and what skin remains is broken up. If any large chunks of skin will not incorporate, remove them.

Add all of the remaining ingredients except the oil, salt, sugar, and extra cayenne. Mix thoroughly. Begin drizzling the oil into the bowl gradually, and with your hand mix and knead until all of the oil has been completely incorporated. It will react rather like mayonnaise; the gradual adding and kneading of the oil into the other ingredients will make a homogeneous substance that is not oily at all.

Now add the salt, additional sugar if needed, and extra cayenne if you want it hotter. You may, of course, leave the sugar out altogether if you wish. Traditionally, it is almost sweet and sour in addition to the hot. Make it as mild or mighty as you wish by the addition of the extra cayenne. Serve chilled.

In the Middle East this is served with leaves of romaine lettuce for scooping; however I often serve it with traditional chips, tortilla chips, raw vegetables, or French bread, as well as leaves of crisp romaine.

CEYLONESE SWEET AND SOUR CURRY DIP
Sri Lanka

Makes about 2 cups
1 cup (8 ounces) sour cream
One 8-1/2-ounce can crushed
  pineapple, drained
1 celery stalk, trimmed and finely
  minced
1 small fresh hot chili, finely
  minced
1 tablespoon minced red onion
1 tablespoon frozen orange juice
  concentrate
1/4 to 1/3 cup brown sugar
2 tablespoons cider vinegar
1 tablespoon Madras-style curry
  powder
1/2 teaspoon cayenne
1 cup (1/2 pint) heavy cream
Fresh mint sprigs and orange slices
  for garnish

Put all of the ingredients except
the heavy cream and garnish in a
bowl and mix well. Whip the
cream to hold peaks and gently
fold into the dip. Chill thoroughly.
Pile into a serving bowl and
garnish with the mint and orange.
Place the bowl in the center of a
platter and surround with a selection
of fresh fruit such as whole strawberries, small sprigs of grapes,
spears of pineapple, melon balls
on picks, slices of peach, orange,
pear, apple and nectarine, etc.
Sprinkle cut fruit with lemon juice
to prevent it from turning brown.

If you really want to put on the
Ritz, pile the dip into the hollowed-
out half-shell of a pineapple or a
jagged-cut melon.

Although I usually suggest beer
with hot foods, this dish goes
exceedingly well with either Gewürztraminer or champagne.

GARDEN FRESH HERB DIP
Family Recipe

All too many people think of hot
foods as being heavy and overcooked. I think you will find that
this recipe delightfully refutes that
concept.

Makes about 3 cups
2 cups (16 ounces) cottage cheese
1/2 cup minced fresh basil leaves
1/4 cup minced fresh chives
1/4 cup minced green onions,
  including tops
1/4 cup minced fresh mint
1/4 cup minced sweet purple onion
1 teaspoon minced fresh cilantro
3 teeth of garlic, minced
1/3 cup hot chunky salsa,
  page 148
Coarsely ground black pepper and
  salt to taste
Tabasco to taste, if you like

Toss all of the ingredients together
and chill. To serve, put into a
serving dish and set on a large
platter or flat basket or tray and
surround with fresh crisp raw
vegetables. And how about getting
out of the carrot stick, radish, and
celery rut? Try sugar peas, slices
of red bell pepper, whole mushrooms, slices of *chayote* or *jícama*,
flowerets of broccoli, and purple
onion rings. The inside leaves of
crisp romaine lettuce make good
scoopers as well.

BAGNA CAUDA
Italy
Hot Anchovy Dip

Makes about 1-1/2 cups
4 tablespoons butter
1/2 cup minced mushroom stems
3 tablespoons finely minced garlic
8 anchovy fillets, drained and
  minced
1 cup (1/2 pint) heavy cream
1 cup shredded mozzarella
1/8 teaspoon cayenne
1/4 teaspoon sugar
1/8 teaspoon coarsely ground
  black pepper
Salt to taste

Melt the butter and gently sauté
the mushrooms and garlic. Do not
let them brown. Add the anchovies
and stir constantly for about a

minute. Add the remaining ingredients and cook over very low heat until the cheese is totally melted, whisking continuously. Pour into a serving dish with its own heat source: candle warmer, electric hot tray, spirit lamp, etc., to keep warm. Accompany with a basket of fresh, crisp, chilled raw vegetables. Celery sticks, cherry tomatoes, raw mushrooms, cucumber, green onions, and red bell peppers are excellent for dipping.

AH, STUFF IT

Take two things that are nice, put one inside the other, and you have something even nicer. Since we aren't exactly snubbing the genus *Capsicum* in this book, I'll begin stuffing with two delicious recipes for stuffed chilies, one Szechwanese and cooked, one Ethiopian and uncooked.

SZECHWANESE FRIED CHILIES
China

Makes 24
24 small fresh hot chilies, seeded (each chili should be about as long as your thumb)

STUFFING
1/2 pound ground pork
1 egg
1 medium onion, minced
1 celery stalk, minced
6 teeth of garlic, minced
1/2 tablespoon grated fresh ginger
1/4 teaspoon Chinese five-spices
1/8 teaspoon cayenne
1 tablespoon soy sauce
1/2 tablespoon sugar
1/2 teaspoon coarsely ground
   black pepper

BATTER
1 egg
1 cup unbleached all-purpose flour
1 cup ice-cold water
1/4 teaspoon baking soda
1/2 teaspoon rice vinegar
Pinch each salt and sugar

Oil for deep-frying

SAUCE
1/4 cup soy sauce
1 tablespoon tomato paste
1/4 cup brown sugar
1/4 cup rice vinegar
4 teeth of garlic, finely minced
1 teaspoon finely grated fresh ginger
1/4 teaspoon cayenne
2/3 cup water

Watercress or parsley sprigs and
   lemon slices for garnish

Cut off the stem end of each chili and remove the seeds and pulp, being careful not to break them. Bring a saucepan of water to the boil and drop in the chilies. Leave just until the water comes to the boil again and then put the chilies immediately into cold water. When cold, drain.

Mix all of the ingredients for the stuffing and gently stuff into the peppers, again being careful not to tear. Set aside while you make the batter.

Beat all of the ingredients for the batter together vigorously and set aside until ready to use. Heat the oil in a deep, heavy pot to approximately 375°, or deep-frying temperature. Dip the chilies in the batter and shake off any excess. Fry 3 or 4 at a time for approximately 5 minutes, or until golden brown. Drain thoroughly on paper towels.

Put all of the ingredients for the sauce into a blender and whir until smooth. Strain into a small saucepan and simmer over a low heat for 5 minutes. The sauce may be served hot or cold. Pour into a small bowl and place on a serving platter. Surround with the deep-fried chilies. Garnish with sprigs of watercress or parsley and slices of lemon.

KIFTO-STUFFED CHILIES WITH BERBERE
Ethiopia

Makes 12 stuffed chilies
1 onion
2 small fresh hot chilies, seeded
6 green onions, including tops
1 bell pepper, seeded
6 teeth of garlic
1 teaspoon finely grated fresh ginger
1/4 teaspoon each ground carda-
    mom, cinnamon, and coarsely
    ground black pepper
1 cup Bereré, page 146
2 tablespoons fresh lemon juice,
    plus 1/4 teaspoon grated lemon
    rind
1 teaspoon sugar
Salt to taste
1-1/2 pounds top-grade lean beef,
    trimmed of all fat and finely
    chopped or coarsely ground
12 large long fresh mild chilies

Watercress or parsley sprigs and
    lemon wedges for garnish

Mince the onion, hot chilies, bell
pepper, and garlic exceedingly fine.
Add the spices, 1 tablespoon of
the Berberé, lemon juice and rind,
sugar and salt. Mix well with the
beef.

Cut each chili in half lengthwise
and remove the seeds. Stuff with
the meat mixture. Put the remaining
Berberé into a serving bowl and
place in the middle of a large
platter. Arrange the stuffed chilies
around it and garnish with sprigs
of cress or parsley and wedges of
lemons.

STUFFED DRUMSTICKS WITH CAPSICUM-GINGER GLAZE
Family Recipe

Makes 12
12 small chicken drumsticks

STUFFING
1/2 pound ground pork
1/2 pound lean ground ham
1 medium onion, minced
4 teeth of garlic, finely minced
1/2 tablespoon minced candied
    ginger
1/8 teaspoon ground cinnamon
1/2 teaspoon cayenne
1/4 teaspoon coarsely ground
    black pepper
1 tablespoon brown sugar
Salt to taste

Capsicum-Ginger Glaze, page 146

You will need an exceedingly sharp
knife, a bottle of good wine, and
the patience of a saint. The knife
hopefully goes inside the chicken
leg and the wine goes inside you,
to help you achieve the patience
of a saint. Holding a chicken leg
by the big end, stand it on a firm
surface. Sort of scraping, sort of
cutting, try to convince the meat
to come away from the bone. Once
you have exposed enough of the
bone at the big end to grab hold
of it gets easier. Continue until all
but about 1 inch of the bone is
free. The meat will have almost
turned inside out. Using a pair of
poultry shears, cut off the freed
bone, leaving that last inch, which
is attached to the meat at the
small end. Turn the empty leg
right side out, pour another glass
of wine, and you now have only
eleven to go. It should get easier.

Using your hands, mix all of the
ingredients for the stuffing together
exceedingly well. Stuff into the
empty chicken legs. Pull the skin
up and close the opening with a
wooden toothpick. Now pretend
you are a sculptor and try to make
these little lumps assume the
shape of chicken legs again.

Place the drumsticks on a rack
over a baking pan and bake at
350° for about 25 to 30 minutes,
painting often with Capsicum-Ginger
Glaze. Serve hot.

WARNING: Remove the toothpicks
before serving the chicken legs.

DIABLE MUSHROOMS
Family Recipe

This dish only whispers an acquaintance with capsicum, boasting more fully of its relationship with garlic and fresh basil.

Makes 12
12 giant, huge, gargantuan, humungous mushrooms*

STUFFING
2 tablespoons butter
2 tablespoons cream sherry
4 teeth of garlic, minced
3 tablespoons minced onion
1/2 teaspoon minced fresh hot chilies
Reserved mushroom stems
1/2 cup chicken livers
1/2 cup ground pork
1/2 teaspoon sugar
1/8 teaspoon fresh-ground black pepper
1 egg
Salt to taste
1 tablespoon shelled pine nuts

An inscription on the Great Pyramid of Cheops records that 1,600 talents of silver was spent on onions and garlic for the workmen in 2900 B.C.

TOPPING
1 tablespoon vegetable oil
1 tablespoon olive oil
4 teeth of garlic, crushed
1/4 teaspoon minced fresh hot chili
1 cup chopped fresh basil leaves
1/4 cup heavy cream
1/4 teaspoon sugar
Salt and coarsely ground black pepper to taste
1/2 cup shredded Swiss cheese

Put a 3- to 4-quart pan of water on to boil. Stem the mushrooms and mince the stems finely. Set aside.

When the water has boiled, drop in the mushroom caps and, as soon as the water comes back to a boil, boil 1 minute longer, then immediately drain the mushrooms and put in running water until they are cold. Drain.

To make the stuffing, melt the butter and sherry together and gently sauté the garlic for about 3 or 4 minutes. Adjust the heat to keep from browning. Add the onion, chilies, chopped mushroom stems, chicken livers, and pork and continue cooking, stirring to break up the meat until the pork is no longer pink but not yet browned. The livers should still show a bit of pink inside. Put this into a blender with all of the remaining stuffing ingredients except the pine nuts. Scrape out into a bowl with a rubber spatula and stir in the pine nuts. Put a dollop into each mushroom cap. Set aside.

Put all of the topping ingredients except the cheese into a blender and whir until well blended. Top each filled mushroom cap with a dollop of the basil mixture and sprinkle with a bit of grated cheese. Put on a baking sheet and bake in a preheated 350° oven until the cheese is melted and slightly bubbling. Serve piping hot.

If there is any of the meat or basil mixture left over, spread it on French bread and toast in the oven.

*You can't find humungous, gargantuan or huge? Big will do, well, even not so big. O.K., so you have to use small, and it's a pain, and of course you will need a bunch more of them, probably about 3 or 4 dozen.

DEVILED CHICKEN NECKS
Family Recipe

Makes 24
24 chicken necks* (be sure they
   have their skins)
2 cups cooked long-grain white rice
1 egg
1 large onion, chopped small
1/2 bell pepper, chopped small
1 celery stalk, chopped small
1 tablespoon minced fresh hot chilies
6 teeth of garlic, minced
1/4 cup minced fresh parsley
1/2 teaspoon mixed dried herbs
   (Italian seasoning)
1/4 teaspoon coarsely ground
   black pepper
1 teaspoon sugar
Salt to taste
Oil for frying
Watercress sprigs or lettuce leaves

Remove the skins from the necks
and set aside. Cover what remains
with water and boil until they are
exceedingly tender. When cool
enough to handle, pick the meat
from the bones and put into a
bowl. Add all of the remaining
ingredients except the skins, oil,
and greens and mix thoroughly
with your hands. Fry a bit to test
for seasoning. Adjust seasoning
for your taste.

Carefully stuff the skins with
this mixture. Skewer each end
shut with a wooden toothpick.
Heat about 1/2 inch of vegetable
oil in a cast-iron or other heavy
skillet and fry the stuffed necks
about 3 minutes on each side, or
until crisp and a delicious golden
brown all over. Drain on paper
towels. Pat off any excess oil with
paper towels and serve on a bed
of watercress or other attractive
greens. If you wish to dress this
dish up a bit more, strew with
cherry tomatoes and a few wedges
of lemon. Serve hot or cold.

*You can usually get chicken necks
at markets catering to an ethnic
clientele.

In the Oxford Book of Oxford,
*T. S. Eliot is recorded as having
said he couldn't see how any
person could put vile mustard on
his food.*

*Now, let's stuff some things we
don't have to cook. That's always a
nice treat for the host or hostess.
After all, you're supposed to enjoy
this party too.*

HORSERADISH BEEF ROLLS
England

Not all hot, hot things contain
capsicum. Horseradish is hot, and
if you manage to get your hands
on a fresh root and grate it
yourself, boy oh boy, is it hot! If
you can't find fresh and don't
grow it, well, you'll just have to
make do with bottled. The recipes
in this book are formulated for
bottled horseradish, so if you
grate your own, disregard any
amounts given here and just begin
adding and tasting a bit at a time
or else you are going to be in big
trouble.

Makes 24
4 ounces cream cheese
1/4 to 1/3 cup prepared horseradish (taste as you go)
2 tablespoons minced fresh chives
1 tablespoon minced red bell pepper
2 teeth of garlic, minced
1-1/2 teaspoons fresh minced dill
   weed, or 1/2 teaspoon dried
1 generous tablespoon chopped
   ripe olives

1/3 cup minced sweet purple onion
1/4 teaspoon coarsely ground
   black pepper
Salt to taste
24 thin slices lean medium-rare
   roast beef
Watercress sprigs for garnish

Put all of the ingredients except
the beef and watercress in a bowl
and blend well with a fork. Spread
each slice of beef with the cheese-
horseradish mixture. It should be
thicker than butter on bread. Roll
up firmly and secure with a cocktail
pick. Stick a tuft of watercress in
one end of each roll and place on
a serving platter. Chill before
serving.

LUMPIA
Philippines
Chicken, Pork, and Potato Rolls

Makes about 20
2 tablespoons vegetable oil
1/4 cup water
1 medium onion, minced
6 teeth of garlic, minced
1 tablespoon finely minced seeded
   fresh hot chilies
1 scant teaspoon grated fresh ginger
1/2 pound ground pork

1/2 bell pepper, preferably red,
   minced
1/2 cup chopped fresh bean sprouts
1/2 cup finely shredded Chinese
   (Napa) cabbage
1/4 cup minced celery
3 green onions, including tops,
   minced
1 tablespoon minced fresh parsley
1/2 teaspoon dry mustard
2 tablespoons soy sauce
1/2 tablespoon sugar
Coarsely ground black pepper and
   salt to taste
1 cup finely shredded cooked chicken
Cayenne to taste (optional)
2 eggs, lightly beaten
1 cup mashed potatoes
1 package egg-roll wrappers
Oil for frying

Heat the oil and water over high
heat in a wok. Add the onion,
garlic, chilies, and ginger and stir-
fry for about 2 minutes. Add all
the remaining ingredients except
the chicken, cayenne, eggs, potatoes,
wrappers, and frying oil. Stir-fry
for another 2 to 3 minutes. The
vegetables should be wilted but
not dead. Remove from the heat.
Add the cooked chicken. Taste the
mixture and, if you want this dish
to be hotter, judiciously add a bit
of cayenne to the mashed potatoes.
Stir the eggs into the mixture.

Lay an egg roll wrapper on a
flat surface in front of you. Spread
it thinly and evenly with the
mashed potato, leaving a 1/2-inch
margin all around the edge. Place
about 1-1/2 tablespoons of the
vegetable mixture in a line along
the edge nearest you. Lift the
wrapper edge near you and begin
rolling. When you have rolled up
half of the wrapper, fold the two
side edges inwards. Then continue
rolling until you reach the end. Set
aside, seam edge down. Continue
until you run out of wrappers or
goop.

Heat about an inch of oil in a
heavy skillet until it reaches 375°,
deep-frying temperature (it should
be hot but not smoking). Place 2
or 3 rolls in the hot oil at a time
and fry on both sides until golden
brown. Remove from the pan with
a slotted spoon and drain thoroughly
on paper towels.

GRILLED MUNCHIES

The technique of grilling was developed by nomadic peoples out of a need for maximum mobility. Desert peoples, following their herds from one scant pasturage to another, had no place in their life style for such cumbersome gear as stoves and a vast array of cooking implements. Fuel was scarce as well, and it didn't take a graduate from the culinary academy to determine that small pieces of meat, threaded onto sticks and held over the fire, cooked quickly and required less fuel than the large roasted joints of Northern Europe where fuel was more plentiful. Not only did this method require less gear to be packed about, but it likewise used little water for washing, an all-important concern in a climate where water was at a premium.

The following recipes, although designed for the open grill, are also tasty if moved indoors and grilled under the broiler or on a rack in a hot oven.

SIS KEBABI
Middle East

Makes 16 to 24 skewers

MARINADE
1/4 cup olive oil
1/2 onion, minced
8 teeth of garlic, finely minced
1/4 cup fresh lemon juice
3 teaspoons minced fresh dill weed, or 1 teaspoon dried
1 teaspoon minced fresh cilantro
1/2 teaspoon crushed dried hot chilies
1/2 teaspoon dry mustard
1/8 teaspoon ground coriander
1/8 teaspoon ground cinnamon
1 teaspoon sugar

2 pounds lean boneless lamb, cut into bite-sized chunks
1 large onion, cut into wedges
1 small eggplant, cut into bite-sized chunks
12 small fresh mild to hot (your choice) chilies
2 or 3 ripe but firm tomatoes, cut into wedges

Mix all of the marinade ingredients together. Add all of the remaining ingredients and toss lightly with the marinade; refrigerate for at least 2 hours.

When ready to cook, thread the meat and vegetables alternately onto skewers and grill about 4 inches from the coals. Turn frequently and paint with extra marinade during cooking. Cook to desired doneness. Serve hot. This is a good cook-saving party dish.

SEAFOOD SIS
Middle East

Makes 12 to 16 skewers

MARINADE
1/4 cup olive oil
1/4 cup fresh lemon juice
3 teaspoons minced fresh dill weed, or 1 teaspoon dried
3 teeth of garlic, minced
1 medium onion, minced
2 bay leaves, crushed
1/2 teaspoon or more crushed dried hot chilies
1/8 teaspoon dried thyme
1/2 teaspoon sugar
1 teaspoon paprika
1/4 teaspoon coarsely ground black pepper

2 pounds assorted firm-fleshed fish and seafood (swordfish, shark, giant prawns, scallops, shucked clams or mussels)*
1 lemon, cut in half

Mix all the marinade ingredients together in a bowl. Add the fish and turn over in the marinade to make sure that all are covered; refrigerate for at least 2 hours before serving. When ready to serve, thread onto skewers and cook as for Sis Kebabi, page 26. Fish are best when cooked lightly. Squeeze fresh lemon juice over while cooking. Again, save yourself the trouble and let your guests fend for themselves, if, that is, they are not the type who will glom up all the prawns and leave nothing but swordfish for the next guy.

*WARNING: Use clams and mussels in the correct season *only*. Call your local health department or department of fish and game.

BEEF TERIYAKI
Japan

Makes 16 to 24 skewers
2 pounds lean high-quality boneless
    beef
Hot Teriyaki Sauce, page 147

Put the beef into the freezer and leave until it is firm but not frozen solid. With an exceedingly sharp knife, cut as thin as possible. Cut these sheets of beef into strips about 1 inch wide and 3 to 4 inches long. Place in Hot Teriyaki Sauce and leave for at least an hour.

To prepare, thread the strips of meat onto short bamboo skewers and grill very quickly over glowing coals on a barbecue or a hibachi. The meat should be placed about 4 inches away from the coals. Turn frequently. The concept of a good teriyaki is to have the thin edges of the meat actually singed and beginning to get crisp while the center is still quite rare. The contrast of textures is part of the essence of this dish. And yet, again, you can let your guests cook their own to their individual preference.

ONION BHUGIAS
India
Fried Onion Fritters

Makes 16 to 20
4 onions, grated
8 teeth of garlic, finely minced
2 tablespoons minced seeded fresh
    hot chilies
1/4 cup minced fresh parsley
1 scant teaspoon grated fresh ginger
1 teaspoon minced fresh cilantro
1/8 teaspoon *each* ground coriander,
    fenugreek, cumin, cayenne, and
    cinnamon

A generous 1/2 teaspoon sugar
1/4 teaspoon coarsely ground
    black pepper
Salt to taste
2 eggs
1/2 cup unbleached all-purpose flour
Oil for frying

Mix all of the ingredients except the oil together well. Fry a small patty in a bit of oil in a skillet to test for seasoning. Add salt and more cayenne at this time if you wish. Divide into 16 to 20 equal portions and form into balls. You may need to lightly dust your hands with flour to prevent sticking.

Put 4 inches of vegetable oil into a deep fryer or wok and heat to 375° (the oil should be hot but not smoking). Fry the *bhugias* a few at a time for 3 to 4 minutes or until golden brown. Fry one first and break open to make sure they will be done on the inside. If it gets too brown on the outside before it is done on the inside, reduce the heat slightly and test again. Drain thoroughly on paper towels and serve hot.

SOME EXTRA THINGS

STEAK TARTAR
Family Recipe

Funny, but a friend of mine who is a Tartar told me that she had never heard of steak Tartar before she came to California.

Serves 8 as a meal,
16 to 20 as a munchy
Leaves of curly endive
2 pounds freshly ground lean
   high-grade beef
1/2 cup mild or hot chunky salsa,
   page 148
1 egg
1 large sweet purple onion, minced
1/2 cup minced green onions,
   including tops
4 small fresh hot chilies, minced
1 tablespoon minced garlic
4 hard-cooked eggs, minced
2 tablespoons capers, drained
One 4-1/2-ounce can chopped
   black olives, drained
1/4 cup minced fresh chives
2 tablespoons minced fresh cilantro
Lemon slices for garnish

Line a serving platter with curly endive. Mound the beef in the center. Make a well in the middle of the beef. Pour the salsa into this and break the raw egg into the middle. Place all the remaining ingredients in small piles around the beef and garnish with thin slices of lemon. Chill before serving.

Provide a basket of RyKrisp, poppy seed crackers, or thinly sliced baguette. I always also provide additional salsa, Tabasco, more lemon and a pepper grinder. Each guest may build a mini-Dagwood of meat and condiments. This is a fine refresher on a hot day.

SASHIMI
WITH THREE SAUCES
Japan

Serves 8 to 12
1/2 pound fresh raw tuna
1/3 pound fresh raw salmon
1/3 pound raw prawns, peeled
1/4 cup grated *daikon* radish
1/4 cup minced green onion tops
1/4 cup finely shredded carrot

SAUCE NO. 1
1/4 cup soy sauce
1-1/2 teaspoons dry mustard
1 teaspoon sugar

SAUCE NO. 2
3 tablespoons soy sauce
1 tablespoon rice vinegar

1-1/2 teaspoons sugar
1/2 teaspoon finely grated fresh
   ginger
1/2 teaspoon peanut oil
4 garlic cloves, finely minced
1/8 teaspoon cayenne

SAUCE NO. 3
2 teaspoons green *wasabi* mustard
3 tablespoons soy sauce

With an exceedingly sharp knife slice the tuna and salmon as thin as possible. Split the prawns in half lengthwise.

Chill a serving plate, then along one side make lines of the *daikon,* the green onion, and the carrot. Now arrange the thin slices of fish and prawns in an attractive pattern beside the vegetables. Refrigerate while you prepare the sauces.

Mix all of the ingredients for Sauce No. 1 together well and set aside in a small bowl; repeat for Sauce No. 2. For Sauce No. 3, mix the *wasabi* with enough water to make a smooth paste. Place in a mound in the center of a small flattish bowl. Pour the soy sauce around it to form a moat.

Serve the plate of *sashimi* accompanied with these three zesty sauces and disposable wooden chopsticks.

MARINATED VEGETABLES
Family Recipe

Serves a bunch
2 quarts water
1/2 head cauliflower, broken into
    flowerets
2 large carrots, peeled and cut on
    the diagonal
20 green beans, cut in half
1/2 pound broccoli, separated into
    flowerets
12 small boiling onions (not pearl
    onions)

MARINADE
2 cups water
2 cups cider vinegar
1/2 cup sugar
1/3 cup salt
20 teeth of garlic, coarsely chopped
1 teaspoon crushed dried hot chilies
1/2 tablespoon pickling spices
3 teaspoons fresh dill weed, or
    1 teaspoon dried
1/4 teaspoon anise seeds
1/4 cup olive oil

1 each red and green bell pepper,
    seeded and cut into strips
12 small fresh mild chilies, seeded
2 celery stalks, washed, trimmed,
    and cut into 2-inch chunks
1 sweet purple onion, cut into rings

Bring the 2 quarts water to a rapid boil. Add the cauliflower and leave only until the water returns to the boil. Drain immediately and put under cold running water until thoroughly cold. Repeat the process for the carrots, green beans, broccoli, and onions. However, leave the broccoli in boiling water for another minute after the water comes to the boil, the carrots and beans 2 to 3 minutes, and the onions just until they can be pierced with the tip of a sharp knife. Drain and cool each in cold running water as you did for the cauliflower.

Put all the marinade ingredients except the oil in a saucepan and bring to a boil. Reduce heat to a simmer and maintain for 5 minutes. Remove from the heat and let cool.

Put the blanched vegetables, together with the bell pepper, fresh chilies, celery, and purple onion, into a large bowl or a crock and pour the marinade over. Stir gently, being careful not to break the vegetables. They can be eaten in a few hours but are best if refrigerated for 2 to 3 days. This will keep for 2 or 3 weeks in the refrigerator. (Actually, I have never had a crock of these veggies keep more than 20 minutes after I set it on the table.)

AARON'S HALLELUIAH GARLIC
Family Recipe

Serves 1 dedicated garlic junky, or 4 to 6 who only have a moderate addiction
20 teeth of garlic, whole but peeled
1/8 teaspoon cayenne
1/2 cup butter
1 baguette

Put the garlic, cayenne, and butter in a small heatproof serving dish. Set the dish inside a steamer and steam for 45 minutes, adding water to the steamer when necessary. When ready the garlic will be soft and sweet. The harshness will have dissipated with the long, slow cooking.

Set in the middle of the table and gather round to tear off chunks of bread, dip in the butter, and spread with the mushy garlic.

Roman legionnaires consumed vast quantities of garlic to increase their prowess on the battlefield and in bed.

INTOXICATED FOWELLE
Elizabethan England

We have some Goodwife late in the sixteenth century to thank for this extraordinary, delicious, and simple dish. The fact that it incorporates the New World capsicum would place it sometime after Captain Francis Drake's circumnavigation of the globe in 1577–1580. The Spanish wine, sherry, was experiencing great popularity at this time. Remember that, until recently, the terms sack and sherry were interchangeable. Sherry was as close as the English tongue could come to wrapping itself around Jerez, the name of the coastal Spanish town where the wine was produced. English merchant-adventurers "liberated" great quantities of the powerful draught after their sack of the town.

Of course ginger had been known in England since the Crusades, and, although many English today feel they have been poisoned if they are asked to eat anything with garlic in it, Medieval/Renaissance man ate it with great gusto. After all, it warded off the plague, guaranteed that your firstborn would be a male, and kept away witches and vampires.

Serves 8 to 12
One frying chicken (the original recipe called for "One Elderly Fowelle")
10 small fresh mild to hot (your choice) chilies (a selection of red, yellow, and green, if available)
20 teeth of garlic
2 cups cream sherry
1 tablespoon slivered fresh ginger
1/2 teaspoon cracked black pepper
1 teaspoon pickling spices
1-1/2 teaspoons minced fresh dill weed, or 1/2 teaspoon dried
Salt to taste

Cut the chicken in half. Then with a heavy, sharp cleaver, take out all your pent-up aggressions and just wallop the blazes out of that poor sucker. You don't want serving pieces, you want 2-inch chunks, any way that cleaver happens to fall. Rinse the chicken pieces under cold running water and put in a pot with water to completely cover. Bring to a boil, then reduce the heat to a rapid simmer and continue to cook 45 minutes to an hour, or until exceedingly tender. Drain, saving the broth for some later use, even if it's only to feed the cats. (Waste it and you will have to do penance; something horrid like reading all of Edmund Spenser's *The Faerie Queene.*) Rinse the chicken pieces and put into a crock or jar large enough to hold them comfortably.

Put a small knife slit into each pepper and slightly crush the garlic cloves. Add the remaining ingredients to the chicken. Refrigerate for at least 2 days before using. Stir occasionally to make sure all the "fowelle" has an equal chance to become intoxicated. This is a wonderful party munchy.

STERLING'S POPCORN DIABLO
Family Recipe

Makes 6 cups
1 cup butter
1 teaspoon curry powder
1/4 teaspoon chili powder
1/4 teaspoon cayenne
Garlic salt to taste
6 cups hot popped popcorn

Put the butter, curry, chili powder, cayenne, and garlic salt in a small saucepan and melt. Drizzle over popcorn and serve hot.

SOUP

I adore soup. Soup with a meal, soup as a meal, soup thick or thin, nothing in it, things in it, hot or cold. I do not like soups from a can, either in my soup bowl or over my noodles with a can of tuna.

The word soup comes from *sop* or *sops,* the chunks of stale or bread that were always served in the Middle Ages for sopping up your broth. Spoons were still a luxury not all households could afford to provide their guests, let alone forks. Incidentally, despite what you may have seen in the movie *Becket,* Thomas à Becket did not introduce the fork to England. It didn't come into common usage until the seventeenth century. Even at the court of Lizzy Tudor it was still considered rather foppish and pretentious. One of her favorites, Robert Dudley, the Earl of Leicester, once said, "A good Englishman hath no need to make hay with his food, pitching it into his mouth with tiny forks."

Ah, but back to soups. Almost everyone ate broth in the Middle Ages. It was an economic necessity. However, the quality of the broth was judged by the quantity of the sops provided to accompany it. When Geoffrey Chaucer was in the employ of John of Gaunt, he recorded an incident when a French dignitary left the dining hall in high dudgeon because no sops had accompanied the broth. John of Gaunt, being quite urbane and in more than comfortable circumstances, provided his guests with spoons, thus making the serving of sops unnecessary. I guess the Frenchman didn't see it that way and thought he had been slighted.

By the end of the fourteenth century, however, everyone who

was anyone at all had ample spoons, thus making sops totally unnecessary. People began to look to the quality of the broth itself, or soup as it had now become known. Soup soon became a fad. People of fashion would show their chef out of the kitchen and try their hand at the creation of new and amazing soups. Things got so out of hand that at one point the Archbishop of Canterbury decreed that only one soup could be served per course. The members of monastic orders were spending far too much time in the kitchen creating soups instead of tending to their matins and vespers.

FOURTEENTH-CENTURY BROTH AND SOPS
England

This soup is a relic from monastic days: it is hot and heady with garlic and mustard, not chilies, which hadn't yet made their journey from the New World.

Serves 6 as a starter, 4 as a meal

BROTH
1 quart rich beef broth
20 teeth of garlic
1 teaspoon dry mustard
1 large potato, peeled and diced (the original recipe called for turnips, potatoes being New World)
2 large leeks, well cleaned and chopped small, including 4 inches of the green
1 large onion, chopped
1 teaspoon sugar
1/2 teaspoon mixed dried herbs (Italian seasoning)
2 tablespoons butter
Salt and fresh-ground black pepper to taste

SOPS
20 teeth of garlic, crushed
1 tablespoon white wine
1/2 teaspoon dry mustard
4 tablespoons butter
1/2 teaspoon sugar
1/3 cup shredded Swiss cheese
Six to eight 1-inch-thick slices French bread

1 cup washed and shredded fresh mustard greens

Put all of the ingredients for the broth, except the salt and pepper, into a saucepan and simmer until the vegetables are tender. Let cool a bit and then whir in a blender. You will probably need to do it in 2 or 3 batches. Rinse out the saucepan and return the soup to it.

To make the sops, put the garlic, wine, mustard, and butter in a small pan and gently cook until the garlic is soft. Do not let it brown. When soft, put into the blender with all of the remaining sop ingredients except the bread and purée.

Toast the bread. In the meantime, bring the broth to a rapid simmer. Add the shredded mustard greens and continue to simmer until the greens are only slightly wilted, no more than 5 to 7 minutes. Pour the broth into a heatproof serving dish. Spread the garlic-mustard butter on the pieces of toast and float on the top of the soup. Sprinkle with the grated cheese and put into the oven at 400° just until the cheese is melted and beginning to bubble and brown. Serve immediately.

SOUP

ASOPAO DE CAMARONES
Puerto Rico
Shrimp Soup

Serves 4 to 6
2 tablespoons oil
1 onion, finely chopped
1 onion, cut into thin rings
1 red bell pepper, seeded and
    cut into thin strips
2 small fresh hot green chilies,
    cut into thin rings
3 tomatoes, chopped
6 to 8 teeth of garlic, minced
1/4 cup tomato paste
6 cups chicken broth
1 cup cooked long-grain white rice
2 pounds shrimp, peeled and
    deveined
1 cup fresh or thawed frozen
    green peas
Salt and coarse-ground black
    pepper to taste
Tabasco for additional hotness,
    if desired
1/3 cup slivered lean cooked ham
2 green onions, minced
One 2-ounce jar chopped pimientos

Heat the oil in a heavy skillet or
wok. Do not let it smoke. Add the
onions, both chopped and rings,
and the pepper, chilies, tomatoes,
and garlic. Stir-fry until the vegetables are tender. Remove to a 2-
1/2- to 3-quart pot and add the
tomato paste and broth. Stir until
all the paste is dissolved. Add the
rice and bring to the boil, then
reduce the heat to a simmer. Add
the shrimp and peas and simmer
for 15 minutes. Add salt, pepper,
and Tabasco to taste. To serve,
ladle into a large heated tureen
and sprinkle with the ham, green
onion, and pimientos.

PEANUT-CHILI SOUP
South Africa

Serves 4 to 6
2 large leeks, including 4 inches
    of the tops, trimmed and washed
    thoroughly
4 cups chicken broth
1 large onion, chopped
1 cup cooked long-grain rice
3 small fresh hot chilies, cut into
    rings, seeds in
1 red bell pepper, seeded and cut
    into thin strips
1 cup roasted salted peanuts
    (not dry roasted)
1 cup fresh or canned okra
Salt, pepper, and cayenne to taste

Cut the leeks into thin rings and
reserve 1/2 cup. Put the broth,
onion, and all the leeks except
the reserved 1/2 cup into a heavy
2- to 3-quart saucepan and bring
to a boil over high heat. Reduce
the heat to low and simmer for
25 to 30 minutes, or until the vegetables are quite tender. Remove
from the heat and whir in a
blender. Return the soup to the
saucepan, reserving 1 cup. Add
the rice, chilies, red bell pepper,
and reserved leek rings to the
saucepan and bring to the boil.
Reduce the heat to a simmer and
cook for about 15 minutes. Meanwhile, put the reserved cup of
soup and the peanuts into a
blender and purée. Stir into the
soup on the stove and continue
cooking for the remainder of the
15 minutes. If you are using fresh
okra, cut it into rings and boil
until tender, about 5 minutes.
Drain and rinse thoroughly. If
using canned okra, drain and rinse
also. Add the okra to the soup,
stir, and remove from the heat.
Season to taste with salt, pepper,
and cayenne if more hotness is
desired. (See, I don't put garlic in
everything.) Ladle into a heated
serving dish and lightly sprinkle
the top with finely chopped peanuts.

SOTO AYAM KUNING
Indonesia
Spicy Chicken-Noodle Soup

Serves 4 to 6
1 frying chicken, quartered
1/2 teaspoon crushed dried hot
  chilies
3 clusters (heads) of garlic, cut in
  half—remove loose outer skin,
  but no need to peel
2 large onions, quartered but not
  peeled
2 celery stalks, coarsely chopped
4 or 5 thin slices fresh ginger
1 small bay leaf
1 star anise pod
1/2 teaspoon ground turmeric
1/2 teaspoon sugar
2 ounces cellophane noodles
  (sometimes called long rice)
1 medium onion, cut into thin
  rings
1 medium leek, including 2 inches
  of the green, cut into thin rings
  and washed thoroughly
1 red bell pepper, seeded and
  cut into thin strips
1 large long mild chili, cut into
  thin rings
1/4 pound snow peas, trimmed of
  any strings

1/4 pound mushrooms, sliced thin
1 egg
Salt and black pepper, to taste
Cayenne (optional)
2 green onion tops, chopped into
  thin rings, for garnish

Put the first 10 ingredients in a large, heavy pot and add just enough water to cover the chicken. Bring to a boil, then reduce the heat to a rapid simmer, and continue to cook for about 45 minutes, or until the chicken is tender but still on the bones. When cool enough to handle, remove the chicken from the pot, drain, and remove the skin. Remove all the meat from the bones. Return the skin and bones to the pot, cover with a lid, and continue to simmer for another 45 minutes to an hour. Cool. Cut the meat into thin strips and reserve.

While the broth is simmering, put the noodles into a bowl and cover with cold water. Leave until soft. When the broth is ready, strain it through a fine sieve. Discard the remains, rinse the pot, and return the strained broth to it. When soft, drain the noodles and add to the broth. Add the vegetables, bring to a boil, immediately reduce the heat to a simmer, and cook for 5 minutes.

Beat the egg and pour into a lightly oiled and heated skillet. Swirl to spread evenly. Continue cooking over a medium heat until the surface is almost dry. Then with a pancake turner, begin to roll. Leave for just a bit longer to ensure that it is dry inside, and turn out onto a cutting surface. With a sharp knife, shred finely.

Taste the broth for seasoning. Add salt and black pepper to taste. If more heat is wanted gradually add cayenne. Ladle into a heated serving dish and add the slivered chicken and stir. Sprinkle over the egg and green onion and serve immediately.

MENUDO
California Farm Workers
Tripe Soup

My Mother and father met while working on Upton Sinclair's campaign for governor of California. The Dust Bowl immigrants of the thirties, wandering their weary way up and down the San Joaquin Valley, were, for the most part, in a sorry plight indeed. My dad spent many a night in a small-town jail for informing the farm workers of their right to strike.

SOUP

This is the *menudo* my dad enjoyed in the home of the family of a farm worker he had marched with. *Menudo* is great stuff. It shows what ingenuity can do when you can only afford the feet and stomach of the pig.

Serves 8

2 pounds tripe, cut into thin strips 3 to 4 inches long
2 pig's feet, split
4 quarts beef broth or water
4 onions, peeled and coarsely chopped
1 bay leaf
1/2 teaspoon cracked black pepper
6 small dried hot chilies
10 teeth of garlic, peeled and crushed
1/2 teaspoon dried oregano
1/2 teaspoon ground cumin
One 14-ounce can hominy
4 tomatoes, chopped
1 green bell pepper, seeded and cut into thin strips
1 red bell pepper, seeded and cut into thin rings
Salt and black pepper to taste

Put the tripe and pigs' feet into a 6-quart stock pot and add water to cover. Bring to a boil, pour off the water, and add the 4 quarts of broth or water, Add the next 7 ingredients and bring to a boil. Reduce the heat to a rapid simmer and continue cooking for 3 to 4 hours or until the meats are exceedingly tender. When cool enough to handle, remove the pigs' feet and bone them. Return the boned meat to the pot, add the remaining ingredients, and simmer for 20 to 30 minutes. Adjust seasoning. Serve hot, accompanied with a basket of steamy-hot flour tortillas. My Chicano friends tell me that *menudo* is excellent for a hangover.

CHEESE AND CHILI SOUP
Zacatecas, Mexico

Serves 4 to 6

4 cups rich beef broth
10 teeth of garlic, peeled
4 large tomatoes, chopped
3 medium onions, quartered
1/2 teaspoon mixed dried herbs (Italian seasoning)
1 scant teaspoon sugar
1/4 teaspoon ground cumin
1 medium onion, cut into rings
1 long mild green chili, cut into thin rings
1 red bell pepper, seeded and cut into thin rings
1 cup shredded sharp Cheddar
1 cup shredded mozzarella
1 cup mild or hot chunky salsa, **page 148**
1 teaspoon minced fresh cilantro for garnish

Put the first 7 ingredients into a pot and bring to a gentle boil. Reduce the heat to a simmer and continue cooking for 30 minutes. Purée in a blender and return to the pot.

Add the onion, chili, and bell pepper to the soup and simmer for about 15 minutes, or until the vegetables are tender.

Toss the two cheeses together. Ladle the soup into a heated serving dish. Add the cheeses and salsa and stir gently. Sprinkle with the cilantro and serve immediately.

Cilantro is sometimes called fresh coriander or Chinese parsley. Many cookbooks say cilantro or parsley. They are not interchangeable. Their flavors are as different as Chardonnay and Zinfandel, Swiss and Cheddar, yogurt and sour cream—each pair related but definitely not interchangeable.

GAZPACHO
Me
Cold Vegetable Soup

So who said soups have to be hot? A cold soup on a hot day can be as refreshing as a hot soup is comforting on a cold day, and in my book (hey, this is my book isn't it), gazpacho is the king of cold soups. And when I say *gazpacho* I don't mean just cold tomato soup, or a puréed glug, or something all watery with an oil slick floating on it, I mean *GAZPACHO!*

Serves 8 for a meal or
16 or more at a party
One 46-ounce can tomato juice
1 cup rich beef broth
1 cup cream sherry
1/2 sweet purple onion, cut into
   thin rings
2 celery stalks, diced
1/2 each green and red bell pepper,
   seeded and cut into thin strips
1 long mild green or yellow chili,
   seeded and cut into thin rings
1/2 large cucumber, peeled and
   diced
1 large tomato, diced
2 avocados, diced
1/2 cup sliced mushrooms
One 2-1/2-ounce can sliced black
   olives, drained

One 4-ounce can diced peeled
   green chilies
4 green onions, including the tops,
   minced
1/4 cup minced fresh parsley
1 tablespoon minced fresh cilantro
1/8 teaspoon ground cumin
Fresh-ground black pepper to taste
1 cup hot chunky salsa, page 148
1/4 cup olive oil
6 to 8 cucumber slices
3 or 4 lemon slices

Put all the ingredients except the last 4 into a large serving bowl and chill thoroughly. Stir the salsa and oil into the gazpacho. Using a sharp knife, firmly drag it down the sides of a cucumber, scoring the skin as you do. Cut into rings. The edge of each slice will be jagged. Float the cucumber rings and lemon slices on top of the gazpacho and serve ice cold. Accompany with additional salsa, Tabasco, and lemon wedges.

NOTE: If you really want to put on the Ritz, try the following. Start with a 50-pound block of ice. Set a stainless steel mixing bowl on top of the block of ice and fill with hot water. When the ice has melted a bit of an indentation into the top of the ice, remove, scoop out the water resulting from the melting, throw out the water in the

bowl (which will now be too cool to continue melting the ice) and replace with more hot water. Continue doing this until you have formed a bowl in the top of the block of ice. Set the entire block on a tray that will catch the drips as the block gradually melts, and use the indentation in the ice as your serving bowl. It makes a spectacular display and keeps the gazpacho beautifully cold as well.

SOPA DE AGUACATE
Mexico
Avocado Soup

Serves 4 to 6
4 cups rich chicken broth
1 onion, chopped
2 small fresh hot chilies, stemmed
   but not seeded
4 teeth of garlic, chopped
1/2 cup cream sherry
3 very ripe large avocados
Salt and fresh-ground black
   pepper to taste
Cayenne to taste (optional)
1 cup (1/2 pint) heavy cream
1/2 teaspoon minced fresh cilantro
1 small avocado

Put the broth, onion, chilies, and garlic into a 2-quart saucepan and bring to a boil. Reduce the heat and simmer for 15 to 20 minutes. Cool. Put into a blender and purée. Pour the mixture back into the saucepan.

Put the sherry and the 3 avocados into a blender and purée until smooth. Whisk into the soup. Season to taste. If you wish more heat, gradually add cayenne to taste. Chill until ready to serve.

Ladle the soup into a chilled serving bowl. Whip the cream and gently fold into the chilled soup. Sprinkle the top with the cilantro. Peel the avocado, slice thinly, and carefully lay on top of the soup. Serve immediately.

CRADLE-OF-THE-DEEP SUMMER SOUP
Family Recipe

Serves 8
6 cups defatted chicken broth
1 pound white fish fillets
6 teeth of garlic, crushed
1 onion, peeled and quartered
3/4 teaspoon fresh dill weed, or
   1/2 teaspoon dried
Juice of 1 lemon
1/2 teaspoon sugar
1/2 pound salmon fillets, poached
   and chilled

1/2 pound firm-fleshed white fish
   (like swordfish or monkfish)
   poached, boned, and chilled
1/2 pound cooked and shelled
   shrimp
1 crab, cooked and shelled
   (see page 14)
1 cup mild or hot chunky salsa,
   page 148
Lemon slices and fresh dill weed
   for garnish

Put the first 8 ingredients into a 2-1/2- or 3-quart saucepan and bring to a boil. Reduce the heat and simmer for 20 minutes. When somewhat cool, purée in a blender. Chill.

Cut the salmon and the white fish into smaller than bite-sized chunks. Pour the soup into a chilled serving bowl. Add all the fish, shellfish, and salsa. Stir gently. Garnish with slices of lemon and sprigs of fresh dill weed. Serve chilled, with a baguette.

SALADS

One of the myriad bits of useless trivia I have picked up in my travels is that we Californians love salads more than most other people, and we are followed closely by our fellow western Americans. And when I speak of salads, I mean *salads,* not a grudging bit of fodder with a smattering of oil and vinegar chucked in its direction. As I was growing up, a meal wasn't complete if there wasn't a salad, and often the meal *was* a salad.

I hear a lot these days about *nouvelle cuisine* and California cuisine, all of which I find quite puzzling because long before such terms were ever coined, my parents, being old Bernaar MacPhadden, Gayelord Houser and Adelle Davis advocates, had thrown the dripping pot and the salt shaker out. I was the first kid on the block with a wok. They didn't have handy-dandy sprouters and yogurt makers in those days, so you sprinkled your alfalfa seeds in wet paper and rolled it up, and a sleeping bag kept your yogurt the right temperature. Have you any idea how hard it was in 1946 to try and talk one of your classmates into trading his balogna sandwich for a jar of homemade yogurt? I was also the only kid in the fourth grade with sandals—did you ever try to play kickball with sandals?

Well, I managed to survive my parents' avant-garde lifestyle, through the forties and, with more difficulty, through the fifties—and, of course, in the sixties that meant I was already where everyone else was trying to get.

But back to salads, which is where it's always really been at as far as my family's eating habits were concerned. We still feel that you can't sit down to dinner without a huge bowl of salad, and that that salad has to have things in it. Not just lettuce, although we never slight lettuce. I usually use a selection of greens; iceberg, romaine, curly endive, perhaps some fresh, crisp spinach, and why not a few nasturtium leaves or even a little fresh basil? What else? Well, a world of thrilling veggies is out there, just waiting to hop into your salad bowl and have a party.

And don't ever think that hot things won't make excellent guests in the salad bowl: chilies, of course, mild or mighty, sweet, fresh, pickled, crushed, sliced, diced; and what's a salad without garlic, unless it's a fruit salad, and then you can invite ginger. What would a party be without ginger? She's a real kick. Grated fresh or slivered candied or the preserved Oriental ginger—they all make a salad bowl party sit up and sing. Horseradish, mustard—they should be on your invitation list as well. It just wouldn't be the same without them.

TABBOULEH
North African Arab States
Bulgur Salad

Serves 4 to 6

1/2 cup fine bulgur (crushed wheat) or commercially prepared *tabbouleh* mix *
2 fresh ripe but firm tomatoes, minced
1 sweet purple onion, minced
6 to 8 green onions, including tops, minced
2 celery stalks, minced
1 each red and green bell pepper, seeded and minced
2 small fresh hot chilies, seeds in, minced
1 cup minced fresh parsley
1 tablespoon minced fresh cilantro
2 tablespoons minced fresh mint (omit if using commercially prepared *tabbouleh* mix)
6 to 8 teeth of garlic, finely minced
1/3 cup fresh lemon juice
1 teaspoon sugar, or more to taste
1/3 cup olive oil
1/3 cup light-flavored vegetable oil
Salt, coarse-ground black pepper, and crushed dried hot chilies for additional heat, to taste

Put the bulgur in a bowl and pour over enough boiling water to cover completely. Let it soak for about 20 minutes or until all the moisture has been absorbed. (If using commercially prepared *tabbouleh* mix, follow the instructions on the package.)

Toss the bulgur lightly with all the remaining ingredients except the oils, salt, pepper, and additional chilies. Mix the oils together and stir in gradually. Adjust seasoning and chill. Serve as is or as individual servings. (I prefer to pile it onto a platter lined with curly endive or escarole, surround it with sliced tomatoes, cucumber, and purple onion rings and scatter black olives about, but don't let me push you into anything. I just don't think it's proper to come to table unless you are dressed for dinner.)

*You will find boxes of this where you find the *couscous* and pilaf, or in the bulk foods section.

GUACAMOLE SALAD
California-Mexican Cuisine

In the first section, I used guacamole and Gobba Ghannouj as party dips. They both make superb salads.

FOR EACH SERVING
Several small inner leaves from a head of romaine
1/3 cup Guacamole, page 18
3 or 4 slices each tomato and avocado
3 or 4 slices fresh mild to hot chili, preferably yellow, seeds removed
1 pickled *jalapeño* chili
Tortilla chips

Arrange the lettuce leaves on the salad plates. If they are a little large, snap off some of the white end, sliver it with a sharp knife, and pile it into the middle of the plate. Put the guacamole in the center of the plate. Arrange the tomato, avocado, and chili attractively around the edge. Add the pickled chili. Serve chilled, accompanied with a basket of tortilla chips.

GOBBA GHANNOUJ SALAD
Middle East

FOR EACH SERVING
A few leaves of curly endive or escarole
1/3 cup Gobba Ghannouj, page 19
3 to 4 slices each ripe tomato, cucumber, and seeded fresh chilies
6 black olives
1 lemon slice

Arrange the greens on individual salad plates. Mound the Gobba Ghannouj in the center. Place alternate slices of tomato, cucumber, and chili along one side. Intersperse the olives and top with the slice of lemon. Chill before serving. Accompany with French bread.

CAPSICUM SALAD
Family Recipe

Serves 4 to 6
1 large green bell pepper, seeded and sliced into thin strips
1 large red bell pepper, seeded and sliced into thin strips
2 long fresh mild chilies, seeded and cut into rings
3 small fresh hot chilies, seeded and cut into thin rings
1 sweet purple onion, peeled and cut into thin rings

One 4-ounce can diced peeled green chilies
1/2 cup julienne-cut lean cooked ham
1/2 cup julienne-cut Gruyère or Swiss cheese

DRESSING
4 teeth of garlic, crushed
1 small fresh hot chili, seeds in (optional)
1/3 cup vegetable oil
1/4 cup cider vinegar
1/8 to 1/4 teaspoon sugar
1/4 teaspoon mixed dried herbs (Italian seasoning)
3/4 teaspoon fresh dill weed, or 1/4 teaspoon dried
1/2 teaspoon Dijon mustard (the type with seeds)

Toss the first 8 ingredients together in a bowl and chill.

Put all the ingredients for the dressing into a blender and whir until creamy. Pour over the salad and toss lightly. Serve chilled, accompanied with a pepper mill, shakers of Parmesan cheese and pepper flakes, and a sour baguette.

POTATO-CAPSICUM SALAD
Family Recipe

Serves 8

6 large boiled potatoes, peeled
and cut into bite-sized slices
1 sweet purple onion, cut into
thin rings
1 green bell pepper, seeded and
cut into thin strips
1 red bell pepper, seeded and
cut into thin rings
2 small fresh hot chilies, cut into
thin rings
2 long fresh mild chilies, seeded
and cut into thin rings
1 teaspoon capers, drained
1/3 cup minced fresh parsley
2 celery stalks, trimmed and cut
across in thin slices

DRESSING
1/3 cup mayonnaise, page 142
4 teeth of garlic, crushed
1/3 cup hot or mild chunky salsa,
page 148
1 tablespoon sweet pickle relish

Combine the first 9 ingredients in
a large bowl. To make the dressing,
put the mayonnaise and garlic into
a blender and purée until the
garlic is incorporated. Stir in the

salsa and pickle relish. Pour over
the salad and toss lightly. Chill
before serving. Accompany with a
pepper mill and a shaker of crushed
dried hot chilies.

RAJMA-CHANA SALAT
India
Chick-pea and Bean Salad

Serves 8 to 10

1 cup each canned or cooked
chick-peas (garbanzos), small
white beans, black beans, small
red beans, and lentils, drained
and well rinsed
1 cup thawed frozen peas
1 cup yellow wax beans, canned,
fresh cooked or thawed frozen
4 to 6 green onions, cut into
2-inch pieces, including tops, then
split 4 to 6 times lengthwise
into slivers
1 medium sweet purple onion,
sliced into rings and the rings
cut in half
1/2 cup minced fresh parsley
1 tablespoon minced fresh cilantro
2 small fresh hot chilies, seeded
and cut into thin rings

1 small ripe lemon, sliced into
thin rings, seeded, and the rings
cut into quarters

DRESSING
1/4 cup light-flavored vegetable oil
1 tablespoon olive oil
2 tablespoons cider vinegar
1/2 teaspoon sugar
6 teeth of garlic, finely minced
1/2 teaspoon minced fresh ginger
1/4 teaspoon crushed dried hot
chilies
1/4 teaspoon ground cumin
1/8 teaspoon ground fenugreek
1/8 teaspoon anise seeds
1/4 teaspoon dry mustard
Salt and coarse-ground black pepper

Toss the chick peas, beans, lentils,
and all of the ingredients up to
and including the lemon together
and chill.

Put all of the ingredients for the
dressing into a jar with a tight lid
and shake vigorously. Set aside for
at least 2 hours, shaking occa-
asionally. Sprinkle the salad with
salt and pepper to taste and
sprinkle over the dressing. Toss
lightly and serve chilled. You may
wish to pile the salad into a bowl
or platter lined with escarole or
curly endive.

CURRIED RICE SALAD
Sri Lanka

Serves 8 as a starter, 6 as a meal
3 cups steamed long-grain white rice
1 large sweet purple onion, diced
4 celery stalks, diced
8 green onions, including tops,
  chopped small
1/2 cup chopped fresh mint leaves
1/4 cup minced candied orange peel
1/4 cup minced crystallized ginger
1/4 cup slivered blanched almonds
1 tablespoon sesame seeds
1/2 teaspoon anise seeds
1 teaspoon minced fresh cilantro
2 seedless oranges, separated into
  segments and cut into smaller
  than bite-sized pieces
1/2 teaspoon crushed dried
  hot chilies

DRESSING
1/3 cup frozen orange juice
  concentrate
1/2 cup plain yogurt
1 teaspoon finely grated fresh ginger
1 teaspoon curry powder
1/8 teaspoon cayenne
1/8 teaspoon ground coriander
1/8 teaspoon ground cinnamon

Oil for deep frying
2 eggs
1/8 teaspoon ground turmeric
1/8teaspoon ground cinnamon
1 teaspoon sugar
1 head curly endive, trimmed,
  washed, and drained
2 oranges, peeled and cut into rings
1 papaya, seeded and sliced thinly
1/2 cantaloupe or other small melon,
  seeded and cut into thin wedges
1 small sweet purple onion, cut
  into rings
Sprigs of mint

Mix the rice and all the ingredients up to and including the crushed chilies together and chill. Put all the ingredients for the dressing into the jar of a blender and whir until creamy. Refrigerate until ready to use.

Heat about 2 inches of oil in a wok or other heavy pan. Beat the eggs, turmeric, cinnamon, and sugar together well. When the oil is deep-frying temperature (375°), use your fingers to drizzle the egg mixture into the hot fat, probably in 2 or 3 different batches. As soon as the egg has solidified, but before it begins to brown, remove from the pan with a slotted spoon and drain on paper towels. Let cool. The appearance of the egg should be that of lace.

Line a serving platter with the lettuce. Pour the dressing into the rice mixture and toss gently. Pile this into the center of the lettuce-lined bowl. Surround with the cut fruits, sprinkle the egg/lace over the top, and garnish with the onion rings and sprigs of fresh mint. This is a most unusual combination of flavors. Do not expect it to taste like Grandma's Thanksgiving Day fruit salad. Accompany with a basket of fried flour tortillas, which are very similar to *chapatis.*

ABALONE SALAD
Japan

Serves 4 to 6
1 can abalone*
1 can smoked oysters*
One 6-1/2-ounce can minced or
  chopped clams
1-1/2 quarts water
1 bunch green onions, trimmed
  of roots but tops left on
2 cucumbers, cut into thin rings
1 small sweet purple onion, cut
  into thin rings

DRESSING
1 tablespoon *miso* paste (soy bean paste)
1/4 cup sake
1 scant teaspoon sugar
1/4 teaspoon cayenne, or to taste
4 teeth of garlic, finely minced
1/2 teaspoon finely grated fresh ginger
1/2 teaspoon sesame seeds
The reserved oyster oil and clam juice

Drain the abalone and cut into long, thin strips, julienne style. Drain the oysters and reserve the oil. Drain the clams and reserve the liquid. Bring the water to a rapid boil and plunge the green onions into this. Leave only until the water reboils. Drain immediately and put into cold running water until thoroughly cold. Drain.

Now, watch my lips. This is tricky. Pick up 1 green onion. At the point about 2 inches from the root end where the white begins to get green, bend the green back and wrap it around the white. When you run out of green, tuck the end under to secure. Continue with each onion. They should look sort of like little messy packages. Set aside.

To assemble, lay a double or triple row of the cucumber rings down the center of an oval or oblong serving platter. Lay a row of purple onion rings along each side of the cucumber slices. Place the green onions in a row down the center of the cucumbers. Lay the abalone spears in a criss-cross pattern over the whole. Strew the minced clams over all. Refrigerate until ready to serve.

Combine all the dressing ingredients and mix thoroughly until the *miso* is totally dissolved. Taste. Add more cayenne if you wish. Drizzle over the salad. Serve chilled.

*Abalone comes primarily in one size of can, which varies in ounces depending on the producer and the size of the abalones. The amount isn't critical. Canned smoked oysters almost always come in the same size of tin, which again can vary in weight.

ENSALADA DE NOPALITOS
Mexico
Cactus Leaf Salad

Serves 6 to 8
1 large jar (16 to 20 ounces) or two 10-ounce cans *nopalitos* (cactus leaves), drained and rinsed thoroughly under cold running water
3 large tomatoes, diced
1 cucumber, peeled and diced
1 red bell pepper, seeded and cut into thin strips
4 to 6 green onions, including tops, minced
1/2 sweet purple onion, cut into rings
1/2 tablespoon minced fresh cilantro
2 celery stalks, trimmed and chopped
2 small fresh hot chilies, seeded and sliced into thin rings

DRESSING
1/4 cup light-flavored vegetable oil
1/4 cup mild or hot chunky salsa, page 148
1/4 teaspoon coarse-ground black pepper
1/8 teaspoon ground cumin
4 teeth of garlic, finely minced
1/8 teaspoon dried oregano
Crushed dried hot chilies (optional)
Salt

Toss all the salad ingredients together in a large bowl and refrigerate. Put all the dressing ingredients into a jar with a tight lid and shake vigorously. If you want it hotter, add crushed chilies to taste. Add salt to taste. Pour over the salad and toss. Serve chilled.

BEAN CURD AND PEANUT SALAD
Thailand

Serves 4 to 6

2 eggs
1/4 teaspoon cayenne
1/2 tablespoon finely minced fresh parsley
Oil
1 cup 1/2-inch cubes bean curd (tofu)
1 cup coarsely chopped *kim chee* (pickled Chinese cabbage)
1 cup fresh bean sprouts
1/2 cup thinly sliced *daikon* (Japanese radish)
1/4 pound snow peas, trimmed and slivered lengthwise
A few thin purple onion rings
1/3 cup chopped roasted peanuts

DRESSING
1/4 cup light-flavored vegetable oil
1/4 cup white vinegar
1/4 cup minced fresh hot chilies
1/2 teaspoon grated fresh ginger
4 teeth of garlic, finely minced
3 tablespoons vinegar
Salt and coarse-ground black pepper to taste
Cayenne to taste (optional)

Beat the eggs, cayenne, and parsley together. Use this to make four thin rolled omelets in a lightly oiled skillet. When cool, sliver the omelets into thin strips. Set aside.

Toss all the remaining salad ingredients except the slivered egg, snow peas, onion rings, and peanuts together in a shallow bowl. Sprinkle the snow peas over the top, then scatter on the onion rings and the slivered egg. Sprinkle the peanuts over all.

Combine all the dressing ingredients in a blender, whir, and drizzle over the salad. Serve chilled.

LOMI-LOMI SALMON
Hawaii

Serves 4 to 6

1 pound beautiful, expensive fresh salmon
6 to 8 green onions, including tops, chopped
1 large sweet purple onion, diced
1/3 cup minced seeded fresh hot chilies
1 tablespoon *kaakuie* nut
Salt, coarse-ground black pepper, and crushed dried hot chilies to taste
2 large ripe tomatoes, diced

Remove any bones and skin from the salmon and dice small. Rinse thoroughly under cold running water. Drain. Combine with all the remaining ingredients except the tomatoes, and *lomi-lomi*. *Lomi-lomi* means to knead or massage. Do this gently to thoroughly incorporate the seasoning into the flesh of the fish, but not to make it into a mush. Add the tomatoes to the bowl and gently toss. This should be served exceedingly cold. I often put the bowl in the freezer until it is absolutely cold but not yet frozen. In Hawaii, the bowl is often served sitting in a tray of chipped ice.

NOTE: Don't panic if you have never heard of *kaakuie* nut. Shell some walnuts and toast slowly in the oven. Pound in a mortar and the result is almost identical.

FISH

When I bite into an oyster I taste all the sea has to offer. I see pirates and pearls, schooners and sea monsters; great crashing waves engulfing a jetty and silent, long, loan stretches of sand where the sea oozes landwards and then—with a sigh and a gentle hiss—rolls back to its bed. The sea was the beginning, and if we don't take steps to save it, it may be the end.

One of the aspects of a polluted world that I find the most disquieting is that we are hovering on the brink of the destruction of our precious seas. When this, the mother of all life on this planet is dead, what will be left?

Think of this when you spray your flies, think of this when you bait your snails, think of this when you wash your clothes, think of this when you vote, and think of life, if indeed there would be life, without the seas, without winter walks on windswept sands, without quiet together times on sunny beaches, without clamming, musseling, without sails on the bay, and Italian fishermen, clambakes, *cioppino*, cracked crab, and *sashimi*. What is a bagel without lox?

It may amaze you to know that I have met some people who do not like fish. I usually find that the only way they have ever consumed this wondrous class of victuals is the requisite Friday-evening hunk of dried-out fried fillet smeared with store-bought Tartar sauce. If that was the only fish I had ever eaten I probably wouldn't like it much either. I find the treasures of the deep among the most varied and versatile of all this earth's harvest, and my feelings are shared by the peoples of many cultures.

CLAMS WITH RICE
Galvanized Gullet Contribution

Galvanized Gullets crop up in the strangest places. How's 30,000 feet in the air for strange?

In my work I spend a lot of time flying. No matter what the ads say, airlines are pretty much the same. It's the law. International rulings very strictly regulate what can and can't be offered. Therefore the main difference is in the service and the attitudes of the ground and air crews. In my ten years as a professional food and travel writer I have run into service that ranged from royal to degrading.

In my experience two airlines stand head and shoulders, or should I say, wings and landing gear above the rest: Aloha Airlines, the inter-island transport in Hawaii, and British Airlines.

From the moment you approach the ticket desk until the muu-muu-clad stewardess sees you off the plane at one of the outer islands, you experience Hawaii's "aloha spirit." British Airlines, and I have flown with them in all classes, treats you with the courteous hospitality you are told you will find in a quaint English country inn. Old World hospitality and contempo-rary technology come together to make my flying time hassle-free and enjoyable.

Once, on striking up a conversation with my flight attendant, we discovered we shared a delight in hot foods and eagerly launched into discussion of our favorite dishes. Another member of the crew was hailed, who likewise confessed to being a hot-food junkie.

A while later the captain came to my seat and said, "I understand you collect recipes for hot foods. I just happen to have a few . . .", and seating himself next to me he plunged headlong into what was obviously a favorite subject, unfor-tunately, he explained, one not shared by his wife. He bestowed upon me five fine recipes, gathered from far-flung places he had visited during his career as a British Airlines pilot, before he grudgingly went back to relieve his co-pilot. I was richer by five excellent recipes and several new friends and Gal-vanized Gullet members. This recipe is one the captain shared with me.

Serves 4
4 dozen small clams
Four 6-1/2-ounce cans chopped clams
2 tablespoons olive oil
1 large onion, minced
4 teeth of garlic, minced
2 cups long-grain white rice
4 small fresh hot chilies, cut into thin rings
3 medium tomatoes, chopped
1 medium bell pepper, minced
3/4 teaspoon minced fresh dill weed, or 1/4 teaspoon dried
1 tablespoon crushed dried chilies
1 tablespoon sugar
2-1/2 cups light chicken broth
1/2 cup dry white wine
1/2 cup minced fresh parsley
2 tablespoons minced fresh cilantro
Salt and coarsely ground black pepper

Wash the whole clams and set aside. Open the cans of clams, drain, reserve the juice and set aside.

Heat the oil in a 5- to 6-quart casserole and sauté the onion and garlic over moderately high heat until the onions are translucent but not yet browned. Add the rice and cook for about 5 minutes, stirring frequently. Add the chilies, tomatoes, bell pepper, dill, crushed chilies, and sugar. Stir into the rice and cook, stirring often, for another 3 to 4 minutes. Add the broth, wine, and reserved clam juice and bring to a boil. Arrange the clams on top of the rice, cover with a tight-fitting lid and put in a preheated 350° oven for 30 to 45 minutes or until the clams are open, the liquid is mostly absorbed, and the rice is tender. Remove from the oven, stir in the canned clams, parsley, and cilantro. Add salt and pepper to taste, cover, and let sit for 5 minutes before serving.

OYSTERS JEAN LAFITTE
Cajun Cuisine
Baked Oysters
with Piquant Sauce

Like a lot of folk heroes, Jean Lafitte was in actuality a rather murderous scalawag, but to a downtrodden people, which the Cajuns were, he represented liberty, rebellion, and freedom of spirit. Is it any wonder that this lusty oyster creation, the product of Cajun artistry, was named in his honor?

Serves 6
1 cup butter
1/2 cup cooked and drained
   frozen spinach
1/4 cup each minced fresh watercress leaves, minced fresh basil
   leaves, minced fresh parsley, and
   minced celery
1/2 cup each minced green onion
   tops and minced onion
4 teeth of garlic, minced
1 small fresh hot chili, minced
1/4 teaspoon cayenne, or to taste
Salt and freshly ground black
   pepper to taste
1/2 cup shredded Swiss cheese
3 dozen fresh oysters in the shell
3 or 4 lean bacon strips

Put the butter in a saucepan and melt. Add all the remaining ingredients except the cheese, oysters, and bacon and simmer just until the greens are wilted and the onion soft. Put into a blender and whir until smooth.

Scrub the shells of the oysters and open. Cut the briny beast free from his home but return him to the deepest half of the shell. If there was any liquid in the shell, pour it into the blender. When finished, whir the ingredients in the blender once again and put a generous dollop on top of each oyster. If any of the mixture is left

over, spread on French bread and toast.

Cut the bacon crosswise into very fine strips. Sprinkle each osyter with a bit of cheese and add a few bits of bacon.

Put the oysters in a preheated 375° oven for about 10 minutes or just until the mixture begins to brown and bubble. Test one part-way through the baking. The size of the oyster will, of course, alter the cooking time, and you *do not* want them overdone. A well-done oyster is the texture of something between raw oatmeal, precipitated chalk, and peanut butter. Serve piping hot with French bread and a good beer.

NOTE: An easy trick for baking oysters in the half shell is to pour rock salt into a flat baking pan and then rest the oysters on this. It will keep them from toppling over. What kind of oysters should you use? Whatever kind you happen to like. I personally prefer the large Pacific oysters for any dish that is cooked, while I adore chucking the tiny Gulf or East Coast oysters down my throat raw.

BUDIN DE PESCADO Y MARISCO
Tehuantepec, Mexico
Shellfish Soufflé

Serves 6
One large cooked crab
1 pound cooked baby shrimp, or
    1/2 pound cooked shrimp and
    1/2 pound cooked scallops
3 tablespoons vegetable oil
1/2 cup minced onion
3 teeth of garlic, minced
1 small fresh hot chili, seeded
    and minced
2 cups milk
1 cup shredded Swiss cheese
1/2 cup ricotta
1/4 teaspoon fresh-ground black
    pepper
1/4 teaspoon dried oregano
1/8 teaspoon ground cumin
1/2 teaspoon sugar
4 eggs, separated
3 green onions, including tops,
    finely minced
1/3 cup hot or mild chunky salsa,
    page 148
1 teaspoon minced fresh cilantro
Cayenne to taste (optional)
Salt to taste
1 tablespoon minced fresh parsley
1 tablespoon grated Parmesan
    cheese
1 teaspoon paprika

Crack and clean the crab (see page 14) and remove the meat. Mince the shellfish finely and set in the refrigerator until needed. Heat the oil in a heavy pan and gently sauté the onion, garlic, and chili until soft but not yet beginning to brown. Remove from the heat. Put the milk and cheeses into a blender and whir. Add the onion mixture, black pepper, oregano, cumin, sugar, and egg yolks and whir again. Pour into a large bowl. Add the green onions, salsa, cilantro, and shellfish. Stir well and add salt to taste. If you want it hotter, very gradually add cayenne. Beat the egg whites until stiff but not dry and gently fold into the milk mixture. Pour into an oiled 2-quart soufflé pan.

Toss the parsley, Parmesan cheese, and paprika together and sprinkle over the top. Put into a preheated 350° oven and bake for 30 minutes or until high, fluffy and golden brown. Test with a bamboo skewer. Serve immediately. Like all soufflés, the elements are out to get you. It will probably fall between the time you take it from the oven and walk it to the table. Don't panic. It will still taste good. And never admit to anything less than perfection. No matter what happens, that's the way it was supposed to be, right? After all, how many of your guests have ever been to Tehuantepec? Tell them *flat* is a characteristic of the *budins* in that region!

END-OF-THE-CATCH PIE
Cajun Cuisine
Fish and Shellfish Pie

Serves 6 to 8
2 tablespoons lard or bacon
    drippings
2 tablespoons flour
2 large cooked crabs
1 pound prawns
2 dozen mussels, if in season (see
    mussel warning on page 13)
1 pint oysters, drained
1 pound scallops
2 tablespoons fresh lemon juice
1/2 teaspoon coarsely ground
    black pepper
3/4 teaspoon minced fresh dill
    weed, or 1/4 teaspoon dried
2 small hot chilies, chopped
1/4 cup minced fresh parsley
1/2 cup fresh or canned chopped
    okra
1 tablespoon vegetable oil
1 large onion, chopped
8 teeth of garlic, minced
4 large tomatoes, diced
4 green onions, including tops,
    chopped small
2 celery stalks, diced

1 medium bell pepper, diced
1/2 teaspoon mixed dried herbs
   (Italian seasoning)
1/4 teaspoon ground nutmeg
1 teaspoon sugar
Salt to taste
Crushed dried hot chilies (optional)
1 recipe pastry, page 113
1 egg white

"First you make de roux." Put the lard or fat into a heavy pan, and over high heat add the flour and stir rapidly until it begins to bubble. Immediately reduce the heat to the lowest setting and continue cooking, stirring constantly, until the mixture is nut brown. (It takes ages.) Scrape into a small bowl and set aside. Since a roux is elemental to Cajun and Creole cookery, you may want to make up more of it and keep it in the refrigerator for future use. It keeps indefinitely. Use the same recipe no matter how much you are making: equal amounts of fat and flour, cooked slowly while stirring until it is a deep nut brown.

Set the roux aside and prepare the shellfish. Crack and clean the crabs (see page 14). Take the meat out of the body and smaller legs of the crabs and put into a bowl. Reserve the large legs and claws. Shell the prawns but leave their tails on. Drop the mussels into a large pan of boiling water and leave just until they begin to open. Remove to cold water and, when cool enough to handle, shuck and add to the other seafood in the bowl. Save 6 of the shells that are still hooked together. Drain the oysters and add with the scallops to the other shellfish. Sprinkle over the lemon juice, pepper, dill weed, fresh chilies, and parsley. Stir and refrigerate until needed.

If you are using fresh okra, wash well in cold water, drain, and slice into rings. Blanch for 3 to 4 minutes and set aside. If using canned okra, rinse well in a strainer and set aside.

Heat the tablespoon of oil in a heavy skillet over moderate heat and add the onion and garlic. Sauté lightly until the onion is translucent but not yet browned. Add the tomatoes and stir for about a minute. Then add the green onions, celery, and bell pepper. Stir well. Add herbs, nutmeg, and sugar. Stir well and continue cooking for another 2 or 3 minutes. Add salt to taste and adjust seasoning to your liking. If you want it hotter at this point, gradually add crushed chilies. Add 1/8 teaspoon at a time, stir, and continue cooking for another minute. Taste and repeat if more hotness is desired.

Scrape the roux into the sauce, stir well, and continue cooking at a rapid simmer until a thick sauce is formed, about 10 more minutes.

To assemble, roll out the pastry and line a 9-inch pie pan. Add all the shellfish except the large claws and legs of the crabs and all but 6 or 8 of the prawns to the sauce and stir gently. Add the okra. Remove from the fire and, when somewhat cooled, pour the mixture into the pie shell. Cover with the top crust and crimp down. Lightly beat the egg white and paint the surface of the pastry with it. Now, with a small sharp knife, make a slit in the pastry for each of the remaining prawns. Insert a prawn into each slit, pushing it down into the pie ingredients below the pastry but letting the tail and about 1/2 to 1 inch of the prawn stick up. Do the same for the crab claws and legs and for the 6 mussel shells.

Put into a 500° oven for 2 minutes. Then reduce the heat to 350° and continue baking for about 30 minutes or until the crust is golden brown and flaky. Served hot it is superb, but it's also worth more than a kick in the shins if you serve it cold with mustard and pickles and good beer on a hot, hot day.

ESCABECHE
Philippines
Spiced Pickled Fish

Serves 4

One 2-1/2- to 3-pound firm-fleshed
    white fish
2 tablespoons butter
2 tablespoons vegetable oil
6 teeth of garlic, cut into thin
    slivers
1 tablespoon grated fresh ginger
4 small fresh hot chilies, cut into
    thin rings
1/2 teaspoon mixed pickling spices
1 large onion, cut into approxi-
    mately 1/8-inch-thick slices
1 each red and green bell pepper,
    cut into rings and seeded
1/2 cup cider vinegar
1/3 cup dark brown sugar
1/2 tablespoon cornstarch
1/2 cup water
Salt, coarse-ground black pepper,
    and cayenne to taste
Watercress or parsley sprigs
    (optional)

Have the butcher clean and scale
the fish but leave the head, tail,
and fins on. Wash thoroughly
inside and out and pat dry. With a
sharp knife, cut off the head and
tail and cut the remaining body
into 1-inch-thick steaks. Reassemble
the fish to look as if it were still
whole on a heatproof serving platter.

Place the platter in a bamboo
steamer over a wok and steam
over high heat until done, approximately 20 minutes. Keep warm.

Melt the butter and oil together
in a heavy skillet over moderate
heat and add the garlic, ginger,
chilies, and pickling spices. Sauté
gently, stirring all the while, until
the garlic and chilies are soft but
not browned. Add all the remaining
ingredients except the cornstarch,
water, seasonings, and garnish,
and cook for no more than 5
minutes or until the vegetables are
just soft, stirring gently and being
careful not to mash the vegetables.
Taste and adjust seasoning. Mix
the cornstarch and water together
and add to the skillet. Continue
cooking, stirring very gently until
the sauce is thickened, translucent,
and glossy.

Remove the vegetables with a
slotted spoon and slip them alternately between the slices of fish.
Pour the sauce over and, if desired,
garnish with fresh watercress or
parsley. Serve hot.

KAN SHAO HSIA JEN
China
Stir-fried Fish with Peppers

Serves 6

2 pounds firm-fleshed white fish
    fillets
2 tablespoons peanut oil
2 tablespoons soy sauce
2 tablespoons rice wine or dry
    sherry
1 tablespoon grated fresh ginger
6 teeth of garlic, finely minced
1/2 teaspoon crushed dried hot
    chilies
1 tablespoon tomato paste
1 teaspoon sugar
6 small fresh hot chilies, seeded
    and cut into thin rings
1 small red bell pepper, seeded
    and cut into thin rings
4 green onions, including the tops,
    cut into 2-inch lengths
1 celery stalk, cut on the diagonal
    into half-inch chunks
1 tablespoon cornstarch dissolved in
    1/4 cup chicken broth

Cut the fish into bite-sized chunks.
Put the oil in a large wok or skillet
and place over high heat until the
oil is very hot. A few at a time, fry
the chunks of fish in the hot oil.
Gently toss for about 2 minutes,
being careful not to break them

apart. Remove the fish from the pan with a slotted spoon and drain on paper towels or a wire rack.

To the oil in the pan add the soy sauce and wine. Stir. Add the next 5 ingredients and toss for about 2 minutes. Add the fresh chilies, bell pepper, green onions, and celery and stir-fry until the vegetables are heated through but not wilted. Pour in the cornstarch and broth, toss lightly, and continue cooking, tossing gently until the sauce is thickened and glossy. Return the fish to the wok and toss gently to coat evenly. Cook, tossing gently but being careful not to break the fish apart, for another 2 minutes. Serve on a bed of steamed rice.

I once judged a dolmas *competition, and when biting into one of the entries I chipped a tooth. The contestant who had created that dish looked astounded and said, "But the recipe didn't* say *to shell the pine nuts." So, in the interest of dental health, please: all nuts in these recipes are* shelled.

CARURU
Brazil
Shrimp and Fish
with Okra and Peanuts

This dish can be traced to its African origins through its use of okra and peanuts, both originating on that continent.

Serves 6
1 coconut
1 cup boiling water
Liquid from coconut
2 tablespoons butter
2 tablespoons vegetable oil
2 pounds shelled prawns, tails left on
2 pounds firm-fleshed white fish cut into bite-sized chunks
1 medium onion, chopped
6 teeth of garlic, minced
1 medium bell pepper, chopped
2 large tomatoes, diced
3 small fresh hot chilies, minced
1/2 cup roasted peanuts, coarsely ground
1 tablespoon finely minced cilantro
1 cup sliced and blanched fresh or thawed frozen okra
Salt and coarse-ground black pepper to taste
4 cups hot steamed rice
Molho de Pimenta e Limao, page 146

Open the coconut and make coconut milk according to instructions on page 13. Add the liquid from the coconut, if necessary, to make 1-1/2 cups of coconut milk.

In a heavy skillet or wok, melt the butter and oil and, a few at a time, fry the prawns, tossing them until pink, about 2 or 3 minutes. Do the same for the fish, being careful not to break it apart. Set aside to drain.

Add the onion, garlic, and pepper to the oil and butter and sauté gently until the onion is translucent but not browned. Add the tomatoes, chilies, and coconut milk and stir. Reduce the heat to moderate and continue cooking for about 30 minutes or until the tomatoes and coconut milk have reduced to produce a sauce. Stir in the peanuts, cilantro, and okra and cook for another 5 minutes. Return the shrimp and fish and stir gently just until all is heated through. Season with salt and pepper. Mound the rice into a heated serving dish and pour the *carurú* over. Serve hot with Molho de Pimenta e Limao.

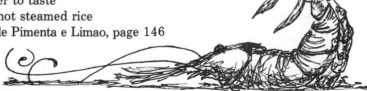

POACHED SHARK STEAKS
with PIQUANT MAYONNAISE
Family Recipe

This recipe isn't really a salad, but it certainly is a refreshing and delightful dish to serve when the temperatures soar and no one really feels like a bowl of chili or chicken and dumplings. This is another dish that is not only easy on heat-frayed palates, but gentle on the cook.

Serves 6
1 tablespoon vegetable oil
1/4 cup distilled vinegar
1 bay leaf
Six 1-inch-thick shark steaks

MAYONNAISE
1 cup mayonnaise, page 142
1/2 cup hot chunky-style salsa, page 148
4 teeth of garlic, finely minced
2 green onions, including tops, minced
1/2 teaspoon minced fresh cilantro
1-1/2 teaspoons minced fresh dill weed, or 1/2 teaspoon dried
2 tablespoons minced fresh parsley

Bibb lettuce leaves
Dijon mustard
Lemon slices
Tomato slices
Sliced hard-cooked eggs
Pitted black olives

Put 1 inch of water in a large skillet, add the oil, vinegar, and bay leaf and bring to a boil. Gently slide in the shark steaks. Let the water return to the boil, reduce the heat to maintain a simmer, and cover with a tight-fitting lid. Poach the fish in this fashion for 8 to 10 minutes, or until the steaks are done through but not falling apart. Slice into one with the tip of a sharp knife; it should be white all the way through.

When done, remove the fish from the water, rinse under cold running water, and let drain. Refrigerate.

Mix all the ingredients for the mayonnaise together well with a fork; do not use a blender or food processor. The mixture should not be homogeneous. Chill.

Put one or two leaves of bibb lettuce on each of 6 salad plates. Add a poached shark steak to each. Put a dollop of the piquant mayonnaise on each steak and spread to cover the surface. Put a dollop of Dijon mustard on each steak. Arrange the slices of lemon, tomato, and egg to form an attractive pattern, and finish with an olive or two. You may prefer to use watercress instead of bibb lettuce. Chill before serving.

PAKKI HUI MACHLI
India
Whole Stuffed Fish
with Coriander Sauce

Serves 6 to 8

STUFFING
2 cups cooked long-grain white rice
1 large onion, diced
6 teeth of garlic, minced
1 teaspoon minced fresh ginger
2 small fresh hot chilies, minced
1/2 cup minced fresh parsley
1/2 tablespoon minced fresh cilantro
1/2 teaspoon sugar
3 eggs
Salt and pepper to taste

One 4-pound sole, flounder, turbot or other firm-fleshed white fish, with head, tail, and fins

FISH

SAUCE

2 tablespoons vegetable oil
2 tablespoons butter
8 teeth of garlic, minced
2 small fresh hot chilies, minced
1 tablespoon minced fresh ginger
1/2 teaspoon each ground
   coriander, ground turmeric, dry
   mustard, ground fenugreek, and
   ground cinnamon
1/4 teaspoon each ground cumin
   and ground cardamom
1/8 teaspoon ground cloves
1 large onion, minced
4 large tomatoes, diced
1 cup minced green onions,
   including tops
2 tablespoons minced fresh cilantro
1/3 cup fresh lemon juice
1/4 cup vegetable oil
1 tablespoon sugar
Salt, fresh-ground black pepper,
   and cayenne to taste

1 egg
2 hard-cooked eggs
1 bunch watercress
1 medium tomato, sliced thin
1 lemon, sliced thin
1 tablespoon minced fresh cilantro

Mix all the stuffing ingredients together in a bowl and set aside. Have the butcher clean and scale the fish but make sure the head, tail and fins are left on. Wash the fish well inside and out and pat dry. Pack firmly with the stuffing and truss shut. Place in a baking dish with a tight-fitting lid.

To make the sauce, heat the oil and butter together over moderate heat. Add the garlic, chilies, herbs, and spices and, stirring constantly, cook for 5 minutes. Add the onion, tomatoes, green onion, cilantro, lemon juice, oil, sugar, and seasonings and, stirring frequently, cook for an additional 10 minutes. Cool slightly, put into a blender, and whir until smooth.

Pour over the fish, cover with the lid, and put in a preheated 350° oven for 30 to 45 minutes. Remove from the oven occasionally and baste the fish with some of the sauce in the bottom of the dish. Remove the fish from the oven, transfer to a heatproof serving dish, and slide under the broiler for just a moment or two.

Beat the raw egg lightly and pour it into a lightly oiled omelet pan over moderate heat. When it has formed a skin on the bottom but is not dry, start at one side and roll into a long omelet. Remove to a flat cutting surface and let cool. Remove the whites from the hard-cooked eggs and chop fine. Put the yolks through a sieve using the back of a spoon to produce a pile of yellow fluffy powder.

Surround the fish with the watercress. Arrange the slices of tomato and lemon alternately among the cress. Slice the omelet roll thinly and sprinkle down the center of the fish. Arrange the egg whites around this. Sprinkle the entire fish with the cilantro.

Put the baking pan on the top of the stove over a moderate heat, add the powdered egg yolks and, stirring all the while, bring to a simmer. Scrape into a small serving bowl and serve as an accompaniment to the fish.

JAMBALAYA
Cajun
Rice and Seafood Pottage

Serves 8
2 large cooked crabs
Chicken broth
1 bay leaf (optional)

1/4 cup vegetable oil
1 large onion, chopped
6 green onions, including tops,
    chopped
3 celery stalks, chopped
1 large bell pepper, seeded and
    chopped
8 teeth of garlic, minced
1/2 teaspoon crushed dried hot
    chilies, or to taste
1/4 teaspoon coarse-ground black
    pepper
1/2 teaspoon sugar
3/4 teaspoon fresh dill weed, or
1/4 teaspoon dried
1/2 teaspoon mixed dried herbs
    (Italian seasoning)
1 cup long-grain rice
2 pounds cooked and cleaned
    shrimp*
2 pounds small fresh clams
1/2 cup minced fresh parsley
1 teaspoon minced fresh cilantro
Salt and coarsely ground black
    pepper
Cayenne (optional)

Crack and shell the crabs (see page 14). Reserve the meat. Do not throw away the liquid and butter from the body cavity. Pound the shells and place with the liquid and crab butter in a large pan. Add enough water to completely cover the shells and bring to a rapid boil. Reduce the heat to a high simmer, cover with a tight-fitting lid, and continue to cook for 45 minutes to 1 hour. Strain through soft muslin and save the liquid. Measure and, if necessary, add enough chicken broth to make 4 cups of liquid. You may add a bay leaf to the crab shells during the boiling if you wish.

In the meantime, heat the oil in a large heavy pan or casserole and add the vegetables, garlic, chilies, pepper, sugar, and herbs. Sauté for about 3 minutes, or until the vegetables are soft but not yet beginning to brown. Add the rice and stir to coat evenly with the oil.

Pour over the 4 cups of the water the shells were boiled in. Bring to a boil, reduce the heat to simmer, cover with a tight-fitting lid, and cook for an additional 30 minutes, or until the rice is almost tender but still *al dente*. It should still have just a bit of tooth.

When the rice is ready stir in the reserved crab meat, shrimp, clams, parsley, and cilantro. Add salt and pepper to taste and additional cayenne if desired. Cover and continue to simmer just until the clams have opened and the rice is tender. It will still be a little soupy. Serve from the casserole or mound into a large deep serving dish that has been heated.

NOTE: In bayou country this dish is *HOT,* and those who consume it are true candidates for admission into the Galvanized Gullet. However, if you haven't spent your days wrestling 'gaters you may prefer this somewhat tamer version. Like almost all the recipes you find here, if you want it several degrees hotter, please, be my guest.

*I didn't realize the term "shrimp" was at all ambiguous until I started traveling. In England what we call "baby shrimp" are called prawns and the critter we call a rather smallish prawn is labeled "scampi." In bayou country, what I was used to seeing labeled as jumbo-giant prawns, they called "little ol' shrimp"!

The Visigoths demanded a ransom of three thousand pounds of pepper to raise the siege of Rome.

TEESRYO
Indian
Steamed Curried Clams

Serves 6
2 tablespoons butter
2 tablespoons vegetable oil
2 large onions, cut into very thin
  rings
2 small fresh hot chilies, cut into
  thin rings
1 tablespoon grated fresh ginger
1/2 teaspoon ground coriander
1/2 teaspoon ground turmeric
1/8 teaspoon ground cinnamon
1/8 teaspoon ground cardamom
1/4 teaspoon cayenne
1/3 cup shredded fresh coconut
  (see page 13)
1/4 cup fresh lemon juice
1/2 teaspoon minced fresh cilantro
1/2 teaspoon sugar
Salt to taste
6 dozen small clams, well scrubbed
Cilantro sprigs and lemon slices
  for garnish

Over a high flame, heat the butter
and oil together in a large heavy
pan or wok with a tight-fitting lid.
Add the onions and fresh chilies
and sauté until the onions are
translucent but not browned. Add
the next 9 ingredients and toss
with the onions and chilies for
about 2 minutes. Reduce the heat
to a simmer and add the sugar
and salt to taste. Add the clams
and cover with a tight-fitting lid.
Steam for 8 to 10 minutes or until
the clams open.

With a slotted spoon, remove
the clams to a deep serving dish.
Turn up the flame and, stirring
briskly, cook the juices in the pan
for about 1 minute. Pour over the
clams. Garnish with cilantro and
lemon and serve immediately.

BAKED CHEESE
WITH SEAFOOD STUFFING
Family Recipe

Serves 6 as an entrée,
12 to 15 as a party nibble
One 4-pound Edam cheese
1/2 pound cooked baby shrimp
1/2 pound cooked crab meat
1 tablespoon butter
1 tablespoon vegetable oil
1 large onion, minced
1/2 cup minced mushrooms
1/4 cup minced fresh parsley
1/4 cup cream sherry
1/4 teaspoon cayenne
1/4 teaspoon coarse-ground black
  pepper
2 tablespoons cornstarch
Salt and cayenne

Cut a slice about 1 inch thick from
the top of the cheese. With a
spoon, scoop out the inside of the
cheese, leaving a shell approximately 1/2 inch thick all around.
Do the same with the top. Set
aside.

Shred enough of the cheese (on
the large holes of a grater) removed
from the inside of the cheese to
make 2 cups and reserve. Mince
the shrimp and crab meat and set
aside.

In a heavy skillet, melt the
butter and oil together over moderate heat. Add the onion and
sauté until translucent but not
browned. Add the mushrooms,
parsley, sherry, cayenne, and pepper.
Sauté gently until the vegetables
are soft but not browned.

In a bowl, toss the cheese with
the cornstarch and add the shrimp,
crab, and vegetable mixture. Add
salt and more cayenne to taste
and pile into the cheese shell. Put
on the lid and set in an oiled
heatproof serving dish. Bake for
about 30 minutes in a 350° oven.
Serve immediately, accompanied
with fondue forks and a basket of
cubes of French bread for dunking.

CEVICHE
Mexico

We have our Mexican neighbors to thank for this delectable host- or hostess-saver. *Ceviche* is one of those dishes that is easy on the cook when temperatures soar, while tempting heat-frayed appetites.

Serves 6 as an entrée or
12 as a party nibble
2 pounds raw firm-fleshed boneless fish or shellfish (butterfish, sole, salmon, scallops, shrimp, or a combination)
2/3 cup fresh lime juice
1 sweet purple onion, half diced and half sliced into thin rings
1 large or 2 small tomatoes, diced
4 green onions, including tops, chopped small
1 small bell pepper, seeded and cut into thin strips
1 to 4 small fresh hot chilies, depending on desired hotness, minced
4 teeth of garlic, minced
1 teaspoon minced fresh cilantro
1/8 teaspoon ground cumin
1/2 teaspoon sugar
1/4 teaspoon coarse-ground black pepper
Salt to taste

Dice the fish into smaller than bite-sized pieces. If the scallops are large, cut in half. Shell the shrimp or prawns. If large, cut into pieces the size of the fish (remember, all this is raw. *Ceviche* is sort of a Mexican *sashimi*). Put into a bowl and cover with the lime juice. Mix thoroughly and refrigerate. Add the vegetables to the fish, add the herbs and spices, season to taste with salt, and refrigerate for at least 1 hour. Taste and, if you want more hotness, add more fresh chilies at this time. Serve chilled.

NOTE: In some regions of Mexico things like clams and cooked baby shrimp are added to the raw fish. This is a dish that can cost as much or as little as you wish.

RUTH'S RECIPE
Family Recipe
Seafood, Chicken, and Rice

Although a quarter of a century my senior, I could never think of Ruth, my ex-mother-in-law, as anything but my contemporary. She never quit learning and never quit teaching. Her educational process took her from rural America to the theaters of London, New York and San Francisco, the galleries of Paris, the kibbutzim of Israel, the sacred burial grounds of India, and along the Great Wall of China. From the pyramids along the Nile to the pyramids of the Yucatán, Ruth was busy feeding her insatiable thirst for knowledge.

A superb cook, part of her travel experiences and educational process was learning the cuisines of the people and places she visited and sharing them with people at home. Here is a zesty New World form of Spanish *paella* that Ruth shared with me after one of her adventures.

Serves 10
1/4 cup olive oil
6 chorizos
1 cup diced lean cooked ham
12 chicken drumsticks
1 large onion, chopped
10 teeth of garlic, minced
4 small fresh hot chilies, minced
1 large tomato, diced
1 each large green and red bell pepper, seeded and cut into thin strips
1/4 teaspoon ground cumin
1/2 teaspoon coarse-ground black pepper

Crushed dried hot chilies to taste
(optional)
1/2 teaspoon saffron
2 cups long-grain white rice
About 6 cups light chicken broth
1 pound cooked baby shrimp
1/2 cup minced fresh parsley
1 tablespoon minced fresh cilantro
1 large crab, cooked and cleaned
12 prawns
12 clams
12 mussels (see warning on
page 13)
1/2 cup thawed frozen peas
2 lemons, cut into wedges

In a large *paella* pan, heavy skillet, or wok with a tight-fitting lid, heat the olive oil. Sauté the chorizos only until browned on all sides. Next brown the ham, then the chicken drumsticks. Set aside. Add the onion, garlic, and chilies to the oil and sauté just until the onions are pink and translucent but not yet browned. Add the tomato and stir the mixture until it begins to form a sauce. Next add the bell peppers, cumin, black pepper, and dried chilies, if desired. Continue cooking over moderate heat for about 5 minutes. Add the saffron and stir.

Turn up the heat and add the rice, stirring to coat it evenly with the oil and tomato/chili sauce. Add the baby shrimp, parsley, and cilantro and toss gently. Pour over enough light chicken broth to reach about 1 inch above the surface of the rice. Continue cooking over high heat until the stock has evaporated to just the level of the surface of the rice. While the stock is evaporating, break the legs off the crab and break the body of the crab into chunks; arrange on top of the rice. Cut the chorizos in half and push each chunk down into the rice. Do the same with the chicken legs, prawns, clams, and mussels. Scatter the peas about the top and randomly arrange the lemon wedges.

As soon as the level of the broth has just barely evaporated to the level of the surface of the rice, cover with a tight-fitting lid, reduce the heat to the lowest setting and leave 30 to 45 minutes, or until the rice is tender. Fluff the rice with a fork, and serve immediately from the pan it was cooked in, accompanied with rich-flavored Mexican beer, and good friends.

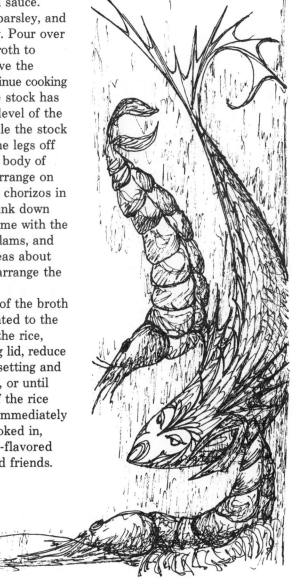

BEEF

It has taken me a long time to come to terms with the fact that by eating meat I am depriving a fellow inhabitant of this planet of its life to make mine a little more enjoyable. People do not need nearly as much meat in their diet as those of us living in western cultures consume, but neither do I think we were intended to do without it totally.

Even though I have been a vegetarian and am still very much in sympathy with those who withhold meat from their diets for either moral or health reasons, I do detest the professional big V vegetarian. A friend of mine had (and I stress the *had)* a wife who wouldn't kiss him for twenty-four hours after he had eaten a Big Mac. This woman was at a party at my house one time and, picking up a cookie, asked if it had been near any meat product during its preparation. "No," answered another friend, "but it was baked in a gas oven. You know, a fossil fuel. Just think of all those poor little pterodactyls and brontosauruses that gave up their lives to cook your cookie!"

And so, from a born-again carnivore, here are the delights of flesh prepared by meat eaters around the world; meat eaters who like it hot!

WOK MEAT
Family Recipe

This is not specifically an Oriental dish. My sons invented it several years ago. Between then and now it has gone through changes and refinements, becoming one of our favorite family dishes, something we serve when there's a flick on the telly that keeps us away from the dining table. (We are addicted Bogey and Hepburn fans. We'll even give up chocolate mousse for *Casablanca*.)

Serves 6
1-1/2 to 2 pounds lean tender beef
1/4 cup light-flavored vegetable oil
1 each medium red and green bell pepper, seeded and sliced into thin rings
10 teeth of garlic, minced
2 large onions, sliced into thin rings
2 small fresh hot chilies, sliced into thin rings (add more if you want more fire)

2 cups sliced mushrooms
1/2 cup tomato catsup
1/2 cup soy sauce
1/3 to 1/2 cup dark brown sugar, or to taste
1 teaspoon mixed dried herbs (Italian seasoning)
1/2 teaspoon coarsely ground black pepper
Salt to taste

Partially freeze the beef. This will enable you to slice it exceedingly thin. With a *sharp* knife, slice the beef across the grain as thin as possible. Then cut the slices into strips about 1/2 inch wide.

Put the wok or large frying pan over a high flame and add the oil. When the oil is almost smoking, add the strips of beef a few at a time and toss about until just seared, only a minute or two for each handful. As each batch is done, remove with a slotted spoon and set aside.

Add the red and green bell peppers and toss until just hot through. Remove with a slotted spoon and set aside. Add the garlic to the pan and sauté for 1 minute. Then add the onions and chilies and sauté until limp. Add the mushrooms and toss gently. Add next 5 ingredients and toss. Return the meat to the wok and reduce the heat to a high simmer. Cook uncovered until a thick sauce results, about 10 minutes. Return the bell peppers to the wok during the last 2 or 3 minutes of cooking time. You want them done but not dead. Add salt to taste.

Place the wok in the middle of the table and accompany with baguettes and lots of paper napkins. Your guests may slice chunks of baguette in half and make sandwiches of this savory, saucy beef. Sometimes my boys serve it with a pile of hot and steamy flour tortillas and let everyone make their own pseudo-burritos, and other times they serve it with pita bread. Any way you serve it, it's yummers. The whole point is, it's not much work and there are no dishes but the wok.

"Upon what meat doth this our Caesar feed, that he is grown so great?"
—Julius Caesar, *Act I, scene ii*

SIK SIK WAT
Ethiopia
Hotter-Than-Hell Beef
and Pepper Stew

Serves 8

20 small dried hot chilies
2-1/2 to 3 pounds boneless beef
1/4 cup peanut oil
10 to 12 teeth of garlic, minced
2 large onions, cut into thin rings
4 small fresh hot chilies, cut into
    thin rings
1 teaspoon crushed dried hot chilies
1 tablespoon grated fresh ginger
1/4 teaspoon ground fenugreek
1/8 teaspoon ground cloves
    (optional; it's traditional but
    I always leave them out)
1/2 teaspoon ground cinnamon
1/4 teaspoon each ground nutmeg,
    cardamom, and coriander
2 tablespoons paprika
1/4 cup Berberé, page 146
2 large ripe tomatoes
1/2 cup dry full-bodied red wine
1/3 to 1/2 cup sugar
1 teaspoon coarsely ground black
    pepper
Salt to taste
1 tablespoon minced fresh cilantro
    and 2 lemons cut in wedges
    for garnish

Put the whole dried chilies in a
bowl and pour boiling water over
them. Leave for an hour, drain, and
repeat. Leave to soak the second
time until you are ready to use
them. Then drain.

Trim the beef of excess fat and
cut into paper-thin strips about 1
inch wide and 2 inches long. Heat
the oil in a large heavy pan or
casserole over moderate heat. Add
the meat and toss about just until
all the pieces are seared. Remove
and set aside. Add the garlic,
onions, and chilies and sauté until
soft but not browned.

Add the ingredients up to and
including *berberé* and, stirring constantly, cook for 2 minutes. Add
all the remaining ingredients except
the garnish, stir, and reduce the
heat to a fast simmer. Cook for 1
to 1-1/2 hours or until the beef is
exceedingly tender. Stir occasionally
to prevent sticking. Taste for salt
and seasonings about halfway
through the cooking and adjust to
your taste.

To serve, line a shallow basket
or serving platter with overlapping
injera (see recipe, page 138) or
large flour tortillas. Pour in the
stew and sprinkle with the minced
cilantro and garnish with the lemon
wedges. Set the basket or platter
in the middle of the table. *Wat* is
traditionally eaten with the hands
by tearing off pieces of the *injera*
and wrapping it around the meat.

PIONONOS
Puerto Rico
Deep-Fried Stuffed Plantains

Serves 6

4 large plantains (no you *can*
    not substitute bananas!)
2 tablespoons butter
4 tablespoons light-flavored
    vegetable oil
1 large onion, chopped
4 teeth of garlic, minced
1 medium bell pepper, chopped
    (preferably red)
2 or more small fresh hot chilies,
    minced
1-1/2 pounds ground lean beef
2 tablespoons flour
1 teaspoon ground turmeric
1 teaspoon mixed dried herbs
    (Italian seasoning)
1/2 teaspoon paprika
1/2 cup minced fresh parsley
2 large tomatoes, chopped
1/2 teaspoon or more coarsely
    ground black pepper
2 tablespoons dark brown sugar
2 tablespoons distilled vinegar
1 cup finely diced lean cooked ham
Oil for deep frying
4 eggs, beaten

Peel the plantains and cut lengthwise into 4 strips. In a heavy
skillet, melt the butter and 2
tablespoons of the oil together.
When the butter is melted and

incorporated with the oil but not browned, add the plantains, a few at a time. Cook them for about 3 minutes, turning with large chopsticks or a slotted spoon or tongs. When they are golden brown, set aside to drain on paper towels.

Using the same skillet, add the remaining 2 tablespoons of oil and, when hot, sauté the onion, garlic, pepper, and chilies just until the onions are translucent but not yet browned. Add the meat and stir briskly to break apart. The meat should be cooked only until no pink shows. Add the flour and stir until thoroughly incorporated. Add all the remaining ingredients except the frying oil and eggs. Stir, reduce the heat to a fast simmer, and continue to cook, stirring, until the mixture thickens enough to hold its shape if you press it together. Remove from heat and allow to cool enough to handle.

Make each strip of fried plantain into a ring, overlapping the ends slightly and securing with a wooden toothpick. Spoon the beef mixture into the center of each plantain ring and, using your hands, pack it firmly.

Heat enough oil for deep-frying in your favorite frying container.

(I always use a wok.) Using a slotted spoon, dip each *pionono* into the beaten egg to coat evenly, then slide carefully into the hot oil. If it browns too quickly, reduce the heat slightly.

GOMEN SEGA
Ethiopia
Beef and Mustard Greens

Serves 6 to 8
2 tablespoons lard
3 pounds boneless chuck
2 large onions, sliced into thin rings
6 teeth of garlic, minced
1 each medium green and red bell pepper, seeded and cut into thin strips
1/2 teaspoon minced fresh ginger
1/4 teaspoon ground turmeric
1/8 teaspoon each ground cardamom, cinnamon, and nutmeg
1 whole clove
1/4 teaspoon coarsely ground black pepper
1 cup beef broth
8 to 10 small fresh hot chilies
2 medium leeks, cut into 2-inch lengths including 4 inches of the greens, and washed exceedingly well
2 pounds fresh mustard greens, including the blossoms, if any
Salt to taste
Injera, page 138

Melt the lard in a large skillet or wok. Cut the meat into 1/4-inch-thick slices. Cut each slice into strips approximately 1/2 inch wide by 2 to 3 inches long. Sauté in the lard only until just browned. Remove and set aside. Sauté the onion rings, garlic, and peppers until soft, probably no more than 2 minutes. Remove and set aside.

Add the spices to the lard in the pan and, stirring over a high flame, cook for about 1 minute. Pour in the broth and bring to a boil. Reduce the heat to a fast simmer and add the chilies and return the meat. Cover and cook for 5 minutes. Add the leeks and cook for another 5 minutes. Then return the onions and peppers and continue simmering while you coarsely chop the mustard greens. Lay the greens on top of the other ingredients, cover, and steam until the greens are tender, approximately 15 minutes.

Line a basket or deep serving platter with *injera* and place the wilted mustard greens on top of this. Add salt to taste to the meat and vegetable mixture, spoon it over the greens, and serve at once.

EMPANADAS
Mexico
Mexican Cornish Pasties*

*Makes about 15 small
picnic-size turnovers*

FILLING
1 tablespoon lard
1 large onion, chopped
6 to 8 teeth of garlic, minced
1 pound ground beef
1 medium bell pepper, chopped
2 large tomatoes, chopped
1/2 cup minced fresh parsley
1/2 teaspoon crushed dried hot
   chilies, or more to taste
1/2 teaspoon dried oregano
1/4 teaspoon ground cumin
1 teaspoon sugar
1/8 teaspoon coarsely ground black
   pepper, or more to taste
1 teaspoon minced fresh cilantro
Salt to taste

A double recipe for pastry, page 113
1 egg white

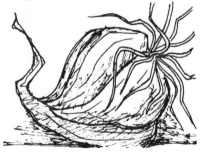

To make the filling, melt the lard in a heavy skillet over medium heat. Sauté the onion and garlic just until the onion is translucent but not yet browned. Add the beef and sauté, stirring to break into small pieces, until just done but not dead and dry. Add all the remaining filling ingredients and stir. Reduce heat to a high simmer, and, stirring occasionally, cook until thick. Cool.

Roll out the pastry to 1/8-inch thickness. Cut into 4- or 5-inch rounds.** Place a heaping table-spoonful of the meat mixture on each pastry round. Fold the pastry in half. Moisten the edges lightly and, using the tines of a fork, press the edges together to seal. Lightly beat the egg white. Paint the surface of each *empanada* with egg white, place on lightly oiled baking sheets, and bake in preheated 350° oven for about 15 to 20 minutes, or until golden brown. Remember, the filling is already done. All you are cooking is the pastry.

An alternative method is to fry the *empanadas* in about an inch of hot lard or vegetable oil until golden brown, then drain on paper towels. I find these a little too greasy.

Hot or cold, *empanadas* are a delight, and please, don't let me be a dictator. Be creative. Fill them with whatever you want. Pork, chorizo, chicken, tuna, cheese, and mushrooms are all fine. Try chucking in some minced black olives or hard-cooked eggs or any combination. Remember, if it's good, it's even better in a pastry shell.

*Almost every culture that uses ovens puts yummy things inside a nice flaky crust and bakes it. There are records of little pies filled with meat, cheese, or vegetables dating as far back as man has had ovens to cook them in. They are tasty, handy, portable, and an excellent way to get your family to eat up things that might otherwise go a-begging. Since these are perhaps the original convenience foods, double, triple, or quadruple the recipe and stuff them in the freezer.

**An empty 2-pound coffee can makes a perfect cutter. With a pair of pliers, carefully pull off the blunt lip. This will leave you with a sharp edge that makes an excellent tool. If you are feeling particularly clever, instead of keeping the whole can, cut it down to be about 3 inches tall. Use a pair of tin snips or an electric saw with a metal-cutting blade.

GRILLADES AND GRITS
Creole Cuisine
Braised Beef Filets in Piquant Sauce with Grits

Serves 4

4 small beef filets or veal steaks
1/4 cup unbleached all-purpose flour
1/2 teaspoon salt
1/2 teaspoon sugar
1/2 teaspoon fresh-ground black pepper
1/2 teaspoon mixed dried herbs (Italian seasoning)
1 teaspoon paprika
1/8 teaspoon cayenne
2 tablespoons lard

SAUCE

2 large onions, chopped
6 teeth of garlic, minced
1 large bell pepper, seeded and chopped
1 celery stalk
2 small fresh hot chilies
2 large tomatoes, chopped
2 cups rich beef broth
1/4 teaspoon each dried thyme, oregano, and sage
1 teaspoon sugar
1 bay leaf

1/2 cup chopped fresh parsley
1/2 tablespoon minced fresh cilantro
Salt, coarsely ground black pepper, and crushed dried hot chilies to taste

4 cups water
1 teaspoon salt
1 cup quick-cooking hominy grits

Trim the meat of all excess fat. Put the flour, salt, sugar, herbs, and spices into a small paper or plastic bag and shake well. Drop in the filets one at a time and shake. Then shake off any excess flour and lay them on a flat surface. Pound lightly on both sides. If you don't have an official meat-pounding thingy, then use the dull edge of a large butcher knife. I said pound it lightly—that means incorporate the flour and seasonings into the meat, not make Spanish lace out of it.

Melt the lard in a heavy skillet and sauté the filets or steaks only until they are browned on both sides. Then set aside.

To make the sauce, put the onions and garlic into the pan the meat was browned in. You may need to add a bit more lard. Sauté until soft but not yet browned. Add the bell pepper, celery, and

chilies and sauté, stirring, for another minute or two. Next add the tomatoes and continue cooking over a high flame, stirring constantly, until the liquid from the tomatoes has been extracted and the mixture is quite saucy. Then add the broth and the remaining ingredients up to and including the bay leaf. Bring to a boil, reduce the heat to a rapid simmer, and, stirring frequently, continue to cook to the consistency of tomato sauce, 20 to 30 minutes. Stir in the parsley, cilantro, salt, black pepper, and chilies and continue to stir and simmer for about 2 more minutes. Return the meat to the pan, reduce to the lowest possible heat, and cover with a tight-fitting lid.

Bring the water to boil in a medium-sized saucepan. Add the 1/2 teaspoon salt and slowly stir in the grits. Cook and stir until thick, about 5 minutes. Mound the grits on a heated serving platter and lay the filets around it. Pour the sauce over all and serve hot. Send to the table accompanied with rich New Orleans coffee with chicory, and you have a perfect beginning to a lazy spring morning in New Orleans, or anyplace else for that matter.

BOBOTIE
South Africa
Meat and Egg Casserole

Serves 6 to 8

4 eggs
1 cup milk
2 slices homemade or French-style white bread
2 tablespoons butter
1 tablespoon corn or other light-flavored oil
2 tablespoons Madras-style curry powder
1 large onion, diced
4 teeth of garlic, minced
2 pounds coarsely ground beef
1 pound lean boneless beef, diced into bite-sized chunks
3 chicken breasts, boned and cut into bite-sized chunks
2 tart cooking apples, peeled, cored, and diced
1/2 teaspoon mixed dried herbs (Italian seasoning)

1 scant teaspoon ground cinnamon
1 tablespoon grated fresh ginger
1/2 teaspoon cayenne, or more to taste
1/2 teaspoon coarsely ground black pepper
3 tablespoons dark brown sugar
1/3 cup fresh lemon juice
1/2 teaspoon grated lemon rind
1/2 cup seedless raisins
1/2 cup slivered blanched almonds
Salt to taste
6 hard-cooked eggs
A few blanched almond halves

Beat the eggs with the milk. Crumble the bread into it and stir well. Set aside. Melt the butter and oil together over moderately high heat. Add the curry powder and lightly singe, stirring rapidly for about 2 minutes. Add the onion and garlic and sauté just until the onions are translucent but not yet browned. Add the ground meat and sauté until just done, stirring well to break apart any chunks. Now add the chunks of meat and sear on all sides. Add the chicken and toss with the other ingredients in the pan to evenly coat and gently sauté. Add all the remaining ingredients except the cooked eggs and almonds, stir, and simmer for 5 minutes. If the mixture seems too dry, add water, a tablespoonful at a time, not enough to make it soupy, but just enough to produce a little gravy.

Meanwhile, peel the eggs and cut them in half lengthwise. When ready, transfer the meat mixture to a 3- or 4-quart casserole. Press the egg halves in among the meat, cut side down, and, with the back of a large spoon, smooth the surface.

Stir the egg and milk mixture again and pour over the top of the meat. Strew the top with the almond halves and put into a preheated 350° oven for 30 minutes or until the top is golden brown and the custard is set. Serve hot from the baking dish. *Bobotie* is traditionally served with steamed rice.

Africans both black and white have traditionally been avid hunters. Bobotie was originally made of a variety of small wild animals and birds and wild birds' eggs; however, with the enforcement of stricter game laws, the same pie is now made, and with great success, from commercially raised products.

KAENG KARI NUA
Thailand
HOT Curried Beef Strips

Serves 6
1 large coconut
3 cups boiling water
2 pounds boneless lean chuck roast
1/4 cup peanut oil
6 small fresh hot chilies, minced
1 medium onion, diced
4 teeth of garlic, minced
1 teaspoon paprika
1/8 teaspoon caraway seeds
1/8 teaspoon coriander seeds
1/2 teaspoon grated fresh lemon
   rind
1 teaspoon grated fresh ginger
1/2 teaspoon ground cinnamon
1 bay leaf
2 teaspoons ground turmeric
3 star anise
1 tablespoon dark brown sugar
1/2 teaspoon shrimp paste (available in Oriental markets), or
   1/4 teaspoon anchovy paste
Reserved liquid from coconut
Salt to taste
1/4 pound snow peas, trimmed
   and blanched
2 medium onions, each cut into
   8 wedges and blanched
2 medium carrots, scraped and cut
   into 2-inch-long julienne strips
   and blanched
1/2 pound Chinese long beans,
   trimmed and cut into 2-inch-long
   strips and blanched
1 tablespoon peanut oil
1/2 cup peanut oil
2 eggs, well beaten
4 cups steamed long-grain white rice

Open the coconut and use the boiling water to make coconut milk according to instructions on page 13.

Cut the beef into paper-thin strips 1 inch wide and 3 inches long. Heat the peanut oil over medium-high heat in a large wok. Add the strips of beef a handful at a time and stir-fry until just cooked but not done. Remove from the oil and drain. Reduce the heat slightly and add the chilies, diced onion, and garlic. Stir-fry until the vegetables are soft but not browned. Add the next 11 ingredients and, stirring constantly, cook with the onion mixture for about 2 minutes. Pour in the coconut milk and the liquid from the coconut, turn up the heat, and bring to a boil. Reduce the heat to a high simmer and cook uncovered until the liquid is reduced by half its original volume, about 30 to 40 minutes. Add the beef and continue cooking for another 15 minutes, stirring frequently. Add salt and adjust the seasoning.

Meanwhile, in another wok or large skillet, heat the remaining tablespoon of peanut oil and stir-fry the snow peas for about 1 minute. Set aside to drain, and continue doing the same with the remaining vegetables.

Heat the 1/2 cup of peanut oil in a small pan or wok until it is deep-frying temperature (375°). With a whisk or your fingers, drizzle the beaten egg into the hot oil, 1 teaspoonful at a time. Cook for only about 30 seconds before lifting out with a slotted spoon; drain on paper towels. Continue until all the egg has been cooked.

Pile the rice on a deep serving platter. Make a well in the center of it and pour in the beef-and-coconut-milk mixture. Place the various vegetables in piles around the edge. Sprinkle the egg lace over the top of the meat and serve immediately.

STIR-FRIED GINGER BEEF AND MUSTARD GREENS
China

Serves 6

2 tablespoons peanut oil
2 pounds lean tender beef cut into paper-thin slices, then into 1/2-by-2-inch strips
6 teeth of garlic, minced
1 tablespoon slivered fresh ginger
1 large onion, cut into bite-sized wedges
10 to 12 very small, thin fresh hot chilies, blanched
2 tablespoons soy sauce
2 tablespoons beef broth
1/4 teaspoon Chinese five-spices
1/4 teaspoon coarsely ground black pepper
1/2 teaspoon sugar
1 tablespoon dry sherry
1 pound mustard greens, washed and shredded
1 teaspoon cornstarch mixed with 1 tablespoon beef broth

Heat the oil over a high flame in a large wok or skillet. Add the meat and stir-fry until browned on all sides. Remove from the heat and set aside. Add the garlic and ginger and stir-fry for about 1 minute. Add the onion and blanched chilies and stir-fry just until the onion is heated through. Add the soy sauce, broth, five-spices, pepper, sugar, and sherry and toss all together. Return the beef to the pan and add the mustard greens. Stir-fry until the greens are wilted. Add the cornstarch mixture and continue stirring gently until the resulting sauce is glossy and somewhat thickened. Serve at once, accompanied with steamed white long-grain rice.

PORK

One of the greatest dietetic disasters for the poor and working classes of Northern Europe was when laws were passed forbidding the keeping of pigs near the house. Previously every cottager was able to keep a pig, and that porker ruled the family's diet the year round. From September on through the autumn, the family could enjoy fresh meat and black puddings. Then through winter there were the salted joints and pickled brawns. Come Christmas, the boar's work was done, and he was served up as the traditional boar's head and mince pies (yes, mincemeat pies really are supposed to have meat in them), the rest of him providing salt meat, pies, boiled pork, ham, bacon, and lard for the remainder of the winter, thus filling in nicely until the first chicks and rabbits of spring were available.

The removal of the cottager's pig was urban legislation forced upon rural populations with rather disastrous effects. The health of poor country families declined rapidly after the passage of the pig acts. Interestingly enough, during World War II many European countries repealed these laws and offered incentives to encourage families to start raising their own pigs again.

CHICHERONES CON SALSA
Mexico
Fried Pork Skins
Served in Chili Sauce

Mazatlan sits on the rim of a long, gently curving, crescent-shaped bay. The north end is gringoland, with its Holiday Inn and other such establishments designed to isolate the traveler from the country he or she is visiting. The south end of the bay is definitely Mexico. Here, less-than-posh open-air cantinas, perched on ancient pilings, cantilever over the bay. Children play in the tide and search the sands for sunbathers' lost treasures. And when the sun goes down, the people come out and you learn the meaning of the word promenade. Young people, old people, lovers and children, families pushing prams and dragging toddlers by the arm fill the streets for the evening's entertainment.

Smells pungent and seductive drift from burro-drawn carts, and the sound of the *mariachis* comes scampering across the water from one of the teetering establishments on the edge of the bay.

I once wandered into a small cantina that looked promising and, mustering my very finest vocabulary of two dozen Spanish words, asked what was cooking. The handsome young man behing the counter of the open-air kitchen managed with his less-than sumptuous English vocabulary to inform me that food would not be ready for about an hour, and offered me a beer.

I seated myself at a table by the arched opening draped with bougainvillea. He returned with two beers and, plopping down across the table from me, sat there grinning like a Cheshire cat. We drank our brews and looked at each other with that embarassment that comes from not being able to communicate. Eventually we managed to exchange names—his was Ramon—and we were soon rescued by the entrance of a friend of his, who possessed considerably more English. The new friend hailed us, went to the bar and returned with three beers, and in exceedingly broken but rather extensive English launched into a dissertation of his philosophy of life. He had gotten as far as his feelings on the space program when a tall gentleman entered the cantina, hailed them with bravado, went to the bar and, returning with four beers, snagged a chair from a neighboring table and joined us. They all raised their bottles and said, "*Sí* Geraldine, *Sí* California, *sí cervesa*. Good," and we drained our bottles, so I figured it was about time for my round. I rose to go to the bar and was forcibly thrust back into my seat. Ramon made the next run.

Several more rounds went down our throats, and then a little man with a huge gunnysack on his back came in. My friends hailed him. He trotted to our table, unshouldered his sack, and produced the biggest *chicherones* I have ever seen. He produced a paper plate, broke the giant pig skins into manageable pieces, and sprinkled them with hot sauce. I eagerly reached for a chunk. I could see the smug smiles begin to creep across the faces of my friends. "Just wait til the gringo tastes that,' they were thinking, each one to himself. Well, I popped down several of the most thoroughly drenched pieces, and their jaws dropped. Needless to say their *machismo* was in significant danger. They had to reclaim their status in my eyes and their own, and snatching up another bottle of sauce from the counter, drenched the *chicherones* and started munching. Much to their amazement I munched with the best of them. This of course called for several more rounds of the fine local brew, Pacifico, and when the little, not-very-good *mariachi* band arrived we were all in a quite jocular mood. Actually, they were far more than not very good. They were wretched. My friends took their instruments away from them. My friends were good.

They played and we sang, and drank more beer, and an American couple who had ventured out of the protective cocoon of the north end of the town sent even more beer to our table.

Sometime after three in the morning, the couple who owned the cantina suggested that we and they would be much happier if we were to take ourselves elsewhere, so with our arms cradling the numerous bottles of beer we had convinced the cantina to sell us, we sang our way up back streets until we came to Ramon's house, where, much to the distress of a sleepy green parrot, we continued our revelry until the sun came up.

Serves 6

One 5-ounce package *chicherones* (Corona brand)
4 large tomatoes, chopped
1 large onion, chopped
6 teeth of garlic, minced
4 small fresh hot chilies, minced
1 medium onion, cut into thin rings
1 each red and green bell pepper, seeded and cut into thin rings
2 celery stalks, chopped
1/2 teaspoon sugar
1/4 teaspoon dried oregano
1/8 teaspoon ground cumin
1/4 teaspoon coarsely ground black pepper
One 4-ounce can diced peeled green chilies
6 to 8 green onions, trimmed and chopped, including the tops
1/2 cup minced fresh parsley
1/2 tablespoon minced fresh cilantro
2 tablespoons olive oil
Salt and coarsely ground black pepper

Break the *chicherones* into bite-sized pieces and place in a heat-proof bowl. Pour over enough boiling water to cover and leave until soft. Put the tomatoes, chopped onion, garlic, and fresh chilies into the jar of a blender and whir. Pour into a saucepan and bring to a boil. Reduce the heat to a high simmer and cook, stirring occasionally, for about 10 minutes. Add the next 7 ingredients and continue simmering for another 10 minutes.

Drain the *chicherones* and put into a serving bowl. Pour over the sauce, add the canned chilies, green onions, parsley, and cilantro and toss. Drizzle over the olive oil and toss lightly. Add salt and pepper to taste. Serve hot or cold.

*I'm not talking about wimpy little pork skins sold in small packages to munch along with drinks, or the small crackling puffs. I'm talking about *chicherones,* big gnarly chunks of pig skin, deep-fried and packaged in large chunks, all wonderful and chewy and salty. They are sold in Latino markets, and in supermarkets in areas with a large Latino population.

STUFFED PORK CHOPS
Family Recipe

Serves 6

6 large boneless pork chops,
  at least 1 inch thick
1 tablespoon corn or other light-
  flavored vegetable oil
1 tablespoon butter
1 medium onion, minced
2 tart apples, peeled, cored and
  finely chopped
3 teeth of garlic, minced
2 small fresh hot chilies, minced
1/4 cup currants
3/4 teaspoon minced fresh dill
  weed, or 1/4 teaspoon dried
1/4 teaspoon ground cinnamon
1/4 teaspoon dried savory
1/4 teaspoon grated fresh ginger
1 teaspoon brown sugar
1/2 cup bread crumbs
1 egg, lightly beaten
Salt and pepper to taste

With a sharp knife, make a deep
incision in the side of each
chop, forming a pocket. Set aside.
   Melt the oil and butter together
in a heavy skillet. Lightly sauté
the onion, apples, garlic, and chilies.
Add the currants, herbs and spices,
and sugar and continue cooking,
stirring gently, until all is blended
and the apples are soft. Remove
from the heat and let cool. Add
the bread crumbs and egg. If the
mixture is not moist enough to
hold together when pressed into a
ball in your hand, add a few drops
of milk at a time until it is the
right consistency. Add salt and
pepper. Pack firmly into the pockets
in the pork chops and truss shut
with a bamboo skewer. Grill to
desired doneness on a charcoal
grill or under a broiler. Serve with
steamed rice and homemade spicy
applesauce.

WEST OAKLAND BARBECUE
Black-American Cuisine

A sojurn to Flint's Barbecue in
Oakland is one of the stops on my
Show My Overseas Guests My
California Tour. It's right up there
at the top of the list with "the
ultimate wine country picnic in
Sonoma," "the Sequoias," "Point
Lobos," and, of course, "Yosemite."
   I have consumed my share of
barbecued pork prepared by numerous ethnic groups around the
world, but none, in my estimation,
can compare with that which is
found within the black community
in West Oakland. Talk about a
party in your mouth!

Serves 8 to 12

SAUCE
One 14-ounce bottle tomato catsup
2 large onions, chopped
2 large bell peppers, seeded and
  chopped
12 teeth of garlic, minced
6 small fresh hot chilies, minced
1 tablespoon crushed dried hot
  chilies
1 cup brown sugar
1/2 cup distilled vinegar
1 tablespoon mixed dried herbs
  (Italian seasoning)
1 teaspoon liquid smoke
10 pounds spareribs

Purée all the sauce ingredients in
a blender. Put into a saucepan and
bring to a boil. Reduce the heat
and simmer, stirring frequently,
until a thick glossy sauce results.
This may be stored for several
weeks in the refrigerator, in a jar
with a tight-fitting lid.
   Paint the ribs liberally with the
sauce and cook to desired doneness
over charcoal, under a broiler, or
in the oven. Paint frequently with
the sauce throughout the cooking.
Serve with *lots* of cold beer!

CARBONADA
Argentina
Meat, Vegetable, and Fruit Stew
Served in a Baked Pumpkin

Serves 6 to 8
One 12- to 15-pound pumpkin
1/2 cup butter, at room temperature
1 teaspoon ground cinnamon
1 teaspoon chili powder
1 cup brown sugar
2 tablespoons olive oil
3 pounds boneless pork loin,
   trimmed and cut into 1-inch cubes
1 medium onion, chopped
6 teeth of garlic, minced
1 medium bell pepper, seeded
   and chopped
2 large tomatoes, chopped
4 cups beef broth
1/2 teaspoon crushed dried hot
   chilies, or more to taste
1 tablespoon brown sugar
1/2 teaspoon dried oregano
1 teaspoon minced fresh cilantro
1/4 teaspoon fresh-ground black
   pepper
2 pounds yams, peeled and cut
   into 1/2-inch chunks
6 to 8 small mild chilies, stemmed
10 or 12 small boiling onions,
   parboiled
2 small zucchini, cut into 1/2-inch
   chunks
2 ears of corn, shucked and cut
   into 1/2-inch slices

4 to 6 small peaches, peeled and
   cut in half
2 small seedless oranges, cut into
   thin slices, peel left on
Salt

With a large knife, cut off the top of the pumpkin in such a manner as to make a lid. Clean the inside of its seeds and pulp. Rub the inside with the butter. Mix the cinnamon and chili powder with the 1 cup of brown sugar and sprinkle inside the pumpkin. Tilt the pumpkin from side to side to coat evenly. Set the pumpkin in a shallow baking pan and put into the oven at 350° for about 30 to 45 minutes or until the inside is tender but the shell is still firm enough to hold its shape.

Heat the olive oil in a heavy pan and sauté the meat until browned on all sides. Remove with a slotted spoon and set aside. Add the onion, garlic, bell pepper, and tomatoes and continue cooking, stirring occasionally, for about 5 minutes or until the vegetables are soft. Pour in the broth. Add the

crushed chilies, 1 tablespoon of brown sugar, oregano, cilantro, and black pepper and bring to a boil. Add the browned meat, boil for about 2 minutes, then reduce the heat to a rapid simmer and continue cooking, stirring occasionally, for about 30 minutes, or until the meat is exceedingly tender. After 15 minutes add the yams, mild chilies, and boiling onions. At the end of the 30 minutes add the zucchini, corn, peaches, and oranges. Continue to simmer for another 5 minutes or until the zucchini is just done. Add salt to taste.

Place the pumpkin on a serving platter* and pour in the stew. Top with the lid and serve immediately. When serving, scoop a bit of the flesh from the pumpkin into each serving.

*If the pumpkin does not have a flat base, wring out a tea towel in hot water and roll it up lengthwise. Then twist it round to form a ring. Set this on the serving plate to form a base for the pumpkin to sit in. Disguise the tea towel with parsley, fresh watercress, curly endive, or even small-leafed ivy and a few flowers like marigolds. This is a festive dish, and often it is served with lighted candles stuck into the pumpkin shell.

SWEET AND SOUR PORK
A LA DR. YUEN
Family Recipe

My first father-in-law was Hawaiian-Chinese and a skilled surgeon. Like many old-world men, regular kitchen work was far beneath his manly dignity, but he did on occasion and with great aptitude find his relaxation by engaging in the culinary arts. When he made sweet and sour pork, he always started with a whole leg of pork. Watching him bone that joint was almost magic. He would insert a long, thin, exceedingly sharp knife into the leg next to the bone, from the large end. Then, holding the knife still, he would grab the knuckle of bone that protruded from the small end and turn it around and around so that the leg of pork rotated on the blade of the knife. Then with no effort whatsoever, he would pull the now meatless bone out of the leg, leaving a solid chunk of meat lying on the kitchen counter.

I have been trying to perfect his technique for over 25 years with no success at all. If you master it, please let me know.

Serves 6 or 8

2-1/2 to 3 pounds boneless pork loin
1 tablespoon soy sauce
1 tablespoon dry mustard
1/2 teaspoon ground ginger
1/2 teaspoon cayenne
1/2 teaspoon salt
1 teaspoon sugar
1/4 cup peanut oil
6 teeth of garlic, minced
1/2 tablespoon grated fresh ginger
1/2 tablespoon tomato paste
1/4 cup soy sauce
1/4 cup chicken broth
4 small fresh hot chilies, cut into thin rings
1 bell pepper, preferably red, cored, seeded, and cut into thin strips
1 large onion, cut into bite-sized wedges
6 green onions, trimmed and cut into 2-inch lengths, including 4 inches of the greens
1/8 teaspoon Chinese five-spices
1 tablespoon sugar
2 tablespoons rice vinegar or distilled vinegar
1 teaspoon cornstarch mixed with 1 tablespoon chicken broth
Salt and fresh-ground black pepper
Crushed dried hot chilies to taste (optional)

Cut the pork into 1/4-by-1/2-by-2-inch strips. Mix the next 6 ingredients together and massage into the pork.

Heat the peanut oil in a large wok and sauté the pork until browned on all sides. Remove from the wok and set aside. Add the garlic and ginger and stir-fry until heated through but not browned. Add the tomato paste, soy, and broth and stir together until well blended. Next add the fresh chilies, bell pepper, and onion, and stir-fry until the vegetables are just heated through, no more than 2 minutes. Return the meat to the pan and toss. Add the green onions and toss again. Next add the five-spices, sugar, and vinegar and continue to stir-fry for another minute or two. Pour in the cornstarch mixture and stir-fry until the sauce is somewhat thickened and glossy. Add salt and pepper to taste. If you want a more distinct sweet and sour flavor add more sugar and vinegar at this time. Also, if you want the dish hotter, gradually add dried red pepper flakes a bit at a time until the desired conflagration is obtained. Serve immediately with steamed white rice.

MU-HSU-JOU
Shansi, China
Stir-fried Pork and Peppers
with Eggs

Serves 6

2 pounds boneless pork butt or loin
1/4 cup peanut oil
1 tablespoon soy sauce
1 tablespoon cream sherry
1 tablespoon beef broth
6 small fresh hot chilies, seeded
   and cut into thin rings
1 large red bell pepper, seeded
   and cut into thin strips
1 cup thinly sliced fresh mushrooms
4 or 5 green onions, trimmed and
   cut into 2-inch-long pieces,
   including the tops, and each
   piece cut into thin strips
   lengthwise
5 eggs, lightly beaten
1 4 cup soy sauce
1/4 cup beef broth
2 tablespoons cream sherry
1 teaspoon smoky Oriental
   sesame oil
4 teeth of garlic, minced
1/2 teaspoon grated fresh ginger
1/2 teaspoon crushed dried hot
   chilies
1/4 teaspoon coarsely ground
   black pepper

1/4 teaspoon dry mustard
1 scant teaspoon sugar (add a bit
   at a time while tasting)
1 teaspoon cornstarch mixed with
1 tablespoon beef stock

Cut the pork into paper-thin slices. Then cut each slice into strips 1/4 inch wide and 2 to 3 inches long. Heat the oil in a large wok or skillet. When the oil is hot, add the pork a handful at a time and stir-fry only until it is lightly browned on all sides. Add the 1 tablespoon each of soy sauce, sherry, and broth and heat until boiling. Add the fresh chilies, bell pepper, and mushrooms and stir-fry for an additional 3 to 4 minutes. Add the green onions and stir-fry for 1 minute more. Scoop the ingredients from the wok with a slotted spoon and arrange on a heated serving plate. Keep warm.

Oil an omelet pan lightly with an oiled brush or paper towel and heat. Pour in half the beaten eggs. Tilt the pan to evenly distribute the egg mixture. As soon as a skin forms on the bottom of the egg, pull it to one side of the pan and tilt the pan again to let the uncooked portion of the egg run to the bottom of the pan. Continue this gentle tilting of the pan and scooping aside of the cooked portion until all of the egg is set but not dry. Remove to a plate and repeat with the remaining egg. Break apart these egg curds and toss them with the vegetables and pork on the serving plate.

Heat the wok again and add all of the remaining ingredients. Bring to a boil, stirring constantly, reduce heat, and stir while simmering until the sauce is somewhat thickened, translucent and glossy. Taste for additional salt. (I find that I seldom use salt when using soy sauce.) Pour over the pork and eggs and serve immediately.

"Look at Pork. There's a subject! If you want a subject, look at Pork!"
Charles Dickens,
Great Expectations

HUNG-SHAO-TI-BANG
Northern China
Red-Cooked Pork

Serves 6 to 8
6 or 8 dried Chinese mushrooms
One 5- to 6-pound fresh pork loin
  or shoulder
1/2 cup soy sauce
1 tablespoon tomato paste
3 tablespoons sugar
2 whole star anise
1/4 cup rice wine or dry sherry
2 cups chicken broth
1 teaspoon crushed dried hot chilies
1 tablespoon slivered fresh ginger
8 teeth of garlic, minced
1 teaspoon dry mustard
1 cup water
4 cups steamed long-grain white rice

Soak the mushrooms in warm
water to cover for 1 hour; drain
and set aside. Put the pork in a
large pot, cover with water, and
bring to a boil. Boil for 15 minutes.
Drain. Return the pork to the pot.
Combine all the remaining ingredients except the rice and add to
the pot with the pork. Bring to a
boil and reduce heat to a simmer,
cover, and continue cooking, turning
the meat occasionally until the
pork is exceedingly tender, about
3 hours. Remove the pork to a
cutting board and allow to cool
slightly. Meanwhile, remove the

star anise pod from the remaining
liquid and, turning up the flame,
reduce to a thick sauce. When the
pork is cool enough to handle, cut
into thin strips and return to the
thickened sauce in the pan. Toss
gently over a high flame to coat
evenly. Pile the steamed rice onto
a serving platter and arrange the
pork on top of it. Drain
the mushrooms and cut into quarters. Toss in the sauce and,
when heated through, arrange on
top of the pork. Spoon any of the
remaining sauce over all and serve
immediately.

SHIH-TZU-TOU
China
Lions' Heads (Meatballs and
Chinese Cabbage
in Savory Gravy)

Serves 6

MEATBALLS
2 pounds ground pork
3 tablespoons soy sauce
2 green onions, including tops,
  minced
6 teeth of garlic, minced
1/2 tablespoon minced fresh ginger
2 small fresh hot chilies, minced
1 medium onion, minced

1/2 teaspoon Chinese five-spices
6 canned water chestnuts, drained
  and finely minced
2 tablespoons cornstarch
1/2 teaspoon sugar
2 eggs, lightly beaten
1/4 teaspoon coarsely ground
  black pepper
2 tablespoons peanut oil

1 head Chinese (Napa) cabbage
1/2 cup light beef broth
3 tablespoons soy sauce
3 tablespoons cream sherry
1 tablespoon peanut oil
3 teeth of garlic, minced
1/4 teaspoon grated fresh ginger
1/4 teaspoon crushed dried hot
  chilies
Salt and pepper and more crushed
  dried hot chilies to taste
1 teaspoon cornstarch mixed with
1 tablespoon beef broth

Mix all the ingredients for the
meatballs, except the oil, together
well and form into 12 meatballs.
Heat the oil in a large heavy
skillet over a high flame. When the
oil is hot, reduce the heat to
moderate and fry the meatballs 3
or 4 at a time, turning them
occasionally to brown well on all
sides. When finished, set aside.
  Cut the head of cabbage crosswise
so that you are left with leaves at

least 5 or 6 inches long. (Reserve the stem end to use another time with stir-fried vegetables.) Separate the leaves of the head end and wash well under running water. (Use only the larger outer leaves. The small inner ones should be used another time with the stem end.) Drain the leaves.

Put all the remaining ingredients except the cornstarch mixture and final seasonings into a large wok over a high flame and bring to a boil. Add the cabbage leaves and toss about gently to coat evenly with the sauce. Cover with a tight-fitting lid and reduce the heat to low. Steam the leaves about 10 minutes or until wilted. Add the cornstarch mixture and stir gently until the sauce is thickened. Add the meatballs and leave just long enough to heat them through. Remove the meatballs to a heated serving plate. Lay the cabbage leaves on the plate and place a meatball on each leaf of cabbage. (This is why they are called lions' heads. The cabbage looks like the mane of a lion's head.) Tuck any extra cabbage here and there among the lions' heads. Pour over the extra sauce and serve immediately.

ROAST PORK CALYPSO
Jamaica
Roast Pork
with Chili-Rum Sauce

Serves 6 to 8
One 6- to 8-pound pork loin
2 cups chicken broth
1 cup dark brown sugar
8 to 10 teeth of garlic, minced
1/2 tablespoon grated fresh ginger
1/8 teaspoon ground cloves
1 medium onion, minced
Juice of 2 oranges
1 teaspoon grated orange rind
1 teaspoon crushed dried hot
   chilies
1/4 teaspoon coarsely ground
   black pepper
1/4 cup fresh lime juice
1/2 cup crushed canned pineapple
Salt to taste
1/3 cup dark Jamaican rum
Watercress sprigs and orange slices
   for garnish (optional)

With a sharp knife, score the pork to make diagonal cuts about 1/4 inch deep at 1-inch intervals on the side with fat or skin. Place the pork, scored side up, in a roasting pan and add the broth. Cover and put in a preheated oven at 350° for 1 to 1-1/2 hours.

Meanwhile, combine all of the remaining ingredients except the

rum, watercress, and oranges in a blender. Remove the pork from the oven and allow to cool just enough to be able to touch it. Drain off the pan juices. Rub the paste you created in the blender into the flesh of the pork and pour any that remains over the top. Return to the oven uncovered and bake for another 45 minutes to 1 hour, basting occasionally with any liquid in the pan.

Degrease the pan juices that were poured off after the first roasting. Put the juices in a pan over high heat and, stirring frequently, reduce to only about 2/3 cup. When the pork is done, remove it from the oven and place it on a heated serving platter; set the pork aside and keep it warm. Skim off the fat from the roasting pan and scrape what juices and marinade remain into the reduced stock. Stir together over a high flame. Add the rum and continue cooking, stirring all the while, for about 3 minutes. Strain and pour over the pork on the platter. Garnish, if you wish, with fresh watercress and slices of orange. Serve hot.

SHADOWPOINT TAMALE PIE
Family Recipe

My parents' home, wherever it was at any given time, always headquartered local artists and intelligentsia. Although my parents never found themselves in opulent circumstances, they entertained often and lavishly, particularly when they were young and living in their "Other Eden" at Lake Elsinore. Shadowpoint was truly a paradise, particularly if you were five years old and didn't have to take care of it. The six acres of chickens, apricots, walnuts, and overgrown lawn rambled down a gentle slope to the lake itself: a warm, still, green lake that beckoned on summer nights when the moon cast its path across the surface.

My father, a powerful swimmer, would put me on his back on those silver nights and together we would swim the shimmering moon path. We never quite reached the moon but it never occurred to me that we wouldn't sooner or later. Tonight just wasn't the right night. Anyway, it would be time to swim back to the ramada where the party was. There might be two hundred Young Democrats, or Friends of Wallace (that's Henry, not George), or perhaps the local

Folk Dance Society. The ramada was built over the water, furnished with a bar, Victorian rattan furniture, and potted palms. The strains of concertina and balalaika would drift out over the lake, and brilliant people, sure of their ability to save the world, laughed and danced and splashed in the lake and ate. Everyone always brought plenty of food, and my mother fixed more, and you can bet your F.D.R. button that one of the things on the groaning board would be this tamale pie.

I have a large sheet of Formica I use for a work surface. It is much easier to keep sanitary than wood and you can usually get one for less than $5 from a contractor who remodels kitchens. They are what is left over after the Formica counters have been cut to accommodate a hole for a sink. It's sort of like buying donut holes.

Serves 12
2 tablespoons lard
3 large onions, chopped
10 teeth of garlic, finely minced
3 small fresh hot chilies, finely minced
2 large bell peppers, seeded and chopped
2 celery stalks, chopped
2 pounds ground pork
2 tablespoons chili powder
1 tablespoon brown sugar
1/2 teaspoon ground cumin
1 tablespoon minced fresh cilantro
1/2 cup minced fresh parsley
1/2 teaspoon coarsely ground black pepper
1 tablespoon tomato paste
1 cup beef broth
Salt and crushed dried hot chilies
3 cups water
1/2 teaspoon salt
1 cup yellow cornmeal
One 6-ounce can pitted black olives, drained
2 or 3 medium tomatoes, sliced into thin rings
1 small onion, sliced into thin rings
1 small bell pepper, seeded and sliced into thin rings
1/3 cup shredded sharp Cheddar cheese
1/3 cup shredded Swiss cheese
2 green onions, including the tops, minced

Place a large heavy skillet over high heat and melt the lard but do not let it smoke. Sauté the onions and garlic until translucent but not browned. Add the fresh chilies, bell peppers, and celery and sauté for another 2 to 3 minutes or until the vegetables are heated through and beginning to soften but are not browned. Add the pork and stir-fry to break into small bits. If it is browning too rapidly, reduce the heat to moderate. Continue to sauté the meat until all signs of pink are gone but it is not brown and hard.

Now add the next 7 ingredients and stir well. Pour in the broth, stir, and bring to a boil. Reduce the heat to a simmer. Season to taste with salt and crushed chilies, and continue simmering until most of the liquid has evaporated and a thick saucy mixture results, about 30 minutes.

Meanwhile, prepare the cornmeal. Put the water into a saucepan and bring to a boil. Add the salt. Slowly stir in the cornmeal. Reduce heat and stir until thick, about 5

minutes. Let the cornmeal mush sit until it is cool enough to handle. When ready to assemble the pie, use your hands to press the cornmeal mush onto the bottom and sides of a 3- or 4-quart casserole. This cornmeal "crust" should be about 1/2 inch thick. Stir the black olives into the meat mixture, reserving a few for garnish. Spoon the meat into the cornmeal-lined casserole. Arrange the tomato slices slightly overlapping each other in a ring around the outside of the dish. Separate the slices of onion into rings and arrange them in a circle just inside of the tomatoes. Place a few of the bell pepper rings overlapping each other in the center. Toss the cheeses and green onions together and sprinkle over the surface of the pie. Place the reserved black olives here and there on the top and place in a preheated 350° oven for 30 minutes or until the cheese is melted and beginning to brown.

(Since I intimated that this was an economy dish that my mother used for entertaining large numbers of people when the cupboard was bare, you may be wondering about the use of expensive olives. My father cured his own. We used

olives like most people use salt. They were in everything, on everything, and with everything. There was a mixing bowl of olives placed on the table at every meal. Olives were a snack in the evening while reading—no TV in those days. We even talked to each other in the evenings.)

You can, of course, make this dish as economical as you wish. Use economy ground beef or chili meat, leftover meats or poultry, or cut down the amount of meat and add more onions, etc. I have even pulled the turkey carcass out of freezer, boiled it, picked off the meat, and used it. (No, I do not make my family eat turkey soup the week after Thanksgiving; I stuff the sad remains in the freezer. Along about February, turkey soup is a real treat.)

CHANCHO ADOBADO
Mexico
Pork and Yams
in Orange and Lemon Sauce

Serves 6

SAUCE
One 6-ounce can frozen
    orange juice
1/2 cup fresh lemon juice
4 teeth of garlic, finely minced
1 teaspoon ground cumin
1 tablespoon minced fresh cilantro
1/2 teaspoon crushed dried hot
    chilies
1/4 teaspoon coarsely ground
    black pepper
2 tablespoons olive oil
1/4 teaspoon dried oregano
Salt to taste

2 tablespoons lard
2-1/2 to 3 pounds of boneless
    pork, cut into 1-inch cubes
2 large yams
1/2 cup water
Minced fresh cilantro (optional)

Put all of the sauce ingredients
into a bowl and mix well. Add the
pork and refrigerate overnight.

Boil the yams until tender, peel,
and cut into 1/2-inch-thick slices.
Set aside.

Heat the lard in a heavy skillet
over a high flame. Do not let it
smoke. Sauté the pork until well
browned on all sides. Reduce the
heat and pour in the orange
marinade. Add the water and
simmer covered, stirring occasionally,
for 45 minutes or 1 hour, or until
the meat is exceedingly tender.
Spoon the meat onto a heated
serving platter. Add the slices of
yam to the orange sauce and
simmer until just heated through.
Place the yams in a ring around
the meat. Pour over the orange
sauce, sprinkle with minced fresh
cilantro, if you wish, and serve
with hot steamed flour tortillas.

LAULAU
Hawaii
Steamed Taro Leaves, Pork,
and Fish

Makes 10
1 pound boneless lean pork
1 pound salmon fillet
1 pound butterfish fillet
3 cups shredded taro leaves or
    fresh spinach, or equivalent
    amount of frozen spinach
Crushed dried hot chilies
Coarse-ground black pepper
Salt

Chop the pork and fish into smaller-
than-bite-sized pieces. Make 10
squares of aluminum foil.* Onto
each foil square place a small pile
each of pork, salmon, butterfish,
and taro. Sprinkle to taste with
crushed dried chilies, pepper, and
salt. Fold the foil to form small,
tightly sealed packages. Place the
packages in a steamer, pour in
boiling water, and steam for 30
minutes. Serve hot.

*If you are able to find *ti* leaves,
for each *laulau* lay one leaf on top
of another to form a cross. Put the
filling at the large end of one leaf.
Roll up until you come to the end
of the leaf. Place the rolled leaf
crosswise on the broad end of the
second leaf and roll again. You
should no longer be able to see
any of the filling. Tie shut by
splitting the fibrous stem and
using it as a string.

LAMB

My great-grandfather, like all cattlemen of the American frontier, had little if anything good to say about sheep or sheepherders. He saw them only as a plague bleating its way across the pastures, rendering them useless to the cattleman. It took many generations before cattlemen and sheepmen were able to cohabit on the same range.

One of our greatest family rows came when one of his sons tried to show the old man how cattle and sheep could indeed graze the same range. Gramps was unmoved by the argument that sheep provided two cash crops and reproduced at a faster rate than cattle, and that his could be the first ranch in the valley to take advantage of this economic windfall.

For many decades the raising of sheep was left to the Basque immigrants of the high-altitude Sierra pastures. Even John Muir referred to sheep as "hooved locusts" when he saw the erosion they were causing in Yosemite Valley. It wasn't until he was able to convince Teddy Roosevelt to create Yosemite Valley as a national preserve that the sheep were evicted from the floor of the valley and the surrounding meadows.

In England, however, the attitude towards sheep was quite different. For centuries the English economy was based on sheep. It was the taxes from wool that sent the armies into battle. It was the revenue from wool that sent Captain Francis Drake around the globe to bring new worlds under the standard of Elizabeth the First, and spices from those worlds into the markets of London.

The disaster of England's loss of Calais during the reign of

Elizabeth's psychotic sister Mary was not because it was a particularly beautiful or valuable piece of real estate, but because it was the seat of the European Wool Staple, which England controlled until that time. As recently as World War I, farmers in the Cotswolds, a major sheep-raising area of England, were buried with a tuft of wool in their hand. This was so God could see they were shepherds and that was why they hadn't been to church on Sundays.

Even today at the joint session of Lords and Commons that opens Parliament, the speaker sits on a wool sack to remind him from whence his power comes.

When visitors from other countries come to the U.S. they are often puzzled by our term *lamb*. What we sell as lamb, most nations call young mutton. They consider lamb to be the very young animals we sell as spring lamb. This should explain to most Americans why so many foreign cookbooks call for mutton. Mutton to us is old, stringy, and very strong-tasting. We are talking about two different beasts. Mutton to someone from Europe or the Middle East means an animal between six months and eighteen months old, as toothsome a treat as our own animals of that age sold under the name of lamb.

Lamb to a Greek or Turk means a nursing animal under six months of age, tender beyond belief, and usually reserved for such very special occasions as weddings and christenings and Easter.

No matter what you choose to call it, an animal that is between six and eighteen months old and goes *baa* is very tasty indeed cooked any number of ways.

LAMB CURRY
Sri Lanka

Serves 6 to 8

4 to 5 pounds breast of lamb, each rack cut into 1-inch strips
1 tablespoon olive oil
1 tablespoon vegetable oil
2 tablespoons Madras-style curry powder
1 teaspoon crushed dried hot chilies
1/2 teaspoon anise seeds
1 scant teaspoon ground cinnamon
3/4 teaspoon fresh dill weed, or 1/2 teaspoon dried
8 teeth of garlic, finely minced
2 tablespoons grated fresh ginger
1 large onion, chopped
2 cups light beef broth
1/2 cup brown sugar
1/4 cup distilled vinegar
Additional crushed dried hot chilies (optional)
2 medium onions, cut into bite-sized chunks
1 large bell pepper, seeded and cut into strips
2 medium cooking apples, peeled, cored, and cut into bite-sized chunks
2 medium seedless oranges, cut into thin slices, peels on
1/2 fresh ripe pineapple, cored and cut into bite-sized chunks
1 tablespoon cornstarch mixed with 1 tablespoon water or broth
Salt and fresh-ground black pepper
1/2 tablespoon minced fresh cilantro
1 heaping tablespoon minced fresh mint leaves
4 green onions, including greens, minced
Pineapple spears and mint sprigs for garnish (optional)

Cut the strips of meat apart between the ribs. Put the meat in a large pot, cover with cold water, and bring to a boil. Boil for 5 minutes and drain.

Heat the oils over high heat in a large skillet. If they begin to smoke, reduce the heat slightly. Add the herbs and spices, garlic, ginger, and onion. Stirring rapidly, cook for about 2 minutes, or until a paste is formed. Add the meat and stir to coat all evenly.

Pour in the broth, reduce to a rapid simmer, and cook, stirring occasionally, until the meat is exceedingly tender. Add the brown sugar and vinegar and taste. If you want a more distinctly sweet and sour taste or more heat, add additional sugar, vinegar, and red pepper at this time.

Add the onions, pepper, and fruit and continue simmering until the apples are tender but not falling apart. Stir in the cornstarch mixture and continue to simmer, stirring gently, until the sauce is thickened and glossy. Add salt and pepper to taste. Add the cilantro, mint, and green onions and stir lightly. Pour into a heated serving platter. You may cut the remaining pineapple into spears to use for garnish along with sprigs of mint. Sometimes I set the spiked top of the pineapple in the center of the dish and ladle the curry around it. This makes an attractive display. Serve with steamed white rice or saffron rice and hot steamed *chapatis*. (*Chapatis* and flour tortillas are very similar.)

BADAMI GOSHT
India
Lamb with Yogurt, Coconut Milk, and Almond Masala

Serves 6

MASALA
1 large coconut
3 cups boiling water
Liquid from the coconut
1 teaspoon saffron
2 tablespoons hot water
1/2 cup unsalted blanched almonds
1 teaspoon caraway seeds
1/8 teaspoon anise seeds
1/2 teaspoon ground cinnamon
1/4 teaspoon ground cardamom
2 teaspoons grated fresh ginger
1/2 teaspoon cayenne, or more to to taste
1/8 teaspoon ground cloves
1 tablespoon sugar
1 cup (8 ounces) plain yogurt
Salt to taste

2-1/2 pounds lean boneless lamb, cut into bite-sized cubes
2 tablespoons peanut oil
2 tablespoons butter
2 large onions, minced
6 teeth of garlic, minced

Open the coconut and use the boiling water to make coconut milk according to the instructions on page 13. Add the liquid from

the coconut, if necessary, to make 3 cups of coconut milk.

Soak the saffron in the hot water for 10 minutes. Put the saffron and its water, almonds, 1 cup of the coconut milk, and the next 8 ingredients into a blender and whir until smooth. Pour into a bowl and add the remaining coconut milk, yogurt, and salt. Stir. Add the lamb and leave to marinate overnight.

When ready to cook, heat the oil and butter together in a large wok or heavy skillet. Sauté the onions and garlic until soft but not yet browned. Remove the lamb from the marinade with a slotted spoon and brown on all sides. Pour in the remaining marinade and let it cook rapidly, stirring constantly, for 1 minute. Reduce the heat to a high simmer and continue cooking, stirring occasionally, until the meat is very tender. Remove the meat to a heatproof dish and set aside. Turn the heat up and cook the remaining masala over a high heat, stirring to prevent sticking, until somewhat reduced and thickened. Just before serving, put the meat under the high flame of a broiler and leave until the edges have just begun to get crisp. Remove from the broiler and pour the reduced masala over it. Serve at once with hot steamed rice.

LANCASHIRE HOT POT
England
Lamb or Mutton Stew
with Oysters and Black Pepper

Serves 6 to 8

1/4 cup unbleached all-purpose
  flour
1 teaspoon salt
1/2 tablespoon coarsely ground
  black pepper
1 teaspoon dry mustard
3 tablespoons paprika
2 pounds lean lamb, cut into
  bite-sized chunks
6 to 8 lamb kidneys, each cut
  in half lengthwise
3 tablespoons lard
1 large onion, chopped
2 cups beef broth
1 scant teaspoon sugar
1/4 teaspoon dried thyme
1/4 teaspoon salt
1/2 teaspoon coarsely ground
  black pepper
4 large potatoes, peeled and cut
  into thin slices
2 pints fresh oysters, drained
12 small boiling onions, peeled
1 pound small fresh mushrooms,
  quartered
1/2 cup shredded sharp Cheddar
  cheese
1/4 cup fine bread crumbs
1/4 cup minced fresh parsley

Put the flour, salt, pepper, mustard, and paprika into a small bag and shake. Drop in the lamb and kidneys and shake to coat each piece. Shake off any excess flour.

Heat the lard in a heavy skillet over a high flame but do not let it smoke. Brown the lamb and kidneys on all sides, remove with a slotted spoon, and set aside. Sauté the chopped onion in the remaining lard and pour in the broth, sugar, thyme, salt, and pepper. Reduce the heat to medium and cook, stirring, for about 2 minutes. Taste and adjust the seasoning. It should be very peppery. Remove from the heat.

Place half the slices of potato on the bottom of a 5-quart casserole with a tight-fitting lid. Place the lamb, kidneys, oysters, boiling onions, and mushrooms in layers over the potatoes. Top with the remaining potatoes. Pour in the broth. Toss the cheese, bread crumbs, and parsley together and sprinkle over the potatoes. Cover with the lid and put in a 350° oven for 1-1/2 hours, or until the meat is exceedingly tender when pierced with the tip of a sharp knife and the liquid is almost all absorbed. Remove the lid during the last 15

minutes to allow the cheese to brown. Serve from the casserole, accompanied with prepared horse-radish, hot brown mustard, and good English beer.

WHOLE STUFFED
LEG OF LAMB
Greece

Serves 6 to 8

STUFFING
2 cups *al dente* cooked bulgur
6 teeth of garlic, minced
1 large onion, chopped
2 celery stalks, chopped
1 large bell pepper, seeded and
  chopped
6 small fresh hot chilies, seeded
  and minced (save the seeds and
  add a few at a time if you want
  the stuffing hotter)
1/3 cup minced fresh parsley
1 tablespoon minced fresh dill weed,
  or 1 teaspoon dried
1/2 teaspoon ground cumin
Juice of 2 lemons
1 teaspoon grated lemon peel
1 bay leaf
1/3 cup pine nuts
1/3 cup currants
2 eggs, lightly beaten
1 teaspoon sugar
Salt and coarsely ground black
  pepper to taste

1 large leg of lamb, 7 to 8 pounds (have the butcher bone it and make sure he gives you back the bone)

MARINADE
1 cup fresh lemon juice
1/4 cup sugar
1/4 cup olive oil
1 tablespoon minced fresh dill weed, or 1 teaspoon dried
4 teeth of garlic, finely minced
1/4 teaspoon cayenne
1 bay leaf
1 teaspoon dry mustard
1/2 teaspoon mixed dried herbs (Italian seasoning)
1/2 tablespoon paprika
Salt and fresh-ground black pepper to taste

1/2 cup beef broth
Lettuce leaves, tomato wedges, and lemon slices (optional)

Combine all of the ingredients for the stuffing and pack them firmly into the leg of lamb. Truss shut with bamboo or metal skewers.

Mix all the ingredients for the marinade together exceedingly well. Put the stuffed leg of lamb in a deep dish, pour the marinade over, and rub it into the meat on all sides. Refrigerate overnight, turning and rubbing several times.

To bake, place the lamb in a roasting pan with a tight-fitting lid. Mix the broth with the remaining marinade and pour over the leg of lamb. Bake at 350° for 1-1/2 hours or until the meat is exceedingly tender. Remove the lid during the last 20 minutes and turn the heat to 400° to brown.

To serve, set on a heated platter surrounded by greens, tomato wedges, and lemon slices, if you wish. Using a sharp slicing knife, cut straight through, making 1-inch-thick slices.

PUMPKIN BREDE
South Africa
Lamb and Pumpkin Stew

Serves 6
3 tablespoons lard
2 to 2-1/2 pounds boneless lean lamb, cut into bite-sized chunks
2 large onions, cut into 1/4-inch-thick slices
4 teeth of garlic, finely minced
1 teaspoon grated fresh ginger
3 to 4 small fresh hot chilies, chopped
1/2 teaspoon ground cinnamon
1/4 teaspoon ground cumin
1/4 teaspoon ground allspice
1/8 teaspoon ground cloves

2 pounds fresh pumpkin, seeded, peeled, and cut into bite-sized cubes (about 5 cups)
1 cup beef broth
3 tablespoons dark brown sugar
Salt and fresh-ground black pepper to taste

Heat the lard in a heavy casserole with a tight-fitting lid. Add the lamb and brown on all sides. Add the onions and, stirring gently, cook until tender but not browned. Add the next 7 ingredients and, stirring, cook over moderate heat for about 2 minutes. Add the pumpkin and toss until evenly coated with the spices. Then pour in the broth, add the sugar, salt, and pepper, bring to a boil, and remove from the heat immediately. Put on the lid and put into a preheated oven at 350° for 45 minutes or until the lamb is tender. Serve hot.

"Roaste or sodden wholesome is mutton and of the bones be made a broth full restorative and a gelly right royalle."
Twelfth-century Discourse on Sheep

LEYLA'S
LAMB SHANK, GARLIC, AND PEPPER CASSEROLE
Turkey

My friend Leyla is a Tartar by race. She was born in Japan and lived there until she moved to Turkey at the age of 17, and now she is a Californian.

For those of you who may not know what a Tartar is, they are the last of the Golden Horde, the decendants of Batu Khan. She taught me that eggplant does not have to be blatchy gray steamed mush. She makes the very best *piroshki* I have ever eaten in my entire life, and her recipes for Gobba Ghannouj, kebobs, and lots of things with yogurt in them are in this book. Leyla taught me that garlic is a staple vegetable, not a creature of dubious character to be used penuriously on occasion, as is illustrated by the following recipe.

Serves 6
6 meaty lamb shanks, sawn into
   2 or 3 sections each
10 boiling onions, or 3 large
   onions cut into quarters
2 large bell peppers, seeded and
   cut into quarters
3 large potatoes, peeled and cut
   into quarters
8 small fresh hot chilies
2 long slim fresh mild chilies
2 large carrots, cut into 2-inch
   chunks
1 cup large fresh or thawed frozen
   lima beans
30 to 40 peeled teeth of garlic, or
   as Leyla says, a double handful
6 tomatoes, each no more than
   2 inches in diameter, stemmed
   but left whole
2 heads (flowerlets) fresh dill, or
   1/2 teaspoon dried
1/2 teaspoon mixed dried herbs
   (Italian seasoning)
Salt and coarsely ground
   black pepper
Cabbage or grape leaves

You are going to need an ovenproof container with a tight-fitting lid that is large enough to accommodate all of the above. A Dutch oven is perfect. Place the lamb shanks on the bottom. Then layer in the vegetables in the order listed. Sprinkle on the herbs and lots of salt and pepper to taste.

Use enough cabbage or grape leaves to make a tight blanket over the top of everything. Cut a double thickness of a brown paper bag that is about 1 inch larger than the lid of the container. Oil it on both sides with vegetable oil until the paper is saturated through. Lay it on the top of the cooking vessel and put on the lid. Put it into a *cold* oven, turn the temperature setting to 300°, and cook for 5 to 6 hours. If everything will fit you can, of course, use an electric crock. To serve, arrange the various items on a heated platter. Strain the pan juices, heat but do not thicken, and serve in a separate boat to pour over each serving if wanted. Perfect accompaniments are fresh French bread and butter and a crisp green salad with a dill vinaigrette.

You are of course questioning the 30 teeth of garlic and no cooking liquid. As I told you in the introduction that you didn't read (I never read them either), when garlic is cooked for a long time over low heat, the harsh acid is dissipated and you are left only with the sweet, wonderful flavor. You need no liquid because, again, this long slow cooking draws the liquid out of the meat and vegetables and they baste themselves. That is why all those cabbage leaves and paper are on the top.

SAUSAGES & VARIETY MEATS

It is conjectured that sometime around 25,000 B.C. humans, or a close approximation thereof, first discovered that a slab of critter chucked into the embers of a fire not only tasted better but was less perishable and more transportable than raw flesh. We are also told that humans did not develop skills as potters until sometime around 6000 B.C. Are we to assume that the culinary development of humankind stood still during the intervening years? Hardly.

There are numerous evidences of ancient pit cookery throughout the world. Foods were cooked not by actual contact with fire, but by filling the pits with water, adding the foodstuffs, and then filling the pits with stones that had been heated in fire. The food was boiled/steamed, an excellent method for rendering hard roots and grains edible—items that were less than delightful when singed in the embers. There is one obvious drawback to this method of cookery. You had to bring your food to the container and heat source, sometimes a problem for a nomadic culture.

Even before the development of pottery, however, there was another cooking vessel readily available to the Neolithic cook. It was waterproof, reasonably heatproof, and ultimately portable: the stomach of the animal itself. It was discovered that animals hunted in the autumn had been eating the ripened grains of their pastures, and that when the stomachs were cooked in the embers or hung over the fire, the result was a palatable and nourishing pottage.

Soon it was learned that the other soft meats—the liver, kidneys, heart, and some of the fat—if chopped up and added to the grains already in the stomach, produced an excellent delicacy, and the first sausages were born, or puddings, as they were called by medieval people. Puddings were originally meat and grain stuffed into the stomach or gut and boiled or steamed. Over the centuries newly available seasonings were added, and eventually so were dried fruits. The Christmas plum pudding we hear so much of did not contain plums; it was plumb full of goodness. In France, the word for one category of sausage is still *boudin*.

MAKING SAUSAGES

Before you begin, we need to have a general talk about sausage making. First, you need hog casings. Yes, indeed, hog casings are the intestines of hogs, thoroughly cleaned and prepared for use. How do you find them? Get out the yellow pages and phone every butcher in town. You won't find them at Lucky or Safeway. Small specialty butchers often have them;

so do butchers catering to an ethnic clientele. They come either prepackaged in cottage-cheese-type containers or in bulk, in which case the butcher will reel you off a few yards. To keep, *do not* freeze. This removes the elasticity from the tissue and guarantees that your sausages will burst during cooking if not before. To keep them, pack them in lots of salt. Put a cup of salt in a bowl, add the casings, and mush them about with your hand. Then put the casings and all of the salt in a refrigerator dish or plastic bag and put them in the refrigerator. They will keep indefinitely.

To use, remove as much as you want and soak in fresh running water for a few minutes. Drain and cut into whatever lengths you need. Slip one end over the water tap and, holding it in place with one hand, turn the faucet on. This washes all the excess salt from the inside of the casing and also opens the casing up to make it easy to use. Hold the rinsed casing by one end and draw it between two fingers of your other hand to wipe off excess water.

Now you must somehow convince your sausage stuffing to climb inside the casing and stay there. This is a significant problem. Most hand or electric grinders have

sausage stuffing attachments. I find them difficult to use because they require three hands: one to continuously pack the meat into the machine, one to operate the machine, and one to constantly keep easing the stuffed sausage along so the meat won't pack up into uneven lumps, making portions get too fat and burst. If you have access to a third hand, or are quite clever, fine; if not, I suggest a hand stuffer. This is a small metal gadget that looks a lot like a funnel except that the nozzle is fatter. They are usually available at super-trendy kitchen supply shops or, in the opposite direction, small hardware stores in ethnic communities.

Given that you cannot find either, you can get by with a two-liter plastic drink bottle, 3 inches of 1-inch diameter plastic tubing, and a super-glue. Cut the pouring end of the bottle off about 3 inches from the opening. Force the tubing over the end of the bottle and glue into place.

Now, let's try to stuff these things. Tie a knot in one end of the casing. Gather it up and slip the open end over the stuffer like you were putting on a pair of nylons, gathering all of the casing onto the end of the stuffer. Begin packing the meat into the stuffer. This is another one of those activities where you have to listen for the sound of one hand clapping, or become one with your subject. Experience will be the best instructor. Gently push the meat into the stuffer. You will notice that as the meat begins to fill the casing, a bubble of air is beginning to form. With a sharp skewer, prick the bubble. Ease the meat along to distribute it evenly along the casing. Be careful not to pack the meat too tightly, or the sausages will burst in the cooking. When you come to within about 3 or 4 inches of the end, remove the sausage from the stuffer and tie off the end.

For some sausages, like Cajun *boudin,* you will leave the sausage in 2- to 3-foot lengths. For others, like chorizo, you want them in individual 3- to 4-inch links. Just putting a twist in the casing every 3 inches doesn't work. As soon as you aren't looking, the sausages proceed to untwist themselves. Using string or thread is an unpalatable idea as well. Use the casing itself. Cut off a 4- or 5-inch length of casing. Gather it up, again like putting on nylons, and run your fingers through the center of what should now look like a fat, wrinkled rubber band. Hold it

open on your fingers and, with a pair of sharp kitchen scissors, cut it into 1/4-inch widths. Stretch these out and you will have several 4- or 5-inch-long strings of gut, the perfect thing for tying off the individual lengths.

CAUTION: If you are making individual lengths, make the sausage a little skinnier than normal. This will allow a little extra room for when the meat gets squeezed down when you tie off the links. Good luck!

CHORIZO
Mexico
Hot and Spicy Pork Sausages

Makes about 3 dozen 4-inch sausages
3 pounds ground pork
1 cup cornmeal
3 large onions, minced
20 teeth of garlic, minced
4 small fresh hot chilies, minced
1/2 cup minced fresh cilantro
1 teaspoon dried oregano
1 scant teaspoon ground cumin
3 tablespoons chili powder
1 scant teaspoon freshly ground
  black pepper
1 teaspoon crushed dried hot chilies
1 tablespoon sugar
1/4 cup distilled vinegar
Salt to taste
3 yards hog casings

Mix all of the ingredients except the casings together exceedingly well. Test for seasoning by frying a small patty. Adjust the seasoning. Pack into the casings following the instructions on page 86. Tie off into individual 4-inch links, but leave each yard in a continuous string. Hang over a wooden dowel to allow the skins to thoroughly dry. The sausages may be stored in plastic bags in the refrigerator for up to 2 weeks or in the freezer indefinitely. Fry or steam to cook, but, like any sausage, be sure to prick the skins to prevent bursting. It is always more successful to cook sausages slowly.

To get maximum heat from dried chilies and cayenne, buy them fresh and keep them in the freezer in a tight moisture-proof container. If you use them rapidly, within a month, this is not necessary.

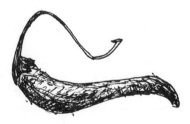

BOUDIN
Cajun Cuisine
(my favorite recipe in this book)
Beef, Pork, and Rice Sausage

In Cajun country *boudin* refers to the finest sausage I have ever eaten. The recipe here is considerably toned down from its original form. I am allowing that all of you may not yet be dedicated members of the Galvanized Gullet. However, if you are made of sterner stuff, then by all means go right ahead and add more chilies, more Tabasco, and more cayenne. A really fine "bate" of Cajun *boudin* will cross your eyes and clear your sinuses.

Makes about 4 yards
2 pounds ground beef
2 pounds ground pork
4 cups *al dente* steamed rice
4 large onions
20 teeth of garlic or more
6 small fresh hot chilies
2 celery stalks
2 large bell peppers, preferably 1 of them red
2 medium leeks, including 4 inches of the green
6 green onions, including the tops
1 cup minced fresh parsley
1/3 cup minced fresh cilantro
1 teaspoon crushed dried chilies

1 teaspoon coarsely ground black pepper
2 tablespoons sugar
1 teaspoon dried mixed herbs (Italian seasoning)
Salt to taste
4 yards hog casings

Put the meats and rice into a large bowl. Very finely mince all the vegetables. *Watch my lips!* I said very finely mince. I *did not* say, make into mush. Therefore, if you have a quick thumb on the button and truly can make your food processor produce a pile of nice fluffy *finely minced* veggies and not baby food, then by all means use it. If not, then put the thing away and use a good knife, a very sharp knife. You will probably have to resharpen it several times during the process. Is all that clear?

Add the finely *minced* veggies to the meat and rice and sprinkle over all of the remaining ingredients, except the hog casings, of course. Mix exceedingly well. The only way you are going to be able to do this is to climb into that bowl with both hands and start kneading. If you have long fingernails you may wish to wear a pair of rubber gloves. To test for seasoning, make a small patty and fry it in a bit of oil. Adjust the seasoning. If you are of stout enough makeup then do by all means add more chilies, either fresh or crushed dried chilies.

Mix thoroughly after adding more seasonings. Cut the hog casing into lengths about 1 yard long. Following the instructions on page 86, stuff the goop in the bowl into the casings, packing it firmly but not tightly, or they will burst in the cooking. Tie off. With a skewer, pierce the *boudin* all over. This also is a precaution to hopefully keep the sausages from bursting.

Using a heavy container—roasting pan, casserole, wok, or Dutch oven—with a tight-fitting lid, coil the *boudin* around themselves so that they lie in flat layers in the container. Pour in water enough to come just level with the top of the *boudin*. Put on the lid and simmer over low heat for 1-1/2 to 2 hours.

Leave the sausage in its cooking liquid until cool. Carefully lift the lengths of *boudin* out of the cooking vessel and place in a colander. Rinse under running hot water to remove the grease that has adhered to them during the cooking. Pat dry. *Boudin* is good at room temperature as a snack like salami, or steamed and served hot as the main course of a meal.

(If you do make this, don't let anyone know you know how. Your life will never be the same. You will be considered a *boudin* machine only.)

CHAURICE
Cajun
Hot Pork Sausage

Makes about 3 yards
4 pounds coarsely ground pork
1 pound coarsely ground pork fat
4 large onions, chopped
1 cup minced fresh parsley
1/4 cup minced fresh cilantro
30 teeth of garlic, finely minced
6 small fresh hot chilies, minced
1 teaspoon crushed dried hot chilies
2 teaspoons freshly ground
   black pepper
2 teaspoons ground thyme
1/2 teaspoon ground nutmeg
1/2 teaspoon ground cinnamon
1/2 teaspoon fennel seeds
2 tablespoons sugar
Salt to taste
3 yards hog casings

Mix all of the ingredients except the casings together well. Cut the casings into 3-foot lengths and proceed as in the directions on page 86. This sausage may be stored as is and cooked fresh or, if you have a home smoker, it is excellent smoked.

HOT ITALIAN SAUSAGES
Lombardy

Makes about 3 dozen 4-inch links
4 pounds coarsely ground pork
1 pound coarsely ground pork fat
4 onions, minced
20 teeth of garlic, minced
1 tablespoon crushed dried
   hot chilies
1/2 cup minced fresh cilantro
1 tablespoon dried mixed herbs
   (Italian seasoning)
1 teaspoon freshly ground black
   pepper
1 teaspoon fennel seeds
1 tablespoon sugar
Salt to taste
3 yards hog casings

Mix all of the ingredients except the hog casings together exceedingly well. Fry a patty to test for seasoning. Adjust the seasoning to your taste. Cut the casings into 3-foot lengths and proceed as in instructions on page 86. Tie off into 4-inch links and leave each yard of links intact.

Again, these sausages are excellent cooked fresh, or they may be smoked if you have access to a home smoker.

VARIETY MEATS

It is an unfortunate circumstance that Americans have traditionally shied away from variety meats, or offal, as it is called in England. It has always pained me to see friends pull the bag of giblets out of a chicken and give it to the cats. Lucky cats. I had a student in one of my cooking classes who, when I made a steak and kidney pie, said, "I didn't know people could eat those!"

One of my joys in shopping abroad is the great abundance of variety meats. Not only is there always liver, kidneys, heart, tongue, fries, tripes, etc., but you can get them from pigs, lambs, cows, calves, chickens and turkeys, ducks and geese. (What are fries? you may ask. Fries are a by-product of gelding the male animal of any species. The cowboys on my great-grandfather's ranch of course knew them as Rocky Mountain oysters.)

Anyone who was raised on a farm as I was is well aware that the finest treat available, the reward for the back-breaking work of butchering day, is the freshly cooked liver and kidneys. There is absolutely nothing that can compare to the liver of any critter, lightly sautéed in butter with a hint of garlic and fresh herbs, within two or three hours of butchering.

There is no getting around the fact that variety meats make for some fine eating, but like many things, it's all in the cooking. I have known many people who vowed that they hated liver and would never touch it again, and at my table were unaware that they were eating it. Liver and onions, fried in grease until the onions are brown threads and the liver is the texture of leather, is an atrocity that shouldn't be foisted off on anyone. However, you will have to go a long way to find a dish as delicate and fine as fresh liver thinly sliced and briefly sautéed in butter, still showing a significant bit of pink in the middle. The traditional scrambled eggs and brains is an abominable dish in my estimation, but poached brains in a zesty vinaigrette is another beast altogether.

I don't know how Americans developed their repugnance for variety meats. Perhaps it was a status thing that developed as those of us who got here first became more affluent. Immigrants who were not yet well established were forced to do the best they could with what they could afford,

and the more opulent perhaps took delight in not having to eat what their poorer neighbors ate. Personally I find *tripe à la mode de Caen* or a fine pâté preferable to a fried steak any ol' day.

MIXED OFFAL SIS KEBAB
Greece

Serves 6 to 8

MARINADE
1/2 cup olive oil
1/2 cup dry red wine
   (generic burgundy will do
   just fine)
1 tablespoon sugar
10 teeth of garlic, minced
1 teaspoon crushed dried hot chilies
1 teaspoon dry mustard
1/2 teaspoon dried oregano
1 fresh rosemary sprig, or
   1 teaspoon dried rosemary
2 bay leaves, bruised
1 tablespoon chopped fresh cilantro
1 tablespoon chopped fresh basil
1/2 teaspoon coarsely ground
   black pepper
Salt to taste

1/2 pound tripe
1 pound lamb liver
1 pound lamb heart
1 pound lamb kidneys
12 to 15 small fresh medium-hot
   chilies

2 small zucchini, cut into 1/2-inch
   slices
1 small eggplant, cut into 1-inch
   cubes
2 medium onions, cut into bite-
   sized chunks
1 large bell pepper, preferably
   red, seeded and cut into bite-
   sized chunks
1 pound small mushrooms

Put all of the marinade ingredients in a glass jar with a tight-fitting lid and shake vigorously.

Cut the tripe into 1/4-inch-wide strips as long as you can make them. Cover with water and bring to a boil. Drain, cover with water again, and boil until exceedingly tender. Drain and pat dry.

Cut the remaining meats into bite-sized chunks. Leave any fat on the kidneys. Place all of the remaining ingredients, including the tripe, in a bowl and pour the marinade over. Turn over to make sure that everything is covered. Leave unrefrigerated for at least 2 hours.

To assemble, pick a piece of tripe out of the marinade and stick one end of the strip onto a skewer, leaving the other end hanging free. Fill the skewer with a selection of the other ingredients, threading alternately. When the skewer is almost full, pick up the loose end of tripe and wrap it spiral fashion up the skewer, securing it on the tip when you reach the end. Continue until you have used all the ingredients.

To cook, place the kebabs on a grill 4 inches above a bed of coals. Cook to desired doneness, turning occasionally. Paint with extra marinade during the cooking. Serve at once with pilaf or steamed rice.

PIGS' FEET
WITH BLACK BEAN SAUCE
China

Serves 4

3 pounds pigs' feet
2 tablespoons peanut oil
3 tablespoons fermented black
    bean sauce
6 teeth of garlic, minced
1 tablespoon grated fresh ginger
1 teaspoon crushed dried hot
    chilies
1 teaspoon dry mustard
1/4 cup soy sauce
1/4 cup cream sherry
2 cups chicken or pork broth
1/3 cup minced fresh parsley

Have the butcher split the pigs' feet and cut them once across as well. Cover them with cold water and bring to a boil. Drain, cover again, and boil for 30 minutes.

Heat the oil in a heavy pan and add the bean sauce, garlic, ginger, and chilies. Sauté for 1 minute, then add the mustard, soy, and sherry. Stir over medium heat to form a paste, then add the pigs' feet and toss them to coat evenly with the bean sauce. Continue cooking in this fashion for 2 or 3 minutes or until they brown slightly. Then pour over the broth, bring to a boil, reduce the heat to a fast simmer, cover with a lid, and continue cooking for 1 hour or until the feet are exceedingly tender. Check occasionally to see if more liquid is needed. Place the feet on a serving dish, spoon over the sauce from the pan, and sprinkle with the parsley. Serve with steamed rice.

ABOUT DUMPLINGS

Now before continuing, we are going to have to have a talk about dumplings. Every culture has them in one form or another, but in my experience only in America are they feather-light, moist clouds of delicate flavor that are likely to float out of the pot if you raise the lid without caution. Other cultures bake them, boil them, steam them, and put liver, cheese, eggs, fish, potatoes, and sour cherries in them. All of these concoctions are delicious but they are not American-style dumplings.

Read some cookbooks and you'll find out why. I guess anyone who can make traditional American dumplings learned how to do it from Mama. In nine encyclopedic tomes by various lauded gods and goddesses of cookery, I could not find one recipe that even approached the way my mother taught me to make dumplings. In these books the batter always contained eggs and a lot of butter or lard. The cooking methods varied from putting the batter or dough on top of water and boiling the hell out of them, to putting the dumplings on top of the stew, boiling them uncovered for 5 minutes, then covering for 5 minutes and considering them done. One recipe had you stand there and turn them over every 2 minutes to cook them on both sides. In the word of Nero Wolf, "Phooey." All this will produce soggy lumps of lead! Eggs make them heavy, too much fat makes them heavy, and *MILK* makes them heavy. And they must have their privacy, 20 to 25 minutes of it. Before that and they will be underdone and fall, more than that and they will begin to absorb too much moisture. You should plop them on top of your stew, put on a tight-fitting lid, and leave them alone for 20 to 25 minutes. It's tempting to lift the lid and take a look, but don't do it. You won't be turned to a pillar of salt like Lot, but you will have to eat soggy dumplings, an even worse fate.

SON-OF-A-BITCH STEW
Family Recipe
(this one is armed and dangerous)
Stew of Chitlins and Chilies
with Dumplings

The buffalo still roamed the short-grass prairie when my great-grand-father crossed this continent to carve out his chunk of California. They were so plentiful that it was not yet an evilness to bring one down to provide the wagon train with fresh meat for the next week. The choicest tidbits—the tongue and the brains—went to the family of the man who fired the shot that brought the beast down. But the next best thing, shared by all who participated in the hunt and the

dressing out, were the intestines, well cleaned and made into Son-of-a Bitch Stew. This zesty concoction with the less-than-puritanical name became a specialty of the table at Packwood Ranch, being made each time there was a butchering. There weren't any buffalo in the San Joaquin Valley, but there were bear, boar, deer, and soon the domestic products of the ranch itself, and Son-of-a-Bitch Stew was just too good to forego because of a little thing like not having a herd of buffalo in the backyard. At Packwood, the con-coction took on a definitely Latin flavor, the influence of the Mexican women who assisted the Chinese cook, but it was always served with a topping of that uniquely American phenomenon, feather-light dumplings.

Serves 6
2 pounds prepared chitterlings
1/2 cup distilled vinegar
2 tablespoons lard
2 large onions, chopped
20 teeth of garlic
12 whole small fresh hot chilies
6 small fresh hot chilies, cut
    into thin rings
1/2 tablespoon crushed dried hot
    chilies, or more*

1 teaspoon mixed dried herbs
    (Italian seasoning)
1 tablespoon chili powder
1 tablespoon minced fresh cilantro
3 celery stalks, chopped
1 large bell pepper, chopped
3 large tomatoes, coarsely chopped
12 small boiling onions, peeled
One 14-ounce can hominy, drained
2 tablespoons sugar
1/2 cup blackstrap molasses
1 scant teaspoon coarsely ground
    black pepper
1 California bay laurel leaf
1/2 cup minced fresh parsley
3 cups beef broth
Salt to taste
1 fistful dried digger weed**
1 tablespoon flour mixed with
    1/4 cup water or broth

DUMPLINGS
1 cup unbleached all-purpose flour
1/2 tablespoon baking powder
1/2 teaspoon sugar
A wee pinch of salt
2 tablespoons butter or lard
2/3 cup *water* mixed with
1 tablespoon distilled vinegar

Wash the chitterlings thoroughly and cut into 2- to 3-inch-long chunks. Put them into a pot with a lid and add the vinegar. Add enough water to cover completely. Bring to a boil over a high flame. Boil rapidly for 15 minutes. Drain and cover with fresh water. Bring to a boil and reduce the heat to a fast simmer. Put on the lid and continue to simmer for 3 hours, or until the chitterlings are exceedingly tender. Add more water from time to time if necessary. Drain and pat dry with paper towels.

Heat the lard in a Dutch oven or heavy casserole. Do not let it smoke. Sauté the chitterlings a few at a time until browned on all sides. Remove with a slotted spoon and set aside. Add the onions and sauté just until the onions are translucent. Return the chitterlings to the pan. Add all of the remaining ingredients except the flour mixture and the dumpling ingredients. Bring to a boil. Reduce the heat and simmer for 1 hour. Stir occasionally to prevent sticking.

Add the flour and water mixture and stir to distribute evenly. Continue simmering over moderate heat until the stew is lightly thickened and the gravy is glossy.

To make the dumplings, mix all of the dry ingredients together and cut in the butter or lard with a pastry cutter. Make a well in the center of the dry ingredients and, using a fork, stir in the water and vinegar mixture. Stir vigorously until the batter is well mixed and comes away from the sides of the bowl, somewhat losing its sticky texture.

Have the stew bubbling over moderate heat but not boiling rapidly or you risk it sticking and burning. Drop the dough by tablespoonfuls onto the top of the stew. Keep the heat at a level that will allow the stew to continue to lightly bubble but will not risk scorching, which is always a problem with a thickened stew. Put a tight-fitting lid on immediately and leave absolutely alone for 20 to 25 minutes, depending on the size of the dumplings.

If you are afraid your lid is allowing steam to escape you can use the old-country trick of kneading up a plain flour and water paste and using it to completely seal the lid.

Dumplings must be served *immediately*. No "Just as soon as Spiderman's over," or "Right after the next inning." When the dumplings are done you either eat them then or you feed them to the dog.

*I have chosen to spare your own chitterlings by not following the original recipe in my great-grandmother's journals. In its original form it called for 1 pound of chopped dried hot chilies. Of course, this was for a quantity to feed the entire ranch. My mother remembered, however, that it was pure fire as it was served at Packwood. Make it as hot as you want. This is a recipe that can be as hot as you can take it. Make sure you have lots of beer and the mild form of *salsa cruda* listed in the section on fire extinguishers.

**Several of the original recipes in my great grandmother's journals call for digger weed. I have consulted with the research department at the Bancroft Library at the University of California, members of the West Coast Indian Council, and the botany department of the University of California at Davis, and no one has the faintest idea what digger weed is. However, it is everyone's educated guess that it must have been something used by the Digger Indians, particularly since my great grandfather was Governor of the Diggers and they had a camp by Packwood Creek on his, at one time their, property. (Incidentally, Digger was a rather derogatory and uneducated term the white man gave to all California Indians, which I, being part Paiute, take as a personal affront.)

LIANG-BAN-YAO-PIAN
Chinese
Marinated Kidneys

Serves 4 to 6

MARINADE
1/4 cup peanut oil
1/4 cup rice vinegar
2 tablespoons soy sauce
1 teaspoon smoky Oriental
  sesame oil
1 tablespoon finely grated fresh
  ginger
6 teeth of garlic, minced
2 small hot chilies, finely minced
1/2 teaspoon crushed dried hot
  chilies
1/2 tablespoon sugar
1/4 cup minced fresh parsley
Salt to taste

6 pork kidneys
1 medium leek
1/2 cup thinly sliced mushrooms
1 red bell pepper, seeded and
  cut into thin rings
Watercress sprigs
1 teaspoon sesame seeds

Combine all of the marinade ingredients in a jar with a tight-fitting lid and shake vigorously. Set aside while you prepare the kidneys.

Slice the kidneys into paper-thin slices and remove any large pieces of fat. Put the kidneys in a strainer and set the strainer in a bowl. Set another large bowl under the tap, fill it with cold water, and leave the tap running. Pour boiling water over the kidneys. Lift the kidneys out of the hot water and set in the cold running water; leave until cold. Empty the hot water. Place the kidneys in the strainer back in the other bowl and pour hot water over them again. Again place the kidneys in cold running water. Repeat the process one more time. Drain thoroughly and place in a large shallow refrigerator dish.

Cut the leek into thin slices on the diagonal, including 4 inches of the green. Wash the leeks thoroughly and blanch them in the same manner as the kidneys, but only put them in one hot-water bath. Drain thoroughly and add to the kidneys in the refrigerator dish. Do the same with the mushrooms. Place the bell pepper rings over all. Shake the marinade vigorously and pour over the kidneys and vegetables. Stir gently to cover all with the marinade and refrigerate for at least 4 hours, turning occasionally to ensure that all is covered with the marinade.

To serve, place on a bed of fresh watercress and sprinkle with the sesame seeds. Serve chilled.

CHICKEN & TURKEY

Jean Anthelme Brillat-Savarin wrote in his *Encyclopedia of Cuisine,* "Chicken is for the cook what canvas is to the painter. It is served to us boiled, roasted, fried, hot or cold, whole or in pieces, with or without sauce, boned, skinned, stuffed and always with equal success."

Some historians believe that the domestic chicken is a descendant of the red jungle fowl of Southeast Asia, and was domesticated around 2500 B.C. Professor Carl Sower, founder of the department of geography at the University of California at Berkeley, believed it to have been domesticated much earlier. The Rhode Island Red, that superb fowl for both meat and eggs, is a New World breed, being a descendant of the Aricana of South America.

Regardless of what academic authorities may have to say on the subject, epicures both ancient and modern have had plenty to say, all of it good. Tomb paintings dating from the middle of the Old Kingdom in Egypt show slaves herding flocks of chickens to accompany the pharaoh into the other world, and numerous small figurines of both chickens and ducks have been found in tombs. Our Egyptian ancestors were, in fact, so fond of chicken that they guaranteed a constant supply by incubating eggs in caves using oil lamps to provide the necessary heat.

Legend tells us that the first of the Three Celestial Rulers of China created chicken and pig so that man would always be happy. In fact, the earliest pictograph in the Chinese language for home is a pig and a chicken under a roof.

The Forme of Cury was the first cookbook produced in England. It was written by the royal chef of King Richard. However, historians differ as to whether this was Richard I, the Lion Hearted, or Richard II. Since Coeur de Lion spent but nine months of his ten-year reign in England, my vote would go to Richard II. Whichever Richard's chef wrote the first English cookbook, one thing is certain, he considered "chekyn" a most noble dish to serve one's lord.

KUMQUAT-MAY CHICKEN
Family Recipe
Sweet and Spicy Baked Chicken

Science fiction and fantasy writer Randall Garrett is an outrageous punster, a punster above and beyond the call of duty. He had this chicken dish at my house one evening and asked for the recipe. After writing it down for him I said that he might find it difficult to find the preserved kumquats, and he answered, "I'll find them, my lady, kumquat-may . . ."

Serves 4
1/4 cup light-flavored vegetable oil
1 roasting chicken, cut into serving pieces

1/2 cup orange marmalade
1/3 cup soy sauce
1/3 cup cream sherry
1 tablespoon minced fresh ginger
10 teeth of garlic, minced
1/2 tablespoon crushed dried hot chilies
1 scant teaspoon dry mustard
1 scant teaspoon dried mixed herbs (Italian seasoning)
1/2 teaspoon ground cinnamon
1/4 teaspoon ground nutmeg
1 scant teaspoon coarsely ground black pepper
1/2 cup brown sugar
1 large onion, cut into thin rings
1 each medium red and green bell pepper, seeded and cut into thin strips
1 small jar preserved kumquats (about a dozen)
Salt to taste
Watercress sprigs and a seedless orange cut into thin slices for garnish (leave the peel on the orange)

Put the oil in a heavy baking pan. Add the chicken pieces and turn them over in the oil. Put the next 12 ingredients (up to and including the sugar) in a bowl and mix thoroughly. Add the onion, peppers, and kumquats, including any jelly that may be with them, and turn over in the sauce to cover evenly. Add salt. Pour all onto the chicken.

Turn the chicken over. Put into the oven at 350° for 45 minutes or until the chicken is done to your liking. Turn occasionally and spoon over the juices from the pan. When done, arrange the pieces of chicken on a serving platter. Strew the onion, peppers, and kumquats over the top. Surround with watercress and orange slices. Accompany with steamed rice, kumquat-may.

(It would be a worthy project to serve this to a group doing a reading of Randall's *Too Many Magicians*.)

POLLO EN MOLE VERDE
Mexico
Chicken in Green Nut Sauce

Serves 4
1 large frying chicken, cut into serving pieces

GREEN NUT SAUCE
1/2 cup pumpkin seeds
1/2 cup blanched almonds
4 small fresh hot chilies
3 tomatoes, preferably green, chopped
1 large onion, chopped
6 teeth of garlic, chopped
1/3 cup chopped fresh cilantro
1 large bell pepper, seeded and chopped

1/2 cup chopped fresh parsley
1/2 tablespoon sugar
1/2 teaspoon freshly ground black
  pepper
1 cup chicken broth (use the
  broth the chicken is boiled in
  and, if it is weak, give it a little
  help with powdered bouillon)
1 tablespoon olive oil
1/4 teaspoon ground cumin

Wedges of ripe tomato and lemon

Cover the chicken with water and
bring to a boil. Reduce the heat to
moderate and cover. Cook for 30
minutes or until tender but not
falling off the bone.

Put all the ingredients for the
sauce in the jar of a blender and
reduce to a purée. You may have
to do it in more than one batch.
Pour the purée into a heavy skillet
and bring to a boil, stirring all the
while. Immediately reduce the heat
and continue simmering for 5
minutes. Remove the chicken from
the pot and place in the skillet
with the sauce. Turn over to coat
evenly. Place in a preheated 375°
oven for 10 minutes or just until
the chicken begins to brown on
the edges. Remove the chicken to
a serving plate and pour over the
extra sauce. Garnish with wedges
of tomato and lemon, to contrast
with the green of the sauce.

SINGGANG AYAM
Sumatra
Broiled Chicken
in Almond and Chili Sauce

Serves 4
1 coconut
2 cups boiling water
Liquid from the coconut
1 frying chicken
1/4 cup peanut oil
1/2 cup blanched almonds
1 medium onion, chopped
4 teeth of garlic, minced
1 teaspoon grated fresh ginger
1/2 teaspoon grated lemon rind
4 to 6 small fresh hot chilies,
  chopped
1/2 teaspoon ground turmeric
1/2 teaspoon ground coriander
1 teaspoon chopped fresh cilantro
1 teaspoon sugar
Salt to taste

Open the coconut and use the
boiling water to make coconut
milk according to the instructions
on page 13. Use the liquid from
the coconut, if necessary, to make
2 cups of coconut milk.

With a pair of poultry shears,
cut along both sides of the chicken
to remove the back. Spread the
carcass open until the breastbone
breaks. Then lay the chicken on a
flat surface, skin side up, and
press the breastbone with the flat
of your hand. When the sharp
breastbone pops up, discard it.
Then, using the flat of a large
heavy cleaver or a steak-pounding
mallet, pound the body of the
chicken until it is flattened but not
mutilated. Set aside.

Put all of the remaining ingredients into the jar of a blender
and whir into a purée. Pour into a
heavy saucepan and bring to a
boil. Reduce the heat immediately
and simmer, stirring occasionally,
for 10 minutes. Sometimes coconut
milk will curdle when it is heated.
If this should happen, purée it in
the blender again.

Paint the chicken on both sides
with the sauce, roll it up tightly,
and lay in a dish. Pour the rest of
the sauce over it and leave it to
marinate for at least 2 hours.

Unroll the chicken, shake off the
excess sauce, and cook under the
broiler or over charcoal to desired
doneness. Turn the chicken occasionally and brush frequently with
the extra sauce. Serve hot with
steamed rice.

BASTILA
Morocco
Flaky Pigeon Pie

Serves 6

1 cup (2 sticks) butter
1/2 cup olive oil
1 large frying chicken, cut into serving pieces, given that you probably won't find pigeon at your local market
1 large onion, minced
1 tablespoon minced fresh cilantro
2 tablespoons minced fresh parsley
1 teaspoon grated fresh ginger
1/4 teaspoon ground cumin
3/4 teaspoon cayenne
1/4 teaspoon ground turmeric
1/4 teaspoon crumbled saffron threads
1 scant teaspoon ground cinnamon
2 tablespoons sugar
1 cup light chicken broth
8 eggs, lightly beaten
Salt and freshly ground black pepper
About 1 pound *filo* dough
Powdered sugar
Ground cinnamon

Melt 1/2 cup of the butter and 1/4 cup of the olive oil together in a heavy skillet over moderate to high heat. Brown the pieces of chicken on all sides, then remove with a slotted spoon and set aside. Add the giblets and onion and sauté just until the onion is soft but not yet browned. Add the next 10 ingredients and stir. Cook for about 2 minutes. Add the cup of broth and bring to a boil, stirring constantly. Return the chicken to the pan and turn to coat evenly. Reduce the heat to low and simmer covered for about 1 hour, or until the chicken is exceedingly tender. Set the chicken and giblets aside to cool. When cool enough to handle, remove all the meat from the bones and cut into very thin strips. Mince the giblets fine.

Bring the sauce to the boil and, stirring constantly to prevent burning, cook for 2 or 3 minutes. Reduce the heat to moderate. Gently stir the sauce while pouring the beaten eggs into it in a thin stream. Continue to stir until the eggs and sauce have formed curds. Add salt and pepper to taste.

Melt the remaining 1/2 cup butter and 1/4 cup of oil together. To assemble, paint the bottom of a 12-inch heavy skillet liberally with the butter and oil combination. Cover the bottom of the pan with an overlapping layer of the sheets of *filo*, letting the edges hang over the side. You should place the *filo* so that about 4 inches hangs over the edge of the pan. Fold 2 sheets and place in the middle of the pan. Paint lightly with the oil and butter mixture. Add another layer of *filo* in the same manner and paint again. Continue until half of the *filo* has been used. Put half of the egg mixture on the pastry and spread evenly. Sprinkle over all of the chicken and giblets. Spread with the remaining egg. Gently smooth the top.

Begin covering the eggs with sheets of *filo* in the same manner as when you covered the bottom of the pan except that you do not let the edges hang over the sides of the pan. Fold them over onto themselves to make them fit. Be sure to place 2 folded sheets in the middle of each layer of pastry and to paint each layer with the butter and oil mixture. When all the sheets have been used, bring the ends of the bottom sheets over the finished pie to seal the edges, and paint with the butter and oil.

Put the pan on the highest heat possible and fry the pie for 3 to 4 minutes or until the bottom of the pie is golden brown. Place a large flat platter on top of the frying pan, hold firmly, and invert the frying pan, transferring the pie to the platter. Paint the pan liberally with the oil and butter again, reheat over a high fire, and slide the pie back into the pan to fry the other side. Again, leave just until golden brown. Transfer the pie to the serving plate, sprinkle the top lightly with cinnamon and powdered sugar and, with a sharp knife or a pizza wheel, cut into wedges. Serve immediately.

SWEET AND SOUR CHICKEN CHICKEN CURRY
Sri Lanka

Serves 6 to 8
2 small frying chickens, cut into
  serving pieces
2 tablespoons olive oil
2 tablespoons butter
2 tablespoons Madras-style
  curry powder
1 teaspoon cayenne
1 tablespoon grated fresh ginger
4 teeth of garlic, minced
1 teaspoon ground cinnamon
1/4 teaspoon fennel seeds
1/2 teaspoon ground cumin
1/2 teaspoon coarsely ground
  black pepper
1 large onion, chopped
Two 20-ounce cans pineapple
  chunks

Juice from the pineapple
  plus enough reserved chicken
  broth to make 1-1/2 cups
1/2 cup sugar
1/2 cup distilled vinegar
Salt
2 medium onions, cut into bite-
  sized chunks
2 celery stalks, cut into bite-sized
  chunks
2 medium bell peppers, preferably
  1 red and 1 green, seeded and
  cut into 1/2-inch-wide strips
2 small seedless oranges, cut into
  thin rings, skin on
1 lemon, cut into thin slices, skin on
1 cup canned litchis, drained
1 cup preserved kumquats, drained
1 teaspoon minced fresh cilantro
2 tablespoons cornstarch
  mixed with
1/4 cup water

Put the chicken backs, necks, and giblets into a saucepan, cover with water, and bring to the boil. Reduce the heat, cover, and simmer until the meat is falling off the bones. Strain and reserve the broth. If it is not very flavorful give it a little help with powdered bouillon.

Melt the oil and butter together in a large, heavy skillet or casserole. Add the curry powder and stir about until slightly singed. Add the next 8 ingredients and sauté until the onions are soft but not yet browned. Add the chicken and brown well on all sides.

Drain the pineapple chunks and reserve the juice.

Pour in the pineapple juice and reserved broth and simmer covered until the chicken is tender. Add the sugar and vinegar and simmer for about 2 minutes. Taste. If you want a more distinct sweet and sour flavor add more sugar and vinegar at this time. Also add more cayenne if you want it hotter. Add salt to taste. Add the pineapple chunks and all the remaining ingredients except cornstarch mixture, stir gently, and simmer for 5 minutes. Add cornstarch mixture; stir and simmer until sauce is glossy and slightly thickened. Serve hot with steamed rice and steamed *chapatis* or flour tortillas.

KISS-THE-COLONEL-GOODBYE CHICKEN
Family Recipe

Serves 4 (if 2 of them aren't my sons)
1/4 cup flour
1/4 cup bread crumbs
2 tablespoons chili powder
1 teaspoon cayenne
1/2 teaspoon coarsely ground
   black pepper
1/2 tablespoon mixed dried herbs
   (Italian seasoning)
1 tablespoon paprika
1/2 tablespoon sugar
1 tablespoon finely minced fresh
   cilantro
1/4 teaspoon ground cinnamon
1 scant teaspoon ground ginger
1 scant teaspoon dry mustard
1 tablespoon finely minced garlic
Salt to taste
1 frying chicken, cut up
Light-flavored vegetable oil
   for frying

Put the flour and all the seasonings into a small paper bag and shake. Add the chicken pieces and shake to cover evenly. Shake the excess flour off each piece.

Heat the oil over high heat but do not let it smoke. Add the chicken. Be careful—it may splutter. Fry over high flame until the chicken is thoroughly browned on both sides, 5 or 6 minutes. When well browned, reduce the heat to medium and continue to fry, turning occasionally for another 12 to 15 minutes. To check for doneness, cut into one of the thighs. If the meat still shows blood at the bone, let it cook a bit longer. Drain off excess oil on paper towels and serve at once. If you want the skin crisp, fry uncovered; if you want it soft, cover during the cooking.

RED CHICK AND DIRTY RICE
Creole Cuisine
Chicken in Piquant Sauce with Seasoned Rice

Serves 6
1 tablespoon lard
1 tablespoon flour
3 tablespoons lard
1 large frying chicken, cut into
   serving pieces
1 large onion, chopped
6 teeth of garlic, minced
4 small fresh hot chilies, minced
1 medium bell pepper, seeded
   and chopped
6 green onions, minced
2 tablespoons paprika
1 scant teaspoon mixed dried herbs
   (Italian seasoning)
1 teaspoon minced fresh dill weed,
   or 1/4 teaspoon dried
1/4 teaspoon coarsely ground
   black pepper
1 scant teaspoon sugar
4 large tomatoes, chopped
2 cups rich chicken broth
Dirty Rice, page 133

Prepare a roux with the lard and flour (see page 49); set aside. Heat the lard in a heavy skillet over moderate heat and fry the chicken until nicely browned on both sides. Remove, drain off excess fat, and set aside.

Add the next 11 ingredients and sauté, stirring frequently, until a sauce begins to form. Add the roux and stir to incorporate thoroughly. Pour in the broth and continue to cook, stirring occasionally to prevent scorching, for about 10 minutes. Add the fried chicken and cook, covered, long enough to heat the chicken thoroughly, about 30 minutes.

Put the Dirty Rice on a serving dish and place the pieces of chicken on top. Pour over any extra sauce and serve immediately.

CHICKEN COUSCOUS
North Africa
Chicken, Vegetables, and Grain with Chili Sauce

Couscous is as ubiquitous in Northern Africa as rice is in the Orient or potatoes in Ireland. This version comes from Algiers.

Serves 10

3 cups packaged *couscous*

2 small frying chickens, cut into serving pieces

15 to 20 teeth of garlic, peeled and crushed

4 large onions, quartered

1 tablespoon crushed dried hot chilies

1 tablespoon mixed dried herbs (Italian seasoning)

1 bay leaf

1 tablespoon sugar

1 teaspoon salt

1 teaspoon dry mustard

1 teaspoon fresh-ground black pepper

1/2 cup chopped fresh cilantro

3 cinnamon sticks

2 whole cloves

3 medium potatoes, peeled and quartered

12 to 15 small boiling onions

1 cup bite-sized chunks of pumpkin

5 large long fresh mild chilies

10 small fresh hot chilies, preferably red

15 dates

2 medium leeks, trimmed and cut into 2-inch lengths, including 4 inches of the green

12 to 15 cherry tomatoes

SAUCE NO. 1

4 cups chicken broth

4 tomatoes, chopped

2 large onions, chopped

10 teeth of garlic, crushed

1/2 cup chopped fresh parsley

1/4 cup olive oil

1 large bell pepper, seeded and chopped

1 large onion, chopped

2 small fresh hot chilies, chopped

1/2 tablespoon sugar

Salt to taste

SAUCE NO. 2

1 cup Sauce No. 1

6 small fresh hot chilies

1 tablespoon grated fresh ginger

1 teaspoon cayenne

1/2 cup sugar

1/2 cup distilled vinegar

1/2 teaspoon ground cinnamon

1/4 cup olive oil

1 cup cooked chick-peas (garbanzo beans)

6 hard-cooked eggs, peeled and cut in half

1/2 cup pitted black olives, drained

1 tablespoon minced fresh cilantro

1 lemon, cut into thin slices

Prepare the *couscous* according to the manufacturer's directions. Put the chickens into a pot large enough to hold them comfortably. Add the next 12 ingredients and cover with water. Bring to a boil and reduce the heat to maintain a fast simmer. Cook the chicken about 45 minutes, or until tender. Let it sit in its liquid while you prepare the other ingredients.

Put the potatoes and onions in a pot, cover with water, and boil until tender. Put the next 5 ingredients in a vegetable steamer and steam only until just tender but not mushy. Add the cherry tomatoes during the last few minutes of steaming. They should be hot through but not cooked to the point where they collapse.

To make Sauce No. 1, put the broths into a saucepan. Put the next 5 ingredients into the jar of a blender and whir to a purée. Add to the broth and bring to a boil. Reduce the heat, add the remaining ingredients, and simmer for 45 minutes, stirring occasionally.

To make Sauce No. 2, put all the ingredients into the jar of a blender and whir. Put into a saucepan and simmer for 30 minutes, stirring to prevent scorching.

Sprinkle the *couscous* evenly over a large serving platter. Arrange the chicken, cooked vegetables, chick-peas, eggs, and olives over the *couscous*. Pour Sauce No. 1 over everything. Sprinkle with the cilantro and scatter the lemon slices over all. Serve with Sauce No. 2 in a separate bowl for each diner to use at his or her own discretion or capacity.

SZECHWAN STIR-FRIED CHICKEN, LEEKS, AND CHILIES
China

Serves 6 as a main course,
8 to 10 as part of a Chinese meal
4 whole chicken breasts
3 tablespoons peanut oil
2 medium leeks, sliced into thin
  rings and blanched
1 red bell pepper, seeded and
  sliced into thin strips
6 small fresh hot chilies, cut into
  thin rings and blanched
1 teaspoon finely slivered fresh
  ginger
4 teeth of garlic, sliced very thin
1 tablespoon soy sauce
1/4 cup rich chicken broth
1/4 teaspoon Chinese five-spices
1/2 teaspoon sugar
1/4 teaspoon coarsely ground
  black pepper
1 teaspoon cornstarch dissolved in
1 tablespoon cold chicken broth
Salt to taste

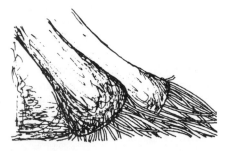

Bone the chicken breasts and remove the skin. Cut the meat into strips 1/4 inch wide by 2 inches long. Shred the skin into slivers.

Heat the oil to very hot in a large wok but do not let it smoke. Add the chicken skin and stir-fry until crisp. Remove with a slotted spoon, drain, and set aside. Begin stir-frying the chicken breasts, a few pieces at a time, just until hot through but not browned. Remove with a slotted spoon and set aside with the skin.

Stir-fry the leeks, pepper, and chilies in the same manner, a few at a time, for no more than a minute. Remove with a slotted spoon and set aside.

Add the next 7 ingredients to the wok and, stirring, cook for about 3 minutes. Return the chicken, skin, and vegetables and stir-fry for 1 minute. Pour in the cornstarch mixture and stir gently until the resulting sauce is thickened and translucent. Add salt. Serve immediately, accompanied with steamed rice.

If you are wondering why there are no recipes for duck, goose, or game hen, in my opinion their flavors just don't lend themselves well to a relationship with hot things, and, after all, it is my book.

KAENG PED CAI
Thailand
Chicken Curry

Serves 6
1 coconut
2 cups boiling water
Liquid from the coconut
4 large whole chicken breasts
2 tablespoons peanut oil
1 tablespoon crushed dried hot
  chilies
6 teeth of garlic, minced
1 teaspoon paprika
1/4 teaspoon grated lemon rind
1/4 teaspoon shrimp paste (available in Chinese markets), or
  anchovy paste
1/8 teaspoon caraway seeds
1/4 teaspoon ground coriander
1/2 teaspoon sugar
4 green onions, chopped
1 teaspoon chopped fresh cilantro
1 red bell pepper, seeded and cut
  into thin sprips
Salt to taste

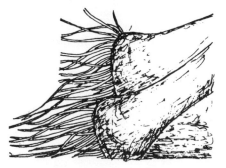

Open the coconut and use the boiling water to make coconut milk according to the instructions on page 13. Use the liquid from the coconut, if necessary, to make 2 cups of coconut milk.

Bone the chicken breasts, remove the skin,* and cut the breasts into strips 1/4 inch wide and 2 inches long.

Heat the oil in a large wok or skillet until it is almost smoking. Add the next 8 ingredients and stir rapidly for 1 minute. Add the chicken breasts and stir-fry for another 2 minutes or just until the chicken is evenly coated with the curry paste and is hot through. Pour in the coconut milk and, stirring constantly, bring to a boil. Stir in the green onions, cilantro, and bell pepper. Add salt. Remove from the heat immediately. Serve with hot steamed rice.

*You shall of course put the skin into the freezer to add to any other bones, giblets, etc., that may accumulate and be used to make stock. I use lots of stock and I find it very handy after I have made it to put it into ice cube trays and freeze. Then I pop out the cubes of stock and put them into plastic bags, ready for use at any time. Just chuck a fistful into the pot.

CHICKEN IN PEANUT SAUCE
West Africa

Serves 6

1 large frying chicken
1 teaspoon salt
1 tablespoon ground ginger
1/4 cup peanut oil
2 large onions, chopped
8 teeth of garlic, minced
4 large ripe tomatoes, chopped
2 tablespoons tomato paste
1 teaspoon grated fresh ginger
1 teaspoon crushed dried hot chilies
1/2 teaspoon fresh-ground
    black pepper
4 cups chicken broth
6 small fresh hot chilies (leave
    the stems on)
1 cup roasted peanuts and
    1 cup water, whirred in a blender
    until a purée is formed
1 teaspoon sugar, or to taste
12 to 15 fresh or thawed frozen
    whole okra
6 hard-cooked eggs
Salt to taste

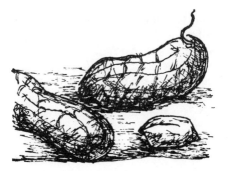

With a cleaver, chop the chicken into bite-sized chunks. Combine the salt and ginger and rub it into the chicken. Heat the oil in a large heavy stew pot or casserole over a moderately hot fire. Brown the chicken. Remove from the oil with a slotted spoon and drain. Set aside.

Add the onions and garlic and sauté until the onions are soft. Add the next 5 ingredients and stir well to blend. Continue to cook, stirring frequently, for another 5 minutes or until a thickish sauce results. Add the broth, chilies, and chicken and stir. Reduce the heat to a simmer and continue cooking for 15 minutes. Stir in the peanut purée and sugar. Add the okra and eggs and cook for 5 minutes longer. Add salt. Mound into a deep platter and surround with small piles of any of the condiments listed below.

Minced onion
Minced green onion
Chopped red and green bell peppers
Diced fresh pineapple
Chopped salted peanuts
Diced tomatoes seasoned with dill
    weed, black pepper, and
    minced fresh chilies
Diced avocado
Diced hard-cooked egg
Minced fresh cilantro

BRILLIANT CAFE-INSPIRED RED BUTTER CHICKEN
London-Indian Cuisine

Southall (pronounced in English fashion Suthal, not South Hall) a suburb of London, is the heart of London's Indian community. Street after street of small shops dispensing all manner of vegetables, herbs, and spices that you have never seen before line the streets. Saris drape sensuously from manikins with bright blue eyes and platinum hair, and tantalizing smells waft from stalls selling samosas and kebabs. The whole effect is that of a bazaar; a delightful experience that unfortunately most visitors to London will never see, opting instead to join the herds shuffling their way through the turnstiles at the Tower of London, or not seeing the Changing of the Guard due to the ten thousand others present each morning.

Down a side street in Southall is the nondescript Brilliant Cafe. Now the rest of their menu is good, very good, but their Red Butter Chicken is something above and beyond. My older son and I spent days in experimentation attempting to re-create the tastes. We are pleased with what we have developed, although it is just a step off the original.

Serves 8

MARINADE
3 tablespoons boiling water
1 tablespoon saffron
1-1/2 cups (3 sticks) butter
1 medium onion, chopped
6 teeth of garlic, chopped
4 tablespoons grated fresh ginger
5 small fresh hot chilies, chopped
4 tablespoons minced fresh cilantro
1 tablespoon grated lemon rind
1/2 cup fresh lemon juice
6 tablespoons Madras-style curry powder
3 tablespoons ground cinnamon
1 teaspoon each ground cumin, nutmeg, cardamom, and turmeric
1 teaspoon anise seeds
6 tablespoons sugar
1 cup (8 ounces) plain yogurt
Salt to taste
Enough red food coloring to turn sauce the color of pomegranate juice

2 frying chickens

Pour the boiling water over the saffron and let it sit. Melt 1/2 cup of the butter. Add all ingredients except the yogurt, salt, food coloring and chickens. Simmer for about 5 minutes but *do not* let it brown. Put into the blender and purée.

Add the yogurt, salt, and food coloring and purée again. Set aside.

Using a cleaver or poultry shears, cut the chicken into bite-sized chunks. Put into a bowl large enough to hold it comfortably and pour the marinade over it. Refrigerate overnight, stirring occasionally to make sure that all is adequately covered.

To cook, use a large basket steamer that fits over a wok, or some similar arrangement. Melt the remaining 1 cup of butter, but do not let it brown. Remove half of the chicken from the marinade and place in a flat heatproof dish that will fit in the steamer and allow at least 1/2 inch around it. Pour boiling water into the bottom of the steamer. Place the dish of chicken on the top of the steamer and pour half of the melted butter over it. Cover with the lid of the steamer and steam over rapidly boiling water for 30 to 40 minutes. Test a piece for doneness. It should be just done, not dry. Top up the steamer with more boiling water if necessary. When the chicken is done, place on a heatproof dish covered tightly with foil and put into a very low oven to keep warm while you repeat the process for the other half of the chicken. Pour any remaining butter from the steaming process into the marinade that is left, put in a small saucepan and bring just to the beginnings of a boil. Pour it into a separate dish and serve with the chicken and steamed rice.

GALINHA CAFREAL ZANBEDIANA
Mozambique
Broiled Chicken Marinated in Lemon Juice with Coconut-Milk Sauce

Serves 4
1 coconut
1-1/2 cups boiling water
Liquid from the coconut
1 cup fresh lemon juice
10 teeth of garlic, finely minced
1 teaspoon crushed dried hot chilies
2 teaspoons sugar
2 tablespoons olive oil
2 small frying chickens, each cut in half

Open the coconut and use the boiling water to make coconut milk according to the instructions on page 13. Add the liquid from the coconut, if necessary, to make 1-1/2 cups of coconut milk.

Mix the lemon juice, garlic, fresh and dried chilies, sugar, and oil together. Place the chickens in a shallow pan and pour the marinade over them. Turn over to coat evenly and marinate for at least 4 hours.

Broil the chickens under moderate heat to desired doneness, turning occasionally and brushing with extra marinade.

Meanwhile, combine the remaining marinade and the coconut milk in a saucepan and, stirring constantly, cook over a low heat for 5 minutes. Try not to let it come to a boil or it may curdle. Salt to taste. Pour the sauce into a separate dish and serve with the chicken.

TURKEY

Come on, sit down. Let's talk turkey. I have spent the day looking through my entire cookbook collection, which is considerable, and I was amazed to find that almost without exception, recipes for whole roasted turkeys call for a small, wimpy 8- to 10-pound bird, hardly worth the effort of hauling it home. A small turkey is not a good thing. First, let's chuck out the misconception that a small turkey is going to be younger and more tender. All turkeys that reach the market in this day of agro-industry are the same age, give or take a week or two. The difference in size is determined by the breed.

So if they are the same, so what's the dif, you ask. The difference is that a small turkey has much more bone per pound than a large turkey. Now if you really have to have a tiny turkey for some purpose, so be it, but you are paying through the nose for that convenience. Well, so once in a while they have little ones on sale to get rid of them. It takes more energy per pound to cook a little turkey than a big turkey. But my family hates leftovers, you are going to say. First, you have a freezer, don't you? Second, I struck the word leftovers from my family's vocabulary years ago. There is no such word. It was invented by the advertising industry as a way to convince you that (1) there was something wrong with food cooked yesterday; and (2) you had to buy some product to make "leftovers" palatable. In our vocabulary there are only "planned-overs." It takes both natural resources and human resources, i.e., your time, to prepare food, and often it is far more "conservative" of both for you to purposefully prepare more food than can be eaten at one meal.

So in my opinion, which you may indeed choose to chuck right out the door, you should go buy the very biggest turkey you can find. Unfortunately, most markets just don't carry truly big turkeys. About twenty-eight pounds is as large as I can usually find.

ROAST TURKEY
WITH CHORIZO STUFFING
Mexican-American Cuisine

The first year my father worked for the California Juvenile Authority correctional facility at Whittier, he was told to make a Christmas party for the boys. Having come to the job with but three weeks until Christmas, this threw my parents into something of a dither. After all, in my family, when we say "Deck the halls," we mean it, and here we were with thirty-six teen-aged boys of mixed ethnic and economic backgrounds to provide a party for, and no budget. My mother and I began baking and my dad got on the phone to the parents of as many of the kids as he could contact. Well, the Mexican-American community of the Los Angeles area came through with flying colors. On Christmas Eve our kitchen was filled with laughing Mexican women roasting chilies, mashing beans, grating cheese,

chopping onions, and tossing tortillas in the air. In a few hours the long trestle table my dad had set up was a cornucopia of gorgeous Latino delicacies, interspersed with such gringo contributions as fruit-cake, frosted sugar cookies, date bars, spiced nuts, and shortbread. But the crowning glory of the feast was several huge roasted turkeys, stuffed with a hot and zesty mixture of chorizos and rice.

Makes about 20 servings
One 16- to 20-pound turkey

STUFFING
3 pounds chorizo
1/3 cup yellow cornmeal
1 cup hot water
3 cups *al dente* cooked rice
3 large onions, chopped
4 celery stalks, chopped
2 bell peppers, preferably one red and one green, chopped
20 teeth of garlic, minced
4 small fresh hot chilies, minced
1 cup seedless raisins
1 cup blanched almonds
1/2 cup chopped candied cactus, if available
1 teaspoon crushed dried hot chilies
1 teaspoon coarsely ground black pepper

1/2 tablespoon mixed dried herbs (Italian seasoning)
1 teaspoon dried oregano
1/2 teaspoon ground cumin
1 tablespoon chili powder
2 tablespoons minced fresh cilantro
1/2 cup minced fresh parsley
2 tablespoon sugar
4 eggs, lightly beaten
Salt to taste

Put the neck and giblets of the turkey in a pan and cover with water. Bring to the boil, then reduce heat to maintain a rapid simmer and cook until all are very tender. When cool enough to handle, pick all the meat from the neck and chop. Also chop the giblets. Put into a large bowl.

To make the stuffing, skin the chorizos, break the meat up into small pieces, and add to the turkey meat and giblets. Soak the cornmeal in the hot water until soft. Add the cornmeal and all the remaining stuffing ingredients to the chorizo-turkey mixture and mix thoroughly. Add just enough of the broth from the giblets to moisten the stuffing a bit. Fry a small amount in a pan with a bit of oil and taste. Adjust seasonings. Pack into the body and neck cavity of the turkey. Truss shut and put on a rack in a large roaster. Bake uncovered at 350° for 12 to 15 minutes per pound.

Remove to a large platter and dress this gorgeous creature appropriately for its exalted station in life before sending to the table. A generous garnish of fresh watercress and slices of orange would be most appropriate.

MOLE POBLANO
DE GUAJOLOTE
Mexico
Turkey in Chocolate
and Chili Sauce

Makes about 20 servings or more
One 16- to 20-pound turkey
2 tablespoons melted lard
1 tablespoon salt
1 tablespoon dried mixed herbs
   (Italian seasoning)
1 teaspoon ground cumin
1 tablespoon minced fresh cilantro
1 teaspoon finely minced garlic
1 teaspoon cayenne
1 tablespoon sugar

MOLE SAUCE
4 cups chicken or turkey broth
1 cup blanched almonds
2 tablespoons crushed dried hot
   chilies
1/2 cup sesame seeds
1/2 tablespoon ground cinnamon

1/4 teaspoon ground cloves
1/2 teaspoon ground coriander
1/2 teaspoon ground cumin
1/2 teaspoon anise seeds
4 large tomatoes, chopped
1 cup seeded raisins
4 small fresh hot chilies
1 large onion, chopped
1 tablespoon sugar
1/2 teaspoon or more coarsely
   ground black pepper
Salt
2 tablespoons lard
2 squares (2 ounces) unsweetened
   chocolate
1 tablespoon coarsely chopped
   fresh cilantro
2 tablespoons sesame seeds

Mix the lard and all seasonings together into a paste and rub onto the turkey, inside and out. Put the turkey into a roasting pan with a tight-fitting lid. Put into the oven (don't bother to preheat it) at 325° until tender, about 3-1/2 to 4 hours. The turkey will steam itself and remain moist. Remember to shake hands with it (see page 108).

To make the *mole,* put 2 cups of the broth and the next 8 ingredients into the jar of a blender and purée. You may need to do it in two batches. Pour the purée into a bowl. Put the tomatoes and next 4 ingredients into the blender and whir. Again you may have to do

this in two batches. Add to the ingredients in the bowl and stir. Add the pepper and salt to taste.

Melt the lard in a heavy skillet, pour in the *mole,* and simmer, stirring constantly, for 5 minutes. Pour in the remaining 2 cups of broth and add the chocolate. Cook, stirring often, until the chocolate is melted.

Check the turkey and when it is tender, remove from the oven and spoon the juices out of the pan. (Save them. They will make excellent soup or gravy for another time.) Return the turkey to the oven uncovered and turn the heat up to 400°. Leave just until the turkey is nicely browned. Pour the *mole* over the turkey and reduce the heat to 350°. Continue to bake for 30 more minutes, basting with the *mole* occasionally.

Remove the turkey to a serving platter and set aside to keep warm. Put the roaster on top of the stove. Stir and cook the *mole* and any juices that may have accumulated in the pan over high heat for 2 or 3 minutes. Pour this over the turkey. Sprinkle with the fresh cilantro and sesame seeds and serve at once.

NOTE: This is usually reserved for very special occasions. *Mole* may also be used for chicken or pork.

TIPS ON COOKING TURKEY

Now, before we end our little talk there is something else we have to discuss. Turkeys, by nature, tend to be dry. After all, they are land birds, unlike a goose or a duck that has to be greasy so it won't drown. A turkey loses natural body juices very easily, and every time you poke a hole in it it makes it a little drier. *Do not* go jabbing at the breast with a fork to see if it is done. Reach in the oven and shake hands with it. When the drumstick moves very easily when you gently move it back and forth, more likely than not the turkey is ready for its coming-out party. This is why you should also avoid those turkeys with the little thermometer that pops up when the turkey is supposed to be done. Well-overdone has been my experience. If when you get your turkey home you find that the skin on the breast has been broken in some way, you can wind up with a turkey whose white meat will be dry and unpalatable. In this case, take a lump of the fat from the flap of skin at the body opening and lay it over the cut in the skin. This will help keep the beast from drying out during the roasting.

RABBIT STEW WITH CORNMEAL DUMPLINGS
Havasupai Indians

The Havasupai are a small nation of Native Americans who inhabit a side valley of the Grand Canyon. In this century most of their cash income derives from leading pack trains to the valley floor for those of us who are either too infirm or indolent to make it down and back up again on our own volition. Their valley is exquisitely beautiful, mostly free from the invasion of twentieth-century luxuries.

Serves 4
1 large stewing rabbit
  (4 to 5 pounds)
1/4 cup lard
15 teeth of garlic
10 small boiling onions
6 small fresh hot chilies
1/2 teaspoon dried sage
1/2 tablespoon chili powder
1 teaspoon sugar
1/2 cup dried pinto beans
Chicken broth
1 cup fresh or thawed frozen corn
1 cup canned diced *nopalitos*
  (cactus leaves)

DUMPLINGS
1 cup yellow cornmeal
1/2 tablespoon baking powder
1 teaspoon sugar
A pinch of salt
1 tablespoon lard or shortening
1 egg
2/3 cup water

Section the rabbit into serving pieces. Heat the lard in a heavy casserole and brown the rabbit on all sides. Add the next 8 ingredients and bring to a boil, stirring to mix thoroughly. Reduce the heat to maintain a fast simmer and cook covered for 1 to 1-1/2 hours, or until the rabbit is exceedingly tender and the beans are done. Add more broth if necessary.

When the rabbit and beans are done, add the corn and *nopalitos,* stir, return the lid and simmer while you prepare the dumplings.

To make the dumplings, work all of the dry ingredients and the lard or shortening together until well blended. Beat the egg and water together and, using a fork, vigorously mix into the dry ingredients. Drop tablespoonfuls of the batter onto the top of the stew. Cover with a tight-fitting lid and continue to simmer for 25 minutes. Remove the lid and serve immediately from the casserole. These will not be the high, light, and fluffy dumplings served with Son-of-a-Bitch Stew, but they are delicious.

EGGS & CHEESE

The egg has always symbolized fertility, longevity, and rejuvenation. In the Orient, weddings, births, and the new year are always enhanced by the distribution of eggs dyed a brilliant red, both the egg and the color being symbols of fertility, longevity, and good luck.

In some English villages, on Shrove Tuesday or Mardi Gras (the day one is shriven or cleansed of sin before entering Lent) children shackle eggs. No, that doesn't mean that they put leg bands and chains on the eggs. Each child brings an egg from home with his or her name written on it. The eggs are placed in a flat basket and shaken. The child whose egg is the last to be cracked wins a prize and is considered to be guaranteed good fortune through the coming year.

In the Ukraine, the child who finds an egg still warm from the hen and is able to bring it to the kitchen to be cooked for his breakfast before it is cold will have good luck all that day.

If a Navajo child finds an egg with a soft shell, unbroken, it is a sure sign that he is favored and life will be easy for him.

OMELETS

You would think that having been raised on a commercial poultry ranch, I might never want to see an egg again in my life. But I adore eggs. I never feel the cupboard is bare if there are eggs. In fact, as much as I enjoy the creation of new dishes, food experimentation, and entertaining, I am sure that I could dine quite sumptuously for the rest of my life if I had nothing but fruit, cheese, and eggs. (Well, I would certainly hope there was a little Hacienda Zinfandel, Buena Vista Gewürztraminer or Stevenot Chardonnay, and a bottle or two of Anchor Steam Beer every now and then.) And so, let us begin this section with that most delightful and adaptable of dishes, the omelet.

I would love to write an entire book on nothing but omelets. Actually, it would be a very short book because it could all be written by just saying, "Pour 2 beaten eggs into an omelet pan and put anything in the world that you like to eat, in any combination whatsoever, on top, fold in half, and serve."

What would not be nice in an omelet? Corn chips might present a problem if served up in an omelet, although the English eat a repulsive thing called a "chip-butty," which is a pile of French fries between the greasy halves of a fried bap (bun). And believe it or not, they sell them from sidewalk vendors in France now as well. I think I probably would not like a Philippine *balut* in my omelet, nor would I enjoy an omelet of sautéed sea cucumber, and I don't think Twinkies or *poi* would make a particularly delightful omelet either. But just about everything else would. So, below are three creations I call, simply, California Omelets. Use them as they are or be creative.

Oh, first, I guess I should enlighten you with my omelet theory. I find that what a lot of people call omelets I call scrambled eggs, and what some people call scrambled eggs I call muck. When I scramble eggs, I heat a lightly oiled pan, pour in the beaten eggs, and let it form a light skin on the bottom. Then I tilt the pan slightly and with the turner, gently pull the skin towards the high side of the pan, letting the uncooked egg run down into the empty portion of the pan. Then set the pan flat again and let a new skin form. I continue in this way until there is no more liquid. I can't stand scrambled eggs that are made by pouring the eggs into a pan and with a fork beating them into curds and whey.

Now for an omelet, I pour the lightly beaten egg into the heated and oiled pan, let it form a light skin, and then begin putting things on top. If I'm using cheese, I always put it on first and, ever so gently, using the back of a fork, agitate the surface of the uncooked egg just until the cheese and uncooked egg begin to achieve some unity. Then I add any other ingredients. When the egg is *almost* set, I fold the whole thing in half, let it sit for a moment, and then slide it onto a heated plate. Now that's an omelet.

CALIFORNIA OMELET NO. 1
Family Recipe

Serves 1
1 teaspoon butter
1 tablespoon cream sherry
2 teeth of garlic, finely minced
2 eggs, lightly beaten
2 tablespoons shredded sharp
   Cheddar cheese
2 tablespoons shredded Swiss
   cheese
2 tablespoon cottage cheese
1 tablespoon finely minced red
   bell pepper or fresh pimiento
1/2 teaspoon finely minced fresh
   chives
1/2 teaspoon minced fresh cilantro

1 teaspoon minced fresh mint
2 tablespoons hot or mild chunky
   salsa, page 148
Salt and pepper to taste

GARNISH
3 avocado slices
2 fresh tomato slices
1 lemon slice
A sprig of fresh cilantro, watercress,
   or parsley

Melt the butter with the sherry over moderate heat and sauté the garlic until soft. Remove from the heat and set aside. Heat an 8- or 9-inch omelet pan or skillet over moderate heat and oil lightly, using an oiled brush or paper towel. Pour in the eggs. When a thin skin has formed on the bottom, sprinkle in the Cheddar and Swiss cheeses and, using the back of the tines of a fork, very gently agitate the surface just until the cheeses have begun to melt and become one with the egg. When the egg and cheese has a custardy appearance but is not totally set and dry, sprinkle the cottage cheese over one half of the surface. Sprinkle on the remaining ingredients, except those for garnish. Gently fold the omelet in half and cook for about 1 more minute. If it appears to be

browning too rapidly, reduce the heat. When done to your liking, slide onto a heated oval plate. Arrange the garnishes in an attractive pattern and serve immediately.

CALIFORNIA OMELET NO. 2
Family Recipe

Serves 1
1 tablespoon corn or other light-
   flavored oil
1 tablespoon butter
1 tablespoon cream sherry
2 tablespoons chopped onion
4 teeth of garlic
1 small fresh hot chili, minced
2 tablespoons each minced celery
   and bell pepper
4 or 5 fresh mushrooms, sliced
2 eggs, lightly beaten
4 tablespoons shredded Swiss
   cheese
1 green onion, minced
1 tablespoon chopped black olives
3/4 teaspoon minced fresh dill
   weed, or 1/4 teaspoon dried
Salt and freshly ground black
   pepper

GARNISH
2 tablespoons Guacamole, page 18
2 tablespoons sour cream
Parsley sprigs
Avocado slices
Tomato slices
Pitted black olives

Melt the oil, butter, and sherry together in a skillet and sauté the onion, garlic, and chili just until soft but not browned. Add the celery, bell pepper, and mushrooms and again sauté just until soft but not browned. Set aside.

Heat an 8- or 9-inch omelet pan or skillet over a moderate heat. Oil lightly, using an oiled brush or paper towel. Pour in the eggs and swirl the pan to coat the bottom evenly with the egg. As soon as they have formed a skin on the bottom, sprinkle the surface with the cheese and agitate the surface gently with the back of a fork just until the cheese and egg begin to become incorporated but are not cooked. Spoon the cooked vegetables over one-half of the surface. Over this sprinkle the green onion, olives, and dill weed. Add salt and pepper to taste and fold the omelet in half. Slide onto a heated plate. Spoon the guacamole and sour cream over the top and garnish with a sprig of parsley, 2 or 3 slices each of avocado and tomato, and a black olive or two. Serve immediately.

CALIFORNIA OMELET NO. 3
Family Recipe

Serves 1
1 tablespoon butter
1 tablespoon oil
1 tablespoon cream sherry
4 teeth of garlic, minced
2 tablespoons chopped onion
2 to 3 stalks of asparagus, cut into
  1/2-inch diagonal slices
1/4 red bell pepper, cut into
  thin strips
3 to 4 mushrooms, sliced thin
2 eggs, lightly beaten
3 to 4 tablespoons shredded
  Gruyère
2 tablespoons hot or mild chunky
  salsa, page 148
1 tablespoon canned diced peeled
  green chilies
1 tablespoon chopped black olives
Salt and freshly ground black
  pepper
2 tablespoons butter
2 tablespoons cream sherry
1/2 tablespoon minced shallots
1/2 teaspoon minced fresh dill
  weed, or 1/8 teaspoon dried
1/2 teaspoon paprika
2 tablespoons sour cream
Coarsely ground black pepper

Melt the butter, oil, and sherry together over moderate heat. Add the garlic and onion and sauté until soft but not yet browned. Add the asparagus, pepper, and mushrooms and sauté until all vegetables are heated through and lightly cooked.

Heat an 8- to 9-inch omelet pan and lightly oil with a brush or a paper towel. Pour in the eggs and swirl to cover the bottom evenly. When a skin has formed on the bottom, sprinkle with the cheese and agitate the top gently to slightly incorporate the cheese and egg.

Spoon the cooked vegetables onto one-half of the surface. Add the salsa, chilies, and olives. Salt and pepper to taste. Fold shut and cook until the eggs are just set but not dry. Slide onto a heated plate and keep warm.

Put the butter and sherry into a saucepan and swirl to melt together over a moderate heat. Add the shallots, dill, and paprika and, swirling, cook for 2 or 3 minutes or until glossy and somewhat thickened. Spoon the sour cream on top of the omelet, pour over the sherry/butter sauce and add a grinding of fresh black pepper. Serve immediately.

HUEVOS RANCHEROS
Mexico
Eggs Poached in Salsa

Serves 4
3 tablespoons corn or other light-
  flavored oil
2 medium onions, chopped
10 teeth of garlic, minced
4 to 6 small fresh hot chilies,
  minced
1 celery stalk, chopped
1 medium bell pepper, seeded and
  chopped
4 large tomatoes, chopped
1 teaspoon mixed dried herbs
  (Italian seasoning)
1/2 teaspoon ground cumin
2 tablespoons minced fresh cilantro
1/2 cup minced fresh parsley
1 teaspoon sugar
2 tablespoons distilled vinegar
Salt and fresh-ground black
  pepper to taste
Crushed dried hot chilies to taste
  if you want it hotter
8 eggs

Heat the oil in a large heavy skillet and sauté the onions and garlic until soft. Add all of the remaining ingredients except the eggs and, stirring occasionally, cook over moderate heat until a thick sauce is formed, 35 to 40 minutes. When ready to serve, turn up the heat for a moment to get the sauce quite hot, stirring all the while to prevent scorching. Crack the eggs on top of the salsa, cover with a tight lid, reduce the heat to moderate, and poach the eggs to desired doneness. Gently spoon the eggs onto a heated serving platter and spoon the salsa around them. Serve with hot corn tortillas and fried chorizo if desired. This makes a robust breakfast and is also excellent for any meal.

NOTE: You don't have to go through all this to have *huevos rancheros.* If you have a brand of chunky salsa you like, just pour it into a pan, heat it and add the eggs. Simple and good. Or, use the salsa on page 148.

CAPSICUM QUICHE
Me
Quiche with Cheese and Three Types of Chilies

Serves 6
1 recipe pastry, following

FILLING
1 tablespoon butter
1 tablespoon cream sherry
6 teeth of garlic, minced
1 medium onion, minced

1 each green and red bell pepper, seeded and cut into thin strips
1 long fresh mild chili, seeded and cut into thin rings
3 small fresh hot chilies, one red, one yellow, one green, seeded and cut into thin rings
3/4 teaspoon minced fresh dill weed, or 1/2 teaspoon dried
1 teaspoon minced fresh basil
1 tablespoon minced fresh cilantro
1-1/2 cups milk
4 eggs, beaten
1 cup shredded Swiss cheese
Salt and fresh-ground black pepper to taste

Prepare the pastry. Roll out and line an 8- or 9-inch quiche pan with removable sides. Refrigerate while you prepare the filling.

To make the filling, melt the butter and sherry in a heavy skillet over moderate heat. Sauté the garlic, onion, peppers, and chilies until soft but not browned. Remove from the heat and cool. Stir in the dill, basil, and cilantro.

Mix the milk, eggs, and cheese together. Remove the quiche pan from the refrigerator and fill with

the vegetables. Pour over the egg mixture and smooth the surface. Add salt and a grinding of fresh pepper to the top.

Put in a preheated 400° oven for 3 minutes. Reduce the heat to 350° and continue to bake until the custard is set, about 20 minutes. Remove the sides of the quiche pan and serve hot or at room temperature. Sour cream is a good accompaniment.

PASTRY
Family Recipe

Makes one 8- or 9-inch pie pastry
1/3 cup lard
1/3 cup butter
1-1/2 cups unbleached all-purpose flour
Pinch of salt
About 4 or 5 tablespoons water

With a wire pastry blender, cut the lard and butter into the flour and salt until all is powdery. Using a fork, mix rapidly as you gradually add the water to form a soft dough. Turn out onto a lightly flowered board and knead the dough sparingly, just until it is no longer sticky and will keep together in a ball. Roll out to a thickness of about 1/8 inch and use to line an 8- or 9-inch pan.

DIABLO MERINGUE PIE
Galvanized Gullet Contribution
Hot and Heady Cheese Sauce
Under a Savory Meringue

My home, where the first meeting of the Galvanized Gullet took place, has to the east a view of Mt. Diablo, a massive solitary mountain rising 3,600 feet from an alluvial plane. It dominates the landscape for hundreds of miles around. When my British Airways 747 brings me home from my various perigrinations, the two sights that tug at my heartstrings are the Golden Gate Bridge and Mt. Diablo. This delightfully devilish concoction was created by one of the charter members of the Galvanized Gullet and named not only for its volcanic use of capsicum but also to honor the extinct volcano in whose shadow we dined.

Serves 6

SAUCE
1 tablespoon butter
3 small fresh hot chilies, chopped
1 medium onion, chopped
6 teeth of garlic, chopped
2 cups milk
1 tablespoon butter
1 tablespoon flour
4 eggs, separated

1/2 cup hot or mild chunky salsa, page 148
1/2 cup shredded sharp Cheddar cheese
1/2 cup shredded Swiss cheese
3/4 teaspoon fresh minced dill weed, or 1/4 teaspoon dried
1 tablespoon minced fresh cilantro
3 green onions, including the tops, chopped small

2 tablespoons freshly grated Parmesan cheese
3/4 teaspoon minced fresh dill weed, or 1/4 teaspoon dried
1 large round loaf of French or rye bread
2 tablespoons melted butter
6 teeth of garlic, finely minced

Melt the butter over moderately high heat and sauté the chilies, onion, and garlic until soft but not yet browned. Put the milk in a blender with the sautéed vegetables and purée.

In a saucepan, blend the butter and flour together over moderate heat for 2 minutes, stirring constantly. Slowly pour the milk mixture into the flour and butter, whisking all the while. Continue whisking over moderate heat until the mixture has begun to thicken.

Remove from the heat and put 1 cup into the blender. Add the egg yolks and whir. Put the saucepan back on the stove over moderate heat and, whisking all the while, very slowly pour in the egg mixture. Continue whisking until the mixture thickens. Continue to whisk while adding the cheeses, dill, cilantro, and green onions. When the cheese is melted and thoroughly incorporated, remove from the heat and set aside.

Beat the egg whites until they hold their shape but are not dry. Gently fold in the Parmesan and dill.

Cut the top off of the bread and remove most of the soft interior, leaving only the empty shell. Paint the inside of the empty loaf of bread with the melted butter and sprinkle on the minced garlic. Put in a preheated oven at 375° until the bread just begins to brown on the inside, no more than 5 minutes. Leave the oven on. Remove the bread shell and put on an oven-proof serving dish.

Fill the bread with the cheese sauce. Let any extra sauce spill over the sides and onto the plate. Pile on the meringue. Put into the oven until the meringue begins to brown and is set. Remove from the oven, garnish with greens or what you will, and serve immediately.

SOUTHALL CHEESE BALLS
London-Indian Cuisine
Fried Cheese, Chili,
and Curry Croquettes

Makes 12
1/2 cup shredded Cheddar cheese
1/2 cup shredded Swiss cheese
1-1/2 cups fine bread crumbs
6 teeth of garlic, finely minced
1 medium onion, finely minced
3 green onions, including tops,
  minced
1 teaspoon finely grated fresh
  ginger
1/2 cup minced fresh parsley
2 tablespoons minced fresh cilantro
1 teaspoon cayenne
1/2 teaspoon ground cumin
1 teaspoon ground turmeric
1 teaspoon sugar
1 teaspoon dry mustard
2 eggs, lightly beaten
Salt and fresh-ground black
  pepper to taste
Light-flavored oil for frying
2 eggs, well beaten
1 cup fine bread crumbs

Mix all the ingredients up to and including the salt and pepper together exceedingly well. If it is not moist enough to hold together when formed into a ball, add another egg and mix again. Form into 12 round balls.

Heat about 1 inch of oil in a heavy skillet to frying temperature; it should be hot but not smoking. Dip the balls into the beaten eggs, shake off any excess, and roll in the bread crumbs. Fry a few at a time, rolling them about to brown evenly until golden brown. If they appear to be browning too fast, adjust the heat. Drain on paper towels and serve hot.

VEGETABLES

While much of Northern Europe was populated by hunter-gatherers, the Indians in the Tamaulipas Mountains of Mexico were engaged in the first struggles of the agricultural revolution, and winning. By 7000 B.C. they were engaged in the domestication of runner beans, aloe, summer squash, chilies, bottle gourds, and a form of the pumpkin.

Somewhat further south in Tehuaca, by 5000 B.C. the native population was well on the way to taming maize, or corn. In its wild state the ears of the indigenous maize were no more than one inch long. By the time Cortez invaded the empire of Montezuma, peoples of the region had succeeded in breeding a plant that produced ears almost as large and tender as those we buy today. By 5600 B.C. the New World was producing beans as a domestic crop, and by 3000 B.C. the potato and tomato had been domesticated.

I am exceedingly glad for our New World harvest, for even though I am no longer a vegetarian, I still carry on my life-long love affair with vegetables. Perhaps it's part of being a California chauvinist.

MIXED VEGETABLE CURRY
Thailand
Vegetables with Red Curry Sauce

Serves 6

SAUCE
2 tablespoons crushed dried hot
   chilies
10 teeth of garlic, minced
2 tablespoons grated fresh ginger
2 tablespoons paprika
1 teaspoon shrimp paste (available
   at Oriental markets)
1 teaspoon caraway seeds
1 teaspoon grated fresh lemon rind
2 tablespoons Madras-style curry
   powder
3 tablespoons sugar
2 tablespoons fresh lemon juice
2 cups light chicken broth
1/4 cup peanut oil
1/2 cup grated fresh coconut
   (see page 13)

12 small dried red chilies
1 cup peanut oil
1 small yam
2 eggs, lightly beaten
3 cups fresh bean sprouts
1 red bell pepper, chopped

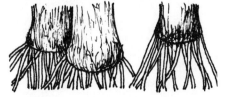

4 green onions, including tops,
   minced
2 cups broccoli flowerets, blanched
4 green onions, cut into 2-inch
   lengths, including tops, blanched
1/4 pound Chinese long beans,
   trimmed, left whole, and blanched
1/4 pound snow peas, blanched
1 large carrot, julienne-cut into
   3-inch lengths and blanched
2 cups coarsely shredded *bok choy*
   greens, blanched
2 medium tomatoes, chopped
1 cup grated fresh coconut (see
   page 13)
1/2 cup chopped raw peanuts
1 lemon, cut into thin slices,
   for garnish

Put all the ingredients for the
sauce into the jar of a blender and
whir. Pour the mixture into a
saucepan and bring to a boil.
Reduce the heat and simmer for
about 15 minutes, stirring frequently to prevent scorching.
Remove from the heat and set aside.

Put the chilies into a bowl and
pour boiling water over them. Let
them sit until the water is cool.
Drain.

Heat the oil to frying temperature.
Peel the yam and cut into 1/4-
inch-thick slices. Fry in the oil for
about 2 minutes. Drain and set
aside.

Wipe the inside of an omelet
pan lightly with oil (use an oiled
brush or paper towel) and pour in
half of the beaten egg. Let it form
a skin and, when almost set, roll it
up. Remove the egg to a cutting
board to cool while you repeat
the process with the remaining
egg. When both rolls are cool
enough to handle, cut into very
thin slivers. Set aside.

Toss the bean sprouts, red bell
pepper, and minced green onions
together. Mound into the center of
a serving platter.

Put all of the vegetables, the
coconut, and peanuts in piles
around the base of the mound of
bean sprouts. Sprinkle the slivered
egg over the bean sprouts. Garnish
with the red chilies and lemon
slices. Drizzle half of the sauce
over the vegetables and serve the
remaining half in a small bowl for
those who wish a more spectacular
conflagration.

"All cooks agree with this opinion,
No savory dish without an onion."
—Nineteenth-century verse

CHILIES AND GARLIC IN OIL
Greece

Serves 6

2 large red bell peppers, or 3 fresh
   pimientos, with stems
6 to 8 fresh hot chilies, preferably
   a mixture of red, green, and
   yellow, with stems
3 long frying chilies, with stems
6 to 8 small boiling onions
20 large teeth of garlic
1 large onion, cut into rings
   1/2 inch thick
6 flower heads of fresh dill if it
   is large and mature, or a small
   bundle of fresh young dill weed
   left whole and tied together as
   for *bouquet garni*
Olive oil

Place all the vegetables in a skillet
(with a tight-fitting lid) large enough
to hold them in a single layer. Lay
the dill on top and pour in enough
olive oil to stand 1 inch deep in
the pan. Put the pan on the stove
and, over moderate heat, bring the
temperature to hot. The instant
the oil begins to simmer, turn the
heat down to the very lowest heat
possible, turn the vegetables over
once, put on the lid, and leave for
45 minutes to 1 hour or until the
boiling onions are quite soft. (If
you have an electric stove, the
lowest setting may not be low
enough. You should try and find a
heat deflector to slightly elevate a
pan and reduce the heat).

When done, remove from the
heat, leave covered, and set aside
until cool. This is good served as a
starter with French bread. Each
diner tears off a piece of French
bread and smears it with some of
the soft chilies, onion, or garlic.
The Greeks drink *retsina* with this.
I can't think of anything that
would go worse. You need, in my
opinion, beer, and not even my
beloved rich and hearty British
brews. I would not like to try and
put out the fire with Guinness,
Old Hooky, Tanglefoot, or Bishop's
Tipple. Normally I adore all these
and I like them served at a
respectable cool, not cold temperature, but with this rich, oily, and
fiery dish I want lager and I
want it *cold*!

FRIED EGGPLANT
WITH YOGURT
Turkey

Remember that not all heat comes
from the genus *Capsicum*. Garlic,
particularly raw garlic, can be hot
indeed. This dish, of Turkish origins,
is yet another that I have Leyla
to thank for.

Serves 6 at a meal,
10 to 12 at a party

1 large eggplant
1/2 cup unbleached all-purpose
   flour
1/2 teaspoon baking powder
Pinch of salt
About 1 cup beer
1 tablespoon olive oil
Light-flavored vegetable oil for
   frying
1 each medium green and red
   bell pepper, seeded and cut into
   strips about 1 inch thick
1 medium onion, cut into bite-sized
   chunks

SAUCE
1 cup (8 ounces) plain yogurt
15 to 20 teeth of garlic, minced

6 or 8 pitted black olives
1 lemon, cut into 6 or 8 wedges

Cut about 1/2 inch from the top
and bottom of the eggplant. With
a sharp knife, peel the eggplant in
strips lengthwise. Leave strips of
skin about 1 inch wide every inch
around the eggplant, then cut the
eggplant into 1/4-inch slices. Cover
and set aside.

Mix the flour, baking powder,
and salt together. Whisking all the
while, pour in enough beer to form
a thin batter, as for pancakes. Add
the olive oil and whisk again.

In a heavy frying pan, heat about 1/2 inch of oil. When it is hot enough for frying but not smoking, dip a slice of eggplant into the batter and fry on both sides until golden brown. If it seems to be browning too quickly, reduce the heat a bit, wait a moment, and then fry another slice of batter-dipped eggplant. When the temperature is correct, fry the dipped slices of eggplant a few at a time, drain of excess oil, and set aside to keep warm.

Add the peppers to the oil and fry just until the skin begins to blister. Drain. Then add the onion and fry, tossing about in the oil until all the pieces are heated through. Drain and set aside with the eggplant to keep warm.

To make the sauce, put the yogurt and garlic in a blender and whir until the garlic is totally dissolved. Arrange the slices of eggplant in a circle around the rim of a serving dish. Scatter the onion and pepper pieces over them and drizzle the yogurt over all. Scatter the olives and lemon wedges about the top. Serve at once.

HOTTER-THAN-HELL SZECHWAN STIR-FRY
China

Serves 6

SAUCE
1/2 cup chicken broth
1/4 cup rice vinegar
1/4 cup dark brown sugar
1/4 cup soy sauce
1/2 tablespoon tomato paste
4 to 6 teeth of garlic, minced
1 tablespoon grated fresh ginger
1/2 teaspoon dry mustard
1 teaspoon crushed dried hot
   chilies, or more to taste
2 tablespoons hoisin sauce
1 teaspoon cornstarch dissolved in
1 tablespoon water or chicken
   broth

12 to 15 very small slim dried
   red chilies
1/4 cup peanut oil
1/4 cup chicken broth
2 teeth of garlic, thinly sliced
1 teaspoon slivered fresh ginger
2 medium onions, cut into bite-
   sized wedges
1/2 pound broccoli flowerets,
   blanched
1 large green bell pepper, cut
   into thin strips
1 large red bell pepper, cut into
   bite-sized chunks

1/2 cup canned water chestnuts,
   drained
1/2 pound snow peas, trimmed
2 medium tomatoes, cut into eighths

Put all the ingredients for the sauce except the cornstarch mixture in the jar of a blender and whir. Pour the mixture into a saucepan and bring to a boil. Immediately reduce the heat to a simmer and cook, stirring occasionally to prevent sticking, for 10 minutes. Add the cornstarch mixture and simmer until thickened and translucent. Set aside.

Put the chilies into a small bowl and cover with boiling water. Let sit until the water cools. Drain. Put the oil in a large wok and heat over a low flame. Add the drained chilies, reduce the heat to the lowest possible setting, and leave them to simmer in the warm oil for 45 minutes to 1 hour, or until soft. Add the broth and turn the heat to high. When hot, add the garlic, ginger, and onions and stir-fry for about 1 minute. Add the broccoli and stir-fry for another minute. Add the remaining ingredients and stir-fry until heated through but still crisp.

Spoon out the excess liquid and discard. Add the sauce, stir-fry to thoroughly coat all the vegetables, and serve with steamed rice.

CHILES EN NOGADA
Mexico
Stuffed Chilies with
Whipped Cream and Nut Sauce

I usually serve this on Cinco de Mayo, Mexico's independence day, since the colors reflect the colors of the Mexican flag.

Serves 4 to 6
1 cup shredded sharp Cheddar
　　cheese
1 cup shredded Swiss cheese
1 cup ricotta
1-1/2 cups finely shredded lean
　　cooked ham
1 tablespoon finely minced
　　fresh hot chilies (no seeds)
1/2 cup currants
1/2 cup slivered blanched almonds
1 tablespoon dark brown sugar
1/2 teaspoon ground cinnamon
1/8 teaspoon ground cloves
1/8 teaspoon ground cumin
Salt to taste
Minced small fresh hot chilies
　　(optional)
8 whole canned peeled green
　　chilies*

SAUCE
1 cup (1/2 pint) heavy cream
1 cup blanched almonds, ground
　　into powder
1 teaspoon sugar
1/4 teaspoon ground cinnamon

1/4 cup tequila
2 tablespoons fresh pomegranate
　　seeds
1 tablespoon coarsely chopped
　　fresh cilantro

Mix all of the ingredients except the salt, minced chilies, canned chilies, and sauce ingredients together in a bowl. Taste and add salt and more minced fresh chilies if you want it hotter. Drain the canned chilies and separate them onto a flat work surface. Carefully run a finger inside each chili to open them, being careful not to tear. Gently pack the stuffing into each chili and place the stuffed chilies in a lightly oiled baking dish. Put into a preheated 350° oven just until the cheeses have melted, no more than 10 minutes. Remove from the oven and arrange on a serving platter.

　　To make the sauce, whip the cream until it will hold its shape. Gently fold in the almonds, sugar, cinnamon, and tequila. Spoon over the stuffed chilies. Scatter the pomegranate seeds and cilantro over the top and serve immediately.

OKRA AND CHILIES
Tex-Mex Cuisine

Serves 4 to 6
2 tablespoons lard
1/2 tablespoon chili powder
1/2 teaspoon ground cumin
1/2 teaspoon mixed dried herbs
　　(Italian seasoning)
6 teeth of garlic, minced
2 medium onions, sliced into rings
2 tomatoes, chopped
6 to 8 small fresh hot chilies,
　　cut into thin rings
1 large bell pepper, seeded and
　　cut into thin strips
1 pound okra, stemmed
Salt and coarsely ground black
　　pepper
1/3 cup shredded sharp Cheddar
　　cheese
2 bacon strips, crisply fried
1 small fresh hot chili, sliced into
　　thin rings and seeded

Heat the lard in a large heavy skillet. When the lard is hot but not yet smoking, add the chili powder, cumin, herbs, and garlic and stir rapidly for about 1 minute. Add the onion rings and toss about in the oil. Add the tomatoes and stir to mix well. Add the chilies, bell pepper, and okra and stir. Reduce the heat to maintain a simmer, cover and continue to simmer only until the okra is tender but not mushy. Add salt and pepper to taste. Transfer to a casserole or other heatproof serving dish. Sprinkle over the cheese. Crumble the bacon and sprinkle over the cheese and scatter the fresh chili over the top. Put in the oven just until the cheese has melted and begun to brown. Serve at once.

GREEN BEANS IN MUSTARD VINAIGRETTE
Creole Cuisine

Serves 6

VINAIGRETTE
1 teaspoon dry mustard
1/4 cup olive oil
6 teeth of garlic, finely minced
1 teaspoon horseradish (if using fresh grated, add to taste)
1/4 cup red wine vinegar
1 teaspoon sugar
1 tablespoon minced fresh parsley
1/2 teaspoon coarsely ground black pepper

1-1/2 pounds green beans, French-cut into lengthwise slivers
1 teaspoon capers, drained
1 teaspoon chopped canned pimiento, drained

To make the vinaigrette, mix the dry mustard with the oil, using the back of a spoon to smooth any lumps. Put this mixture, along with all of the remaining vinaigrette ingredients, into a jar with a tight-fitting lid and shake vigorously until thoroughly mixed.

Fill a large pan with water and bring to a boil. Add the beans and leave only until the water reboils. Remove the beans with a slotted spoon, drain, and put into cold running water until cool. Bring the pan of water to a boil again. Add the beans and boil only until just tender, about 3 minutes. Drain and place on a serving plate. Pour the vinaigrette over and scatter the capers and pimiento on top. Serve hot or cold.

LEEKS VINAIGRETTE
Creole Cuisine

Serves 4 to 6
4 to 6 medium leeks
3 tablespoons red wine vinegar
1 teaspoon paprika
1 teaspoon Dijon mustard with seeds
1/2 teaspoon cayenne
1/4 teaspoon sugar
8 to 10 teaspoons olive oil
Salt and coarsely ground black pepper to taste

Trim the root end off the leeks and trim off all but 4 to 6 inches of the green. Split the leeks in half lengthwise. Rinse well under cold running water. Tie back together with string. Fill a large saucepan with water and bring to a boil. Gently drop in the leeks and leave until the water reboils. Drain immediately and run the leeks under cold running water until they are cold. Refill the pan and bring the water to the boil. Add the leeks and reduce the heat to a simmer and continue to cook until the leeks are just tender. Test by cutting off a bit of green and tasting it. Drain and soak in running water until cold. Drain and set aside.

With a fork, mix the vinegar, paprika, mustard, cayenne, and sugar together well. Then with a fork or wire whisk, blend in the olive oil a very few drops at a time until a thickish sauce is formed. Add salt and pepper.

Arrange the leeks attractively on a serving plate and drizzle the vinaigrette over. Refrigerate for at least 1 hour before serving.

CHORIZO-AND-CHEESE POTATO PANCAKE
Oaxaco, Mexico

My great-great-ever-so-great-grandfather was Johan Wyss, the author of *Swiss Family Robinson.* I still have relatives in and about Bern. On my first trip to Switzerland these distant cousins introduced me to *rösti,* a traditional potato dish of that region.

You can imagine my amazement when, some years later, while staying with a friend in Oaxaca, Mexico, my breakfast one morning was a *rösti,* topped with perfectly prepared sunny-side-up eggs. Well, it wasn't quite a *rösti.* If anything, it was better, for, sandwiched between the crisp golden outer layers of potato was a layer of zesty cheese, chilies, and chorizo; a grand way to start a day.

Serves 6
4 medium potatoes
2 or 3 links chorizo
1 medium onion, minced
6 to 8 teeth of garlic
4 small fresh hot chilies, seeded and cut into thin rings
1/2 cup sliced mushrooms
1/4 teaspoon ground cumin
Oil for frying
1/2 cup sharp Cheddar cheese
2 green onions, including the tops, minced
1 tablespoon minced fresh cilantro
Salt and coarsely ground black pepper

Peel the potatoes and put into a pan large enough to hold them comfortably. Cover with water and parboil 10 or 15 minutes, just until a small sharp knife can easily pierce the outer 1/4 inch but meets with considerable resistance further in. Drain, rinse in cold water, and set aside to drain.

Remove the skin from the chorizo and sauté the meat lightly in a heavy skillet. Add the onion, garlic, and chilies and sauté until soft. Add the mushrooms and cumin and continue to sauté over moderate heat until all the vegetables are tender.

Remove from the heat and set aside. Generously oil a large skillet, at least 9 inches in diameter, and put on high heat. Meanwhile, shred the potatoes on the large end of a grater. When the pan is hot, put half of the shredded potatoes into it and distribute evenly. With the back of a large spoon or pancake turner, pat the potatoes down so that they are somewhat compressed and even. Reduce the heat to medium and fry the potatoes undisturbed for about 2 minutes.

Sprinkle the surface of the potatoes evenly with the chorizo and vegetable mixture. Sprinkle the cheese over this, and over the cheese sprinkle the green onions and cilantro. Sprinkle with salt and pepper to taste. Cover all with the remaining half of the grated potatoes. Make sure that the potatoes are evenly distributed and all of the cheese is covered. With the palm of your hand, flatten and even the potatoes. Lift an edge of the cake with a turner and check for doneness. When golden brown, remove the pan from the heat and set on a flat work surface. Cover the pan with a flat plate large enough to completely cover the surface. Holding both plate and pan firmly, invert and remove the pan, hopefully leaving the browned side of the potato cake up on the plate. Wipe any bits of food from the pan, oil again, and reheat. Carefully slide the potato cake, raw side down, into the hot pan and cook until done, about 10 minutes. Slide onto a heated serving plate. Serve hot.

This is traditionally a breakfast dish served with fried eggs sitting on top and accompanied with salsa in a bowl.

HOMINY IN CHILI SAUCE
Native American Cuisine

A food dislike is a perfectly valid emotion. You try it, you hate it, and you say, "Thank you very much. That was an interesting experiment and I think I'll pass on seconds." That is reasonable. I *hate* hominy. There aren't many things that I don't like. I will not willingly eat most people's potato salad or most people's pineapple-upside-down cake, I hate gin, and I *hate* hominy. I get a tight feeling in my throat when I smell the stuff. My parents, however, loved it and would have it when I wasn't home.

Hominy was developed by Native Americans. Dry kernels of corn were soaked in a solution of lye until they had swollen up more than twice their size. Then the lye was removed with fresh water baths and the result was large, soft, tender kernels of corn that could be prepared in a number of ways, all of them detestable as far as I am concerned, but for those of you who enjoy the stuff, I think you will enjoy this recipe of Southwest Native American origins with a few white man's additions.

Serves 4 to 6
SAUCE
1/4 cup lard
10 teeth of garlic, minced
2 large onions, chopped
1 large bell pepper, seeded and chopped
6 small fresh hot peppers, cut into thin rings
4 large tomatoes, chopped
1/2 teaspoon mixed dried herbs (Italian seasoning)
1 bay leaf
1/2 teaspoon ground cumin
1/2 teaspoon dried oregano
1 teaspoon sugar
2 tablespoons minced fresh cilantro
1/2 teaspoon coarsely ground black pepper
One 6-ounce can pitted black olives, drained
Salt to taste
Crushed dried hot chilies (optional)

One 29-ounce can hominy, drained
1/2 cup shredded sharp Cheddar cheese
1/2 cup shredded Swiss cheese
6 or 8 pitted black olives, sliced thin
1 tablespoon chopped fresh cilantro

To make the sauce, heat the lard over high heat in a heavy skillet. Add the garlic and onions and sauté until lightly browned. Add all the remaining sauce ingredients except the olives, salt, and crushed chilies. Stir and bring to a boil. Reduce the heat and simmer, stirring occasionally, until a thick sauce is formed. Add the olives and salt to taste. If you want it hotter you may add crushed chilies a bit at a time, stirring and simmering for a few minutes after each addition.

Stir the hominy into the sauce and pour into an ovenproof serving dish. Toss the two cheeses together and scatter over the top of the hominy. Strew the olives and cilantro over all and put into a preheated oven at 350° until the cheese has melted and is beginning to bubble and brown. Serve hot.

VARIATION Sauté 3 or 4 lengths of chorizo, cut into 1/2-inch pieces, and stir into the hominy and sauce before baking.

BRUSSELS SPROUTS IN CHEDDAR-HORSERADISH SAUCE
Shipton-under-Wychwood, Oxfordshire, England

In my British travels I have discovered some indigenous dishes that are candidates for membership in the Galvanized Gullet: delightful and zesty offerings usually given their depth of personality by mustards. England has always had a comfortable relationship with mustard and horseradish, using both to create sauces and side dishes guaranteed to add interest to any meal.

Serves 4 to 6

SAUCE
2 tablespoons butter
2 tablespoons unbleached all-purpose flour
1 teaspoon dry mustard
2 cups milk
2 eggs, well beaten
1 cup shredded sharp Cheddar cheese, preferably white
3 tablespoons prepared horseradish, or fresh grated to taste
1-1/2 teaspoons minced fresh dill weed, or 1/2 teaspoon dried
1 teaspoon chopped canned pimiento
Salt to taste

1-1/2 pounds firm fresh Brussels sprouts, well trimmed
Parsley sprigs and pimiento (optional)

To make the sauce, melt the butter in a saucepan over a medium heat. Add the flour and mustard and stir briskly until a paste is formed. *Do not* let it brown; adjust heat if necessary. Begin adding the milk in a thin stream, whisking all the while. Never let it boil or even simmer, just keep whisking over a low heat until the mixture is smooth and thickened. If for some reason it should lump, just bung it into the blender, whir, and return to the saucepan.

Pour half of the mixture into a small bowl and whisk to cool a bit. Whisking all the while, slowly pour the beaten eggs into the bowl of white sauce. When thoroughly incorporated, slowly pour the eggy mixture back into the white sauce in the saucepan, whisking continuously. Continue whisking until thickened. This may take as long as 20 minutes. Again, if it lumps or curds, let your blender rescue you.

When thickened, smooth, and glossy, add the remaining sauce ingredients, stir to blend, and taste for seasoning. Add salt and more horseradish if desired. Set aside and keep warm.

Fill a large pan with water and bring to a boil. Add the sprouts and boil gently just until a small sharp knife can readily pierce them, but beware of overcooking sprouts. (An overcooked Brussels sprout ought to be deported right back to Brussels, taking overcooked cauliflower with it.)

Put the Brussels sprouts in a serving dish and pour the sauce over. Garnish with sprigs of parsley, and more pimiento if desired.

ALU KA RAYTA
India
Potatoes with Yogurt Sauce

Serves 4 to 6
4 to 5 medium potatoes, or 1-1/2 to 2 pounds very small new potatoes
3 tablespoons light-flavored vegetable oil
1 teaspoon each cumin and anise seeds
1 medium onion, chopped
4 teeth of garlic,
3 small fresh hot chilies, preferably both red and green, cut into thin rings
1 cup plain yogurt
2 tablespoons minced fresh cilantro
1 tablespoon minced fresh mint
1/4 cup minced fresh parsley
2 green onions, minced
Salt

If using medium potatoes, cut into 1/2-inch slices. Cover the potatoes with water and boil until tender but still showing some resistance when pierced with the point of a small sharp knife. Drain and peel.

In a heavy skillet or wok, heat the oil over a high heat. Add the cumin and anise seeds and stir in the oil until they begin to crack and pop—almost like popcorn. Add the onion, garlic, and chilies. Stir-fry only until the onions are translucent but not yet browned. Add the potatoes and stir-fry until they are evenly coated with the spice mixture and lightly browned.

Put into a serving bowl and add the yogurt, cilantro, mint, parsley, and green onions. Stir and add salt to taste. Chill for at least 1 hour before serving.

AVIYAL
India
Stir-fried Vegetables
in Coconut Masala

Serves 6

MASALA

2 cups chopped fresh coconut (to open the coconut, see page 13)
1-1/2 cups water
2 tablespoons peanut oil
2 tablespoons butter
2 tablespoons grated fresh ginger
6 teeth of garlic, minced
1 medium onion, chopped
1 tablespoon crushed dried hot chilies
1/2 tablespoon ground coriander
1 teaspoon dry mustard
1 teaspoon ground cinnamon
1/2 teaspoon ground turmeric
1/2 teaspoon ground cumin
1/2 teaspoon fennel seeds
1/2 tablespoon sugar
1/4 cup water
Salt and crushed dried hot chilies to taste

2 tablespoons peanut oil
2 tablespoons water
1 large carrot, cut into 1/4-inch diagonal slices and blanched
10 to 11 stalks of broccoli, cut into approximately 3-inch lengths and blanched
1 small yellow summer squash, cut into 1/4-inch slices
2 small slim dried red chilies
1 red bell pepper, seeded and cut into thin rings
2 small fresh hot chilies, seeded and cut into thin rings
1 small yellow summer squash, cut into 1/4-inch slices
6 green onions, including 3 to 4 inches of the green, cut into 2-inch lengths
3 tablespoons minced fresh cilantro

Put the coconut and 1-1/2 cups of water in the blender and whir until a purée is formed. Set aside.

Melt the oil and butter together in a heavy saucepan or skillet over moderate heat. Add the ginger, garlic, and onion and sauté until the onion is translucent. Adjust heat to prevent browning. Add all the remaining *masala* ingredients except the water, salt, and crushed chilies and stir to incorporate with the oil and onions. Cook for about 1 minute. Add the water and, stirring constantly, cook over low heat for about 5 minutes. Add the coconut purée, stir well, and cook for another 2 to 3 minutes, stirring to prevent scorching. If it appears too dry, add water 1 tablespoonful at a time until a very thick sauce results. Taste and add salt and more chilies to taste.

To cook the vegetables, heat the oil and water in a large wok or skillet over high heat. Add the vegetables one at a time in the order given and stir-fry each for about 40 to 60 seconds before adding the next one. Add the cilantro and toss. Spoon in the *masala,* toss gently, and taste again for seasoning. Stir gently over high heat, for about 1 minute, spoon into a bowl, and serve hot.

NOODLES, BEANS, RICE & BREAD

Most people with a weight problem revel in sweets. Sure, I like chocolate mousse. Strawberries and cream are great, and a root beer float, made with really good old-fashioned root beer and excellent rich vanilla ice cream—well, that's pretty good, and speaking of ice cream: home churned fresh peach or berry ice cream—give me strength. But none of these can beguile me, keep me from a new pair of Levi's that I can't quite get into like a fresh loaf of sourdough French bread, or a hot baked potato dripping with butter. Rice! Rice almost any way except in a rice pudding will lead me off the straight and narrow. Beans, pasta, lentils, dumplings, pot stickers, linguine with clam sauce, pasta with *pesto,* tortillas—ah, yes tortillas. A tortilla dripping melted cheese and salsa; a tortilla spilling minced onion, tomato and chilies out the end; a crisp flour tortilla doing its best to wrap itself around guacamole, refried beans, salsa, chilies, lettuce, onion, garlic, and lots of freshly minced cilantro. Oh well, sweat pants are more comfortable than Levi's anyway. Pass the starch, please.

MEE KROB
Thailand
Crisp Noodles
with Shrimp and Pork Sauce

Serves 6
8 green onions
1/2 pound thinnest Oriental wheat
   noodles available
Light-flavored vegetable oil
   for deep-frying
2 eggs, lightly beaten
1/2 pound lean pork, cut into
   2-inch strips no more than
   1/4 inch wide
1 pound cooked baby shrimp
1 medium onion, chopped
8 teeth of garlic, minced
1 tablespoon grated fresh ginger
1/2 tablespoon crushed dried
   chilies
1/4 cup black bean paste (available in Oriental food stores)
1/2 teaspoon shrimp paste (available in Oriental food stores)
2 tablespoons tomato paste
3/4 cup sugar
1/2 cup fresh lemon juice
1 tablespoon fresh lemon rind,
   cut into the thinnest slivers
   possible
3 small fresh hot chilies, preferably
   red, seeded and cut into the
   thinnest slivers possible
1/2 pound fresh bean sprouts

1 small fresh hot red chili, seeded,
   the flesh cut into a fringe and
   left attached at the stem end

Make the green onions into brushes
for garnish by trimming off the
root and cutting off the tops, leaving the trimmed onions 4 inches
long. Save the tops for use later.
Hold each onion by its root end,
and with a small, sharp knife,
begin cutting 1 inch from the end
and slice through lengthwise all
the way to the other end. Place in
water and refrigerate until needed.
Mince the remaining green parts
fine and reserve.

Bring 2 or 3 quarts of water to
the boil and add the noodles. Boil
until just tender. These thin noodles
will cook quickly, in 3 to 5 minutes.
Drain and leave in a colander to dry.

In a large wok, heat enough oil
for deep-frying, 2 to 3 inches.
When the oil is hot but not
smoking, drizzle in about 1 tablespoon of the beaten egg with your
fingers. It will congeal immediately.
When it is lightly browned, remove
with a slotted turner and place on
paper towels to drain. Repeat
until all the egg is used. Set aside.

Let the oil become hot again
and begin deep-frying the noodles,
a few at a time. If they do not puff

up and dance about in the oil,
becoming crisp almost immediately,
then you are probably frying too
many at one time. Remove the
soggy mess, let the oil get hot
again and try another batch, this
time just a few. Remove from the
oil with a slotted spatula just as
soon as they are golden brown and
crisp. Set aside to drain on paper
towels. Continue until all the
noodles are fried.

Remove all but about 1/4 cup of
the oil from the wok. Heat. Add
the pork and shrimp and toss in
the oil for about 2 minutes. Now
begin adding all the remaining
ingredients in the order given,
except the bean sprouts and fringed
chili. Stir-fry for about a minute
after each addition. Reduce the
heat to low and simmer for 15 to
20 minutes, stirring occasionally.

To assemble, put the fried noodles
in a deep serving plate and pour
the sauce over. Toss very gently
so as not to break the noodles.
Mound it up and place the bean
sprouts in a ring around it. Lay
the egg lace on the top of the
noodle-sauce mixture. Set the
brushes of green onions around
the edge of the dish, sprinkle the
minced onion tops over the dish,
and place the fringed chili on top
like a cap.

KAENG CHUD WOON SEN
Thailand
Cellophane Noodles
with Shrimp and Pork

Serves 6

1/4 cup dried cloud ears (tree
    fungus)
2 tablespoons peanut oil
1/4 pound lean pork, cut into
    very thin strips 2 inches long
1 tablespoon shrimp paste (avail-
    able at Oriental food stores)
6 teeth of garlic, sliced thin
1 tablespoon finely slivered fresh
    ginger
1 large onion, cut into thin rings
6 cups light chicken broth
1 cup sliced fresh mushrooms
4 small fresh hot chilies, cut into
    thin slices
3 tablespoons sugar
1/4 cup fresh lemon juice
The rind of 1/2 lemon, cut into
    the thinnest slivers and blanched
2 tablespoons soy sauce
1/2 pound small shelled shrimp
6 green onions, including the tops,
    cut into 3-inch lengths
2 eggs, lightly beaten
Salt, freshly ground black pepper,
    and cayenne
1 tablespoon minced fresh cilantro
    for garnish

Soak the mushrooms in warm water to cover for 1 hour. Cover the cellophane noodles with water and let sit for 30 minutes. Heat the oil in a wok and sauté the pork until well browned on all sides, 3 to 4 minutes. Add the shrimp paste and stir to thoroughly coat all the pieces of pork. Add the garlic, ginger, and onion and toss with the pork for another minute. Set aside.

Bring the broth to a boil. Reduce the heat to moderate and add the next 7 ingredients. Stir in the pork and onion mixture. Drain the cellophane noodles and cloud ears, add to the pot, and gently stir. Simmer for about 2 more minutes. Add the green onions and, while stirring very gently, drizzle in the beaten egg, a bit at a time. Add salt, pepper, and cayenne to taste. As soon as the egg is set, transfer to a serving dish and sprinkle the cilantro over the top.

HOT POT STICKERS
China
Spicy Stuffed Dumplings

Makes about 24

DOUGH

1 cup unbleached all-purpose flour
1/4 cup water, or more
1 tablespoon peanut oil

FILLING

1/2 pound ground lean pork
1/2 cup minced cooked cabbage
1/2 cup minced onion
6 teeth of garlic, minced
1/2 tablespoon finely grated fresh
    ginger
1 teaspoon crushed dried hot chilies
1/4 teaspoon Chinese five-spices
1 tablespoon brown sugar
1 tablespoon cornstarch
1 egg
2 tablespoons soy sauce
4 green onions, including tops,
    finely minced
1/4 cup minced fresh parsley
1/4 teaspoon coarsely ground
    black pepper

3 tablespoons peanut oil
1 cup chicken broth

Mix all the dough ingredients together exceedingly well with a fork. If the dough is not soft and pliable, add more water 1 teaspoon at a time until the dough is soft and comfortable to work with. It should feel like any good pastry. Knead on a lightly floured surface until soft and glossy.

Form into a snake 1 inch in diameter. Cut this into 1/2-inch chunks. One at a time, place a chunk of dough in front of you on a lightly floured surface. Flatten it with the palm of your hand. Then, using a lightly floured rolling pin, roll each piece of dough into a circle about 3 inches in diameter. When finished, stack them lightly and cover with a slightly dampened cloth to keep them from drying out while you make the filling.

Mix all the filling ingredients together exceedingly well. Make a small patty and fry in a bit of oil to test for seasonings. Add more chilies, pepper, sugar, etc., to taste and test again. When ready, put about a tablespoon of meat mixture in the center of a round of pastry. Fold the pastry in half and, using thumb and forefinger together, press the edges together. Then fold the edge over to make a seal. Secure by either crimping with fingers or laying the pastry on a flat surface and sealing with the tines of a fork. Continue with the remaining ingredients.

Put 2 tablespoons of the oil in a heavy cast-iron skillet. When it is hot, lay the pastries in it and fry undisturbed for 2 minutes. Pour in the broth, reduce the heat to a simmer, cover, and cook until almost all the liquid is absorbed, about 10 minutes. Remove the lid, add the remaining tablespoon of oil, swirl it about in the pan to cover all the pot stickers and continue to fry uncovered for about 2 minutes longer. Scoop from the pan with a pancake turner and put on a serving plate brown side up.

STEAMED CHILI NOODLE
Chinese-American Cuisine

Makes 4 to 6 large noodles
1 cup unbleached all-purpose flour
1/4 cup water
1 tablespoon peanut oil
2 green onions, including tops, finely minced
1/4 cup finely minced cooked ham
1/2 tablespoon finely minced fresh hot chili
Oil

Mix the flour, 1/4 cup water, and oil together well with a fork. If the dough is too dry, add more water, 1 teaspoon at a time until a soft, workable dough is formed. Knead well on a lightly floured board. Divide into 4 to 6 equal pieces. Place one piece on the work surface and, using as little flour as possible, roll out exceedingly thin, no more than 1/16 inch thick. Try to keep as close to a rectangle as possible.

Lightly sprinkle half of the surface with green onions, ham, and chilies. Fold in half and roll again to press the ingredients into the dough and to press the 2 halves of dough back together. Turn the dough over once and roll again. With a sharp knife or pizza wheel, trim it into a rectangle. Put a few drops of oil on the surface and spread it evenly over the surface. Turn the dough over and oil that side too. Roll the dough up jelly-roll fashion in the direction that will produce the longest noodle roll. Place on a plate and continue with the remaining pieces of dough. When all are finished, place them in a Chinese steamer over boiling water in a wok or large pot, cover with the steamer's lid, and steam for 30 minutes. To serve, place on a heated plate and slice into 1-inch chunks on the diagonal. Serve hot with heated smoky Oriental sesame oil for dipping.

UDON
Japan
**Noodles in Chili- and
Ginger-Flavored Stock**

Serves 4 to 6
3 large dried Japanese mushrooms
One 14-ounce package *udon* noodles,
  (no, you can't use spaghetti)
6 cups light chicken broth
2 tablespoons *katsuobushi**, or
  1 cup chowder scraps
6 teeth of garlic, crushed
1 onion, quartered
1 tablespoon chopped fresh ginger
2 sheets *nori* (dried seaweed)
2 tablespoons crushed dried chilies
1 tablespoon sugar
Salt, pepper, and crushed dried
  chilies
2 eggs, lightly beaten
3 green onions, chopped small
1 each small red and green fresh
  hot chili, seeded and cut into
  the thinnest possible strips
1 cup 1/2-inch tofu cubes
1 sheet *nori,* crumbled
12 snow peas, stemmed and cut
  lengthwise into thin slivers

Soak the mushrooms in warm
water to cover for 1 hour. Drain
and set aside. Bring 2 or 3 quarts
of water to a boil and add the
noodles. Continue cooking at a
rapid boil for about 10 minutes or
until the noodles are soft but not
squashy. Drain, rinse in cold water,
and set aside.

Put the next 8 ingredients in a
large pot and bring to a boil.
Reduce heat to maintain a low boil
and cook for 45 minutes. Taste
and add salt, pepper, and more
chilies to taste. If you add more
chilies, continue to cook for another
10 minutes.

Strain the broth, bring it to a boil,
and add the noodles. Reduce heat
and simmer for 5 minutes. Cut the
mushrooms into quarters. In a
lightly oiled omelet pan, make the
eggs into 2 or 3 small rolled
omelets. Remove to a flat surface
and sliver finely. Add with all the
remaining ingredients to the noodles
and broth, stir gently, and simmer
for another minute before putting
into a large bowl or 6 individual
serving bowls. Serve hot.

*Dried bonito flakes, available in
Japanese markets.

PASTA E FAGIOLI
Italy
**Pasta and Beans in
Spicy Tomato-Herb Sauce**

Serves 6
1 cup dried pinto beans

RED SAUCE
4 bacon slices
2 tablespoons olive oil
10 teeth of garlic, chopped
1 large onion, chopped
1 tablespoon crushed dried chilies
3 small fresh hot chilies, sliced
  into thin rings
1 large bell pepper, chopped
4 large tomatoes, chopped
1/2 teaspoon mixed dried herbs
  (Italian seasoning)
1 tablespoon sugar
1/2 cup dry red wine
Salt and pepper to taste

1-1/2 pounds vermicelli or angel
  hair pasta
Olive oil

GREEN SAUCE
1/2 cup butter
1 cup fresh basil leaves
1 medium onion, quartered
2 small fresh hot green chilies, chopped
1 cup shredded mozzarella
1/2 teaspoon sugar
Salt and pepper to taste

Cover the beans with water and bring to a boil. Reduce heat to moderate and cook until the beans are tender. You may have to top up the water occasionally. When tender, drain and set aside.

In a large, heavy skillet, fry the bacon until crisp. Remove from the pan and set aside. Add the olive oil to the pan, let it heat, then add the garlic and onion. Sauté gently until the onion is soft but not yet browned. Add the next 8 ingredients and bring to a boil, stirring frequently. Reduce the heat to maintain a rapid simmer and cook until a thick sauce results, about 45 minutes.

Put the pasta into a large pot of boiling water and boil rapidly until the pasta is just tender. Drain, return to the pot, add a few drops of olive oil, and cover. Leave until ready to assemble the dish.

Melt the butter but do not allow it to brown. Put the butter and all of the remaining ingredients into a

blender and purée. Return to the saucepan you melted the butter in and simmer for no more than 5 minutes.

Add the drained beans to the red sauce and cook just long enough to heat the beans thoroughly. Pile the beans and sauce into the center of a large serving platter. Use tongs to arrange the pasta around the edge of the beans. Drizzle the green sauce over it and serve.

GARBANZOS CON CHORIZO
Basque-American Cuisine
Garbanzo Bean and
Sausage Stew

When Basques began immigrating to California, they found that the eastern slope of the Sierras reproduced the geography of their own Pyrenees. They engaged in the business of herding sheep in this new land as their forefathers had done for generations in the tall mountains on the French and Spanish border. Like the numerous other immigrant populations that have added to the rich texture of American culture, the Basques brought the foundations of their cuisine with them, nudging it a bit to accommodate its new environs. The end result may be seen in a number of robust, yet subtle dishes

that blend Old World concepts with New World vitality.

Serves 6
1-1/2 pounds chorizo
3 tablespoons olive oil
10 teeth of garlic, chopped
3 medium onions, chopped
4 small fresh hot chilies, chopped
3 large tomatoes, chopped
2 celery stalks, chopped
1 scant teaspoon dried mixed herbs (Italian seasoning)
1 tablespoon sugar
Salt, pepper, and crushed dried hot chilies to taste
4 cups cooked garbanzos (chick-peas)
2 tablespoons minced fresh cilantro

Sauté the chorizos in a heavy skillet until well browned on all sides. Prick them several times to prevent bursting. When done, set aside. Add the olive oil to the pan and sauté the garlic and onions until translucent but not yet browned. Add all of the remaining ingredients except the garbanzos and cilantro and cook over moderate heat, stirring occasionally, for 30 to 45 minutes or until a thick sauce is formed. Slice the chorizo into 1/2-inch chunks and add to the sauce with the garbanzos. Simmer for an additional 5 minutes before transferring to a serving plate. Sprinkle with the cilantro.

NEW ORLEANS
RED BEANS AND RICE
Creole Cuisine

Years ago I was a partner in a magnificent, grand disaster. The New Orleans House featured Victorian decor, New Orleans food, and my partner's traditional jazz band. Most such ventures fail and so did ours, but red beans and rice survived. Red beans and rice is a New Orleans tradition, beans for the protein and rice for bulk to fill you up. Poor folks' food. Now everyone knows that musicians are traditionally poor or, at least, they start out that way, and Louis Armstrong was no exception. He grew up with red beans and rice from his mama's kitchen. Well, Louis was destined not to stay poverty-struck, and when he got his first paying gig or two he brought home a ham hock for his mama to put into the beans, and when things got better yet the ham hock was replaced with a nice pork butt.

Red beans and rice holds such a strong place in New Orleans culture, and therefore in the hearts of New Orleans jazz musicians, that there is hardly a Dixieland musician about who can play a sweet note without a good "bate" of red beans and rice under his or her

belt. Well, the recipe grew and developed through the success and failure of most of the great names in jazz. Billie Holiday's mama added a thing or two, Kid Ory changed the seasonings for the better, someone added the tomato sauce, someone else the okra. Bob Scoby had a hand in its development, as did Lou Waters and Turk Murphy. Our vocalist was married to Bessie Smith's daughter, and he claimed that Bessie herself had had a hand in the creation of this tasty pottage.

Now, whether this is all history or legend, here is not "a" but "the" recipe for New Orleans red beans and rice.

Serves 12, at least
4 cups small dried red beans or pinto beans (not kidney beans)
1 large onion, quartered
2 whole heads garlic, each peeled of outer skin and cut in half
1 bay leaf
1 tablespoon mixed pickling spices

SAUCE
1/4 cup lard or bacon drippings (drippings are traditional)
One 2-1/2- to 3-pound pork butt or boneless shoulder, cut into thin strips (1/4 inch wide and 2 inches long)
2 large onions, chopped
10 to 15 teeth of garlic, chopped
6 large tomatoes, chopped
1 cup beef broth
4 small fresh hot chilies, cut into thin rings
2 large bell peppers, seeded and cut into thin strips
6 celery stalks, chopped
1 pound mushrooms, sliced
1/2 pound okra, cut into 1/4 inch rings
1/2 cup minced fresh parsley
1/2 tablespoon mixed dried herbs (Italian seasoning)
3 tablespoons chili powder
2 bay leaves
3 tablespoons sugar
1/2 cup dry red wine
Salt, coarsely ground black pepper, and crushed dried chilies to taste

2 cups long-grain white rice
1 teaspoon oil or butter
Minced fresh parsley for garnish (optional)

Put the beans, onion, garlic, and bay leaf in a large pot and add enough water to cover the beans by 3 or 4 inches. Put the pickling spices in a large tea ball and add to the pot. Bring to a boil and reduce the heat to maintain a slow boil or fast simmer until the beans are quite tender. The time will vary depending on the condition of the beans. Top up the water level from time to time with boiling water from a tea kettle. When the beans are tender, turn off the heat and leave them sitting in the water until ready to use.

To make the sauce, melt the lard or drippings in a large heavy pan. A Dutch oven is perfect. Sauté the pork until browned on all sides but not dry and hard. Add the onions and garlic and sauté just until the onions are soft. Add the tomatoes and stir. Cook for 2 or 3 minutes, then add all the remaining ingredients up to and including the red wine. Bring to a boil, then reduce the heat and simmer, stirring frequently, for 1-1/2 to 2 hours, or until a thick, rich sauce is formed. During the last half hour of cooking, add the salt, black pepper, and crushed chilies.

Put the rice in a pot with a tight-fitting lid and cover with cold water to a depth of one thumb knuckle above the level of the rice. Add the oil or butter. Put on the stove over a high flame and bring to a boil. Boil until the water has

evaporated just to the level of the surface of the rice. Put on the lid, remove from the heat, and leave *undisturbed* 45 minutes. At this time, stir gently to put what was on top on the bottom, return the lid, and leave for another 15 minutes.* Drain the beans and add to the sauce. Stir and simmer together for about 10 minutes or until both are hot.

Put the fluffy rice in a ring around the outside of a large deep serving platter. Pour the saucy beans into the center. If you wish, sprinkle the top with some minced parsley. Serve up with corn bread, greens, and sweet, sweet jazz, and the saints may come marching in just to dish themselves up a plate.

*This method of cooking rice will work no matter how much rice you are cooking or what size or shape pot you are using. The proportions and times are always the same. Cover the rice with water to the level of your first thumb knuckle, cook uncovered until the water is just level with the surface of the rice, cover and let it have some privacy while it steams itself to perfection. This is how to have very happy rice. Aren't you happy when you come out of a sauna?

DIRTY RICE
Cajun Cuisine

Serves 6 to 8
1 pound pork liver
10 teeth of garlic, minced
1 large onion, minced
1 tablespoon crushed dried chilies
1 tablespoon sugar
6 cups water
2 cups long-grain white rice
1 tablespoon butter
1/2 cup minced fresh parsley
Salt and freshly ground black
    pepper to taste

Chop the liver into small pieces. Put in a pot with the garlic, onion, chilies, and sugar. Add the water and bring to a boil. Reduce heat to a fast simmer, cover with a tight-fitting lid, and cook until the liver is practically disintegrated, about 2 hours. Taste the liquid and if it seems a little peaked, make it richer with powdered beef bouillon to taste.

Add the rice, stir, and bring to a boil. Continue to boil until the liquid is reduced to just the level of the top of the rice. Reduce the heat to the lowest possible setting. Add the butter, cover with a tight-fitting lid, and let sit undisturbed for 45 minutes. Just before serving, add the parsley, salt, and pepper and toss lightly. Serve hot.

ORANGE RICE
WITH ALMONDS
Iran

Serves 4 to 6

2 large seedless oranges
4 teeth of garlic, minced
1 tablespoon grated fresh ginger
1 teaspoon saffron
1 tablespoon crushed dried chilies, or more to taste
1 tablespoon Madras-style curry powder
1/2 teaspoon ground cinnamon
3/4 teaspoon minced fresh dill weed, or 1/4 teaspoon dried
1/4 cup frozen orange juice concentrate
3 tablespoons sugar
1/4 teaspoon anise seeds
1/2 cup butter
1 cup light chicken broth
2 cups long-grain white rice
1 cup slivered blanched almonds
1/2 cup chopped pistachios
1/2 cup minced fresh parsley
Salt and coarsely ground black pepper

Peel the oranges. Remove as much of the white as possible from the inside of the rind by scraping gently with a sharp knife. Sliver the rind as thinly as possible. Blanch the rind and set aside.

Chop the oranges and put them and the next 10 ingredients into a blender and whir. Melt the butter in a large heavy skillet or casserole with a tight-fitting lid. Gently sauté the orange rind for 1 minute. Adjust the heat to keep the butter from burning. Pour in the contents of the blender and the cup of broth and simmer, stirring occasionally, for 5 minutes. Add the rice and stir. Smooth the top of the rice and gently pour in enough water to bring the level of the liquid one thumb's-knuckle-depth above the level of the rice. Raise the heat and rapidly simmer until the level of the liquid is just barely level with the top of the rice. Cover with a tight-fitting lid and turn the fire to the lowest possible heat. Leave for 45 minutes to 1 hour, or until the liquid is totally absorbed and the rice tender.

Stir gently to fluff and add the almonds, pistachios, and parsley and fluff again. Add salt and pepper to taste, pile into a serving dish, and serve hot.

NASI KUNING LENGKAP
Indonesia
Coconut-Flavored Rice

This is a recipe given to me by a British Airlines pilot at an unofficial Galvanized Gullet meeting 30,000 feet in the air.

Serves 8

1 whole coconut
1/4 cup peanut oil
1 large onion, minced
8 teeth of garlic, minced
1 tablespoon ground turmeric
2 tablespoons grated fresh ginger
2 tablespoon crushed dried hot chilies
1 teaspoon ground cinnamon
1/2 teaspoon fennel seeds
1 tablespoon dry mustard
3 tablespoons sugar
1/4 teaspoon ground cloves
3 cups long-grain white rice
4 green onions, minced
Salt and pepper

Shred the coconut (see page 13) and set aside. Heat the peanut oil in a large skillet or casserole. Sauté the onion and garlic until the onion is translucent but not browned. Add the next 8 ingredients and cook over high heat, stirring constantly for 2 minutes. Add the rice and stir to coat evenly. Pour over enough water to stand one thumb knuckle above the level of the rice. Simmer until the water is absorbed just to the level of the rice. Cover with a tight-fitting lid and reduce the heat as low as possible. Leave for 45 minutes or until the liquid is totally absorbed and the rice tender. Gently stir in the shredded coconut and green onions. Add salt and pepper to taste, cover again, and leave for 5 minutes before serving.

NOTE: Sorry, but this is another non-specific recipe. You may serve the rice just as it comes out of the pot, or you can make it into a one-dish feast. In its homeland, when served for special occasions, the rice is molded into a tower and surrounded by any number of things, either meat or vegetable. You may decorate the tower with thin strips of marinated barbecued meat, chicken, shellfish, raw vegetables, cooked vegetables, eggs, peanuts, toasted coconut, etc. The decision is yours.

ARROZ VERDE
Mexico
Green Rice

Serves 6
2 large green bell peppers
6 small fresh hot green chilies
5 cups chicken broth
1 cup chopped fresh parsley
1 large onion, chopped
8 teeth of garlic, chopped
1/4 teaspoon freshly ground black pepper
1/2 tablespoon sugar
1/2 teaspoon dried oregano
1/4 teaspoon ground cumin
5 cups chicken broth
1/4 cup corn or other light-flavored oil
2 cups long-grain white rice
Salt to taste
1/4 cup minced fresh cilantro

Roast all the peppers and chilies over a gas flame or under a broiler until the skins blister. Turn to roast all sides. Wrap in a damp towel and leave for 5 minutes. Use the towel to rub off the scorched bits of skin. Stem, seed, and chop the peppers and chilies. Put 1-1/2 cups of the chicken broth in a blender and add the chilies, peppers, parsley, onion, garlic, black pepper, sugar, oregano, and cumin. Whir until a smooth purée is formed.

Heat the oil in a large, heavy skillet or casserole with a tight-fitting lid. When the oil is hot but not smoking, add the rice and stir continuously for a few minutes to coat the rice with the oil, but not long enough to let it brown. Add the purée and simmer, stirring occasionally, for 5 minutes. Add the remaining broth and bring to a boil. Reduce the heat to moderate, add salt, and continue cooking until the liquid is just level with the top of the rice. Cover with the lid and reduce the heat as low as possible. Leave undisturbed for 30 minutes. Turn off the heat and leave for another 15 to 20 minutes or until the rice is tender. Add the cilantro and fluff with a fork. This is excellent served with a variety of Mexican dishes.

The Cajuns say, "A day without rice is a day without eating." In some Chinese provinces a common greeting is, "Is your rice well?" while in other areas of China they speak of the worth of a young woman as, "She knows rice." "He shares his rice," is a Japanese expression that indicates one's philanthropic value, while the Argentines will sadly shake their heads when talking of a friend who has hit the skids and say, "Poor man, he has lost his rice."

PRE-DUNE FRIED RICE
San Francisco Chinese Cuisine
Stir-Fried Rice and Chilies

Remember when I told you about
the New Orleans House? Well,
what I didn't tell you was that,
long before his *Dune, Dune, Dune,*
and then some more *Dune* days,
Frank Herbert worked for a San
Francisco newspaper and knew a
lot about advertising and P.R. He
had my partner and me over to
dinner and a discussion on how to
handle the P.R. for the New
Orleans House.

Now I am not particularly fond
of science fiction, so Frank's talents
in that direction are strictly lost
on me, but he is one of the finest
practitioners of Northern Chinese
cuisines that I have ever had the
great pleasure to cross chopsticks
with. That night he served, in
addition to oodles of other wonderful things, this out-of-the-ordinary
dish.

Serves 6
2 eggs, lightly beaten
1/4 teaspoon ground ginger
1/4 teaspoon Chinese five-spices
1/4 teaspoon sugar
1/8 teaspoon cayenne
1/2 medium onion
1/4 cup peanut oil

4 teeth of garlic, minced
  exceedingly fine
1 teaspoon finely grated fresh ginger
4 cups cooked long-grain white rice
3 tablespoon soy sauce
3 tablespoons *hoisin* sauce*
6 snow peas, steamed and slivered
  lengthwise into the finest of
  threads
6 small fresh hot chilies, seeded
  and cut into paper-thin rings
1/2 cup cooked ham, slivered
  exceedingly fine
2 green onions, including the tops,
  sliced into the finest rings
Salt and freshly ground black
  pepper to taste

Beat the eggs, ginger, five-spices,
sugar, and cayenne together. Oil
an omelet pan lightly, using a
brush or paper towel dipped in oil.
Heat the pan. Pour in half of the
egg mixture and form into a rolled
omelet. Set aside. Repeat with the
remaining egg. Using a sharp knife,
sliver into thin shreds and set
aside. Slice the half onion into the
thinnest rings possible. Cut these
half rings in half once. Set aside.

Heat the peanut oil in a large
wok. Add the garlic, ginger, and
onions and toss for no more than
1 minute, just until heated through.
Add the rice. Mix the soy and
hoisin sauce together and add to
the rice. Stir-fry until the rice is
evenly coated with the sauce.

Add all the remaining ingredients,
including the slivered omelet, and
toss gently. Cover and let sit
without heat for 5 minutes. Toss
gently before serving.

*If *hoisin* sauce is not available,
use 2 additional tablespoons of
soy. It's not the same, but if none
of your guests have had dinner at
Frank Herbert's house, how will
they know?

BREAD

SALSA LOAF
Family Recipe

Makes 1 large round loaf
1 cup lukewarm water
1 package (1 tablespoon) active
  dry yeast
1/4 cup sugar
4 or more cups unbleached all-
  purpose flour
1/4 cup light-flavored vegetable oil
1 teaspoon salt
1 cup hot or mild chunky salsa,
  page 148
2 tablespoons minced fresh cilantro
4 teeth of garlic, minced
1 egg white, beaten (optional)

Mix the water, yeast, and sugar together well in a large bowl. Add 2 tablespoons of the flour, mix, and leave in a warm place to work. It will become frothy and begin to bubble. Add another cup of flour, the oil and salt. Beat well and leave to become bubbly. This can take from 1 hour to 3, depending on the temperature of the room and the age of the yeast (this, incidentally, is called the sponge method of bread baking). When the sponge is light and "spongy," begin adding the remaining flour, stirring well after each cup is added. Your goal is a soft workable dough. When your flour, water, and yeast have reached that august state, turn out onto a lightly floured surface and begin kneading, and kneading, and kneading. When working with yeast breads the major difference between failure and success is insufficient kneading. However, you must at the same time be careful not to work too much flour into the dough or you are in big trouble. Keep your work surface very lightly floured and your hands only lightly dusted with flour as well. If they become too sticky, wash all the dough off, dry thoroughly and pat with flour again.

Your dough should be soft and elastic with a satiny sheen. When the dough is ready, roll it out into a rectangle, keeping the dough about 1/2 inch thick.

Spread the salsa over the surface of the dough, leaving a 1-inch border all around. Sprinkle the cilantro and garlic over the salsa. Starting with the edge that will produce the longest roll, begin rolling jelly-roll fashion. Pinch the length of the seam to make a seal. Then, seam side down, wrap the roll around itself like the shell of a snail. Set on an oiled baking sheet. Paint the surface with lightly beaten egg white if you wish a glossy finish. Leave in a warm place until doubled in bulk. The time will depend on the temperature. Put into the oven at 350° for 45 minutes to an hour, or until the loaf is well browned and sounds hollow when tapped lightly.

NOTE: This is good hot or cold. If you are going to eat the bread hot from the oven, *do not* slice it. Just tear off chunks and stuff it into your mouth, with or without butter. If you try to slice hot bread it will squash and become doughy. If you want to be able to slice the loaf with ease, rub the top with a buttered paper or brush with melted butter or margarine, then wrap in a clean cloth and leave until cool. This makes a soft, tender crust that will slice easily. If you want a crunchy crust, let the bread cool uncovered on a rack.

Incidentally, you *do not* have to preheat the oven when making most yeast breads. Quick breads are a different matter.

VARIATION: After spreading the dough with salsa, sprinkle 1/2 cup of shredded Swiss or mozzarella cheese over the surface and proceed as above.

SALSA LOAF WITH CHEESE AND ONIONS
Family Recipe

1 recipe Salsa Loaf, preceding
1/2 cup shredded sharp Cheddar cheese
1/2 cup shredded Swiss cheese
1/2 cup minced onion
3 tablespoons finely minced garlic
1 teaspoon finely minced fresh dill weed

Follow the recipe for Salsa Loaf, preceding, sprinkling the above ingredients on top of the salsa.

CHILI CORN BREAD
Family Recipe

Corn bread at our home has always been a glorious gastronomic experience: light, crumbly, moist, and yummy, usually dripping butter and honey, but occasionally containing other things. Sometimes my mother would fold chunks of very ripe avocado into the batter, and sometimes cheese.

Serves 6
2 cups yellow cornmeal
1/2 cup unbleached all-
   purpose flour
2 teaspoons baking powder
2 tablespoons chili powder
1/4 cup sugar
1/8 teaspoon salt (optional)
1/4 cup light-flavored vegetable oil
1 cup water (for almost all baking,
   milk is not necessary unless you
   have someone in the family who
   really needs the extra calories)
2 eggs, separated

Put all the ingredients except the egg whites into a bowl and beat together well. Beat the whites until they are high and fluffy. Fold gently into the corn batter. Oil a 10-inch cast-iron frying pan and pour in the batter. Put into a preheated 350° oven for 40 to 50 minutes or until the top is well browned and the corn bread is light. Stick a skewer into the center. When it comes out clean the bread is done.

SALSA-BACON CORN BREAD
Family Recipe

Serves 6
1 recipe Chili Corn Bread,
   preceding
1 cup hot chunky salsa, page 148
3 strips crisply fried bacon

Prepare the batter for Chili Corn Bread and pour it into the frying pan. Just before baking, put tablespoonfuls of salsa about the surface of the corn bread. Crumble the bacon and sprinkle on top. Bake as for Chili Corn Bread.

CHILI-CHEESE CORN BREAD
Family Recipe

Serves 6
1 tablespoon light-flavored
   vegetable oil
3 small fresh hot chilies, cut into
   thin rings
1 medium onion, cut into thin
   rings
6 teeth of garlic, minced
1/2 cup shredded sharp Cheddar
   cheese
1/2 cup shredded mozzarella
   cheese
2 tablespoons minced fresh cilantro
1 tablespoon chili powder
1/2 teaspoon sugar
1/4 teaspoon salt
1 recipe Chili Corn Bread, preceding

Heat the oil in a skillet and add the chilies, onion, and garlic. Sauté until just soft but not yet beginning to brown. Toss all of the remaining ingredients, except for the corn bread, in a bowl. Prepare the cornbread batter and pour into the baking pan. Spread the sautéed vegetables on top of the corn bread batter and sprinkle with the cheese mixture. Bake as for Chili Corn Bread.

INJERA
Ethiopia

Serves 8
1 cup millet
1 cup boiling water
2 cups unbleached all-purpose
   flour
1/2 tablespoon baking powder
1/4 cup sugar
1/4 cup peanut oil
Salt to taste
Approximately 1 cup cold water
   (the amount will vary greatly,
   depending on the quality of the
   millet)

Put the millet in a bowl and pour the boiling water over it. Let it sit until the water is cool, then put it into a blender and whir until a smooth paste results. If necessary add more water.

Put this into a bowl and add all the remaining ingredients except the cold water. Begin stirring, then gradually add water until you have a batter the same consistency as for pancakes.

To bake, heat a large skillet, omelet pan, or griddle and lightly oil. The cooking surface should not be as hot as for pancakes. You don't want the *injera* to brown, just to set. Pour on enough batter to coat the surface and make a cake about 1/8 inch thick and 9 inches in diameter. Let it cook slowly until the surface is dry. If the bottom browns, reduce the heat before baking the next *injera*. As each bread is finished, set on a large plate and cover with a damp cloth. Traditionally, the Ethiopian stew called *wat* (see page 60) is served in a tightly woven basket that is lined with overlapping *injera*. Each diner tears off pieces of the bread and wraps it around a bit of the *wat* to eat it.

YEWOLLO AMBASHA
Ethiopia
Spice Bread

Makes 1 large round loaf

2 packages (2 tablespoons) active dry yeast
2 cups lukewarm water
1/2 cup sugar
1/2 cup butter
2 tablespoons ground coriander
1 teaspoon ground cardamom
1 teaspoon crushed fenugreek seeds
1/2 teaspoon freshly ground black pepper
2 teeth of garlic, minced
1/2 cup minced onion
1 tablespoon finely grated fresh ginger
1/2 teaspoon ground cinnamon
1/4 teaspoon ground nutmeg
1/8 teaspoon ground cloves
1/2 teaspoon cayenne
2 tablespoons paprika
1 teaspoon salt
5 to 6 cups unbleached all-purpose flour
Melted butter (optional)

Mix the yeast, water, and 1 tablespoon of the sugar together in a large bowl and let sit while you melt the butter. While the butter is cooling, measure and add all the remaining ingredients except the

flour and optional melted butter to the bowl with the yeast. Stir well. Add 1 cup of the flour, stir well, and leave until bubbling and spongy (1 to 3 hours). When the sponge is quite active, begin adding the remaining flour, stirring well after each 1/2 cup. Your goal is a soft dough. When enough flour has been added, turn out onto lightly floured surface and knead exceedingly well. Pinch off a small piece of dough about the size of a golf ball and set aside. Form the remaining dough into a large round and place on a lightly oiled baking sheet. With a sharp knife, made a shallow cut, no more than 1/4 inch deep, in the form of a cross across the top of the loaf. Roll the small piece of dough into a ball and set in the middle of the cross. Let the loaf sit in a warm place until doubled in size. Bake at 350° for 50 to 60 minutes or until crispy and golden brown. Slide the loaf onto a wire rack. If a soft crust is desired, paint with butter and wrap with a clean cloth. For a crisp crust leave to cool.

SAINT GYLES
FAIRE GINGERBREAD
Oxford, England

In the late Middle Ages and the Renaissance in England, gingerbread was sold at all the great country fairs. Each fair had its own recipe, and the merchants at that particular fair were licensed to sell breads made from that fair's recipe only. In my travels in England I have collected over fifty of these gingerbread recipes. They range from something akin to the light fluffy cakes we are familiar with to gummy steamed puddings. They are all delicious despite often being outside anything we have experienced.

Saint Gyles was the patron saint of beggars and thieves, who were not allowed inside the gates of most cities. Therefore, all fairs named in honor of St. Gyles, like the one in Oxford, were held just outside the walls. Oxford's fair continues today; however, don't expect to find goats, pigs, or sheep! Like almost all of the fairs, it is now nothing more than a carnival with rides and shooting galleries. And you have to make do with caramel corn and cotton candy instead of the wonderful heady gingerbread that was once sold by the vendors.

Makes about 3 dozen drops

1 cup dark molasses
1 cup dark brown sugar
1 tablespoon cider vinegar
1/2 cup butter
1 teaspoon baking soda
2 tablespoons ground ginger
1 tablespoon ground cinnamon
1/2 teaspoon anise seeds
1/4 teaspoon ground cloves
A pinch of salt
3 cups unbleached all-purpose
  flour

Mix all the ingredients except the flour together exceedingly well. Begin working in the flour until it is all used. Hands may be the best tool. If necessary add water a spoonful at a time to achieve a workable consistency. Work until well blended, then drop by tablespoonfuls onto a lightly oiled baking sheet. Bake in a preheated 350° oven for about 20 minutes. Remove from the pan to cool. The texture should be slightly chewy, not crisp.

SAUCES, PICKLES & CHUTNEYS

The recipes in this section are for a variety of tasty, zesty things. Some may stand alone and be used as munchies, snacks, or accompaniments to meals, like the pickles. Some may form a happy adjunct to another dish, like the sauces and salsas, while some—the mustards, chutneys, etc.—are designed to accompany and enhance other foods.

SAUCES

BASIC
ONE-EGG MAYONNAISE
Family Recipe

Have you given mayonnaise any serious thought lately? No? Well, you really should, you know. After all, when something is that good and all you have to do to get it that way is put out a little elbow grease, well, the least you can do is think about it for a while. A lot of other people have, some of them with less time than you. Caesar gave it quite a lot of thought, and Cleopatra, and Alexander the Great, Thomas Jefferson, Mary Queen of Scots. According to legend they all found it a very worthy subject for contemplation.

The first mayonnaise legend to be lobbed in my direction concerns "Mary, Mary, quite Contrary," or Mary Queen of Scots, who, after all, are one and the same person. We are told that her personal physician invented mayonnaise as a cure for seasickness—mariner's malady or mal de mer—which, when corrupted by the English and Celtic tongues became *mayonnaise*. Personally, I can't think of anything less likely to make me feel better when bobbing across the English Channel in a royal barge than a nice oily spoonful of mayonnaise.

One of my favorite stories says that Caesar, while trekking across the deserts in hot pursuit of Pompey, took time out, right there in the middle of the sand, to invent mayonnaise as a quick energy food for his legions. Or perhaps you prefer the story that it was mayonnaise, not her Nile-green eyes and full-blown body, that bound Caesar to Cleopatra. But then Cleo never did have to worry much about Caesar's love. After all, he gave her back Egypt, had her brother murdered for her, and then even forgave her when he caught her entertaining that mess-a-potaneums!

One story goes that, during Alexander's conquest of Persia, eggs were often carried in the leather bags of olive oil, the dual function being that the thick oil cushioned the eggs, preventing them from breaking, and also sealed the pores of the shells and retarded spoilage.

The story says that a few of the eggs broke in the oil, anyway, and after a day's jostling in a wooden-wheeled cart, the result was mayonnaise.

The above tales may be legend. However, in my mayonnaise days I have discovered a few absolute facts. First, you may use the yolk, white, or whole egg. The result is perfect, creamy, and delicious mayonnaise. You may use a fork, wire whisk, hand rotary beater, electric beater, or blender. The ingredients may be chilled or at room temperature and the mayonnaise will work. The one rule that *must not be broken* is that it is *absolutely necessary* to add the first half of the oil no more than 1/2 teaspoon at a time and mix thoroughly between additions. Once it thickens up you may begin adding the oil faster. And, just as you are about to pour the whole ugly mess down the drain thinking that it is never in all the world going to turn into mayonnaise, *splupe,* it gets thick and really does look like mayonnaise.

My favorite of all mayonnaise stories is true and it happened in London. A friend was so impressed by my just whipping up a bowl full of mayonnaise while we were chatting over tea that she asked for the recipe. The next morning she called me in tears. She had made batch after batch, she said, and none of them had worked. Did I think that, perhaps, she wasn't boiling the egg long enough?

Makes about 2 cups
1 egg
1 teaspoon fresh lemon juice or
   cider vinegar
1/4 teaspoon sugar
Salt to taste
1/2 teaspoon dry mustard
2 cups vegetable oil*

Blend the egg, juice or vinegar, sugar, salt, and mustard together exceedingly well. Begin adding the oil, 1/2 teaspoon at a time, beating well between each addition. When the mixture begins to thicken, you may begin adding the oil 1 teaspoon at a time, and after it has thickened, add the oil 1 tablespoon at a time. After it is thick, taste and adjust seasonings. You will want to alter the flavorings depending on what you are going to use it for. If, for instance, it's for a fruit salad, add a little more sugar. If you're using it for tuna, you probably want more mustard and less sugar. Suit yourself. Covered and refrigerated, it will keep for at least a week. It does need refrigeration because it, of course, contains no preservatives.

*Don't ask me what kind. Any kind will do. Some people insist on olive oil. I think it's far too heavy. I have used peanut oil, corn oil, safflower oil, and I am currently using generic oil with no less success. Sometimes when I want the flavor of olive oil, but not the heaviness, I use a blend. Use whatever oil you like or can afford.

AIOLI DE PROVENCE
Southern France
Garlic Mayonnaise

You don't have to fly to Provençe to have perfect *aïoli* for your artichokes. Just use this simple recipe.

Makes about 2 cups
6 to 8 teeth of garlic,
1 recipe basic mayonnaise,
   page 142

Mince the garlic very fine. Before you begin to make the basic mayonnaise, put 1/2 cup of the oil in the blender with the crushed minced garlic. Set aside. Continue on as for basic mayonnaise. When the mayonnaise has thickened and you have used all of the plain oil, begin adding the oil with the garlic in it. This zesty, velvet-smooth sauce may be used in a variety of ways. It is perfect with artichokes, asparagus, and broccoli. Use a bit as a topping for omelets.

VARIATION NO. 1: Follow the instructions for standard Aïoli de Provençe except separate the egg. Make the *aïoli* as described above, using the yolk of the egg. When the *aïoli* is finished beat the white and gently fold into the *aïoli*. The result is a velvety, fluffy sauce that is absolutely yummers.

VARIATION NO. 2 Try making either version of the *aïoli* and blending with the 1/2 cup of oil and the garlic either 1/3 cup minced fresh parsley, 1/4 cup minced fresh mint leaves, 1/2 cup minced fresh basil leaves, or 2 tablespoons Dijon mustard. All are worthy additions to your repertoire.

CAPSICUM MAYONNAISE
Family Recipe

Makes about 2 cups
1 recipe basic mayonnaise, page 142
4 teeth of garlic, minced
3 small fresh hot chilies, minced

As with the *aïoli,* before beginning to make the basic mayonnaise, put the garlic, chilies, and 1/2 cup of the oil in a blender and whir into a purée. Add to the mayonnaise at the end of the process.

HORSERADISH MAYONNAISE
Family Recipe

Makes about 2 cups
1 recipe basic mayonnaise, page 142
1/2 cup prepared horseradish or
   fresh grated to taste

Proceed as with Capsicum Mayonnaise, preceding.

PUB MUSTARD
England

Makes about 1/2 cup
1/3 cup dry mustard
1 teaspoon sugar
1 teaspoon malt vinegar
Enough brown beer to make
   a thick paste

Mix the mustard and sugar together. Add the vinegar and begin stirring with a fork. Gradually pour in the beer, stirring all the while. When it is the consistency you desire, mix well, cover and set aside for 30 minutes. Check it again for consistency. You may find that after it sits you will want to add just a bit more beer. Add more salt and vinegar if you want a zestier, piquant flavor. This is extremely good with cold meats and cold meat pies and pasties; in other words, the things served in an English pub!

FIREHOUSE MUSTARD
England

Makes 1/4 cup
3 tablespoons dry mustard
1/2 teaspoon cayenne
1/2 teaspoon grated fresh ginger
1 tablespoon dark brown sugar
Cider vinegar

Mix the mustard, cayenne, ginger, and sugar together and gradually add the cider vinegar, stirring all the while until it is the desired consistency. This is particularly good with cold ham.

PACKWOOD RANCH MUSTARD
Family Recipe

The cowboys and ranch hands on Packwood Ranch loved to spread this mustard liberally on cold beef or cold chicken pie.

Makes about 1/2 cup
3 tablespoons mustard seeds
1/3 cup dry mustard
1 teaspoon sugar
Cider vinegar

In the jar of a blender or in a mortar, crush the mustard seeds. Add to the dry mustard and sugar. Stirring all the while, add enough cider vinegar to make into a spreadable paste.

WINE MUSTARD
Sonoma, California

Makes 1/2 cup
1/3 cup dry mustard
1 teaspoon ground turmeric
3 teeth of garlic, forced through
   a garlic press
Cream sherry

Mix the mustard, turmeric, and garlic purée together and add enough cream sherry to make into a paste.

VINEGAR HORSERADISH
England

When fresh horseradish root is available or you grow it yourself you are in for a dimension in heat that is hitherto unexperienced, to say nothing of never again having your sinuses clogged. Whereas the heat of capsicum rests on the tongue and tingles the lips, horseradish goes for the nose. The instant the fumes of freshly grated horseradish touch your tongue they race up your nose and lodge in the sinus cavity behind your eyeballs.

I make fresh horseradish by two methods. Both are quite good; it's just a matter of preference.

Makes 1/2 cup
1/2 cup grated fresh horseradish
  root
1/4 cup cider vinegar
1 teaspoon sugar

Put all the ingredients into a
blender jar and whir to a smooth
purée. If you wish it thinner, add
more vinegar, 1 teaspoon at a
time. Add more sugar to taste.

HORSERADISH CREAM
England

Makes 1/2 cup
1/2 cup grated fresh horseradish
  root
1/4 or more heavy cream
1 teaspoon sugar

Proceed as for vinegar horseradish,
above. When using fresh horseradish it is best to make just what
you are going to use that day.
What's the use of going to the
trouble of making it fresh if you
let it sit about and lose its zap and
become just like store-bought?

SALSA MAYONNAISE
Aaron, my younger son

Makes 1/2 cup
1/2 cup mayonnaise, page 142
1/2 cup hot or mild chunky salsa,
  page 148
6 teeth of garlic, finely minced
2 tablespoons finely minced onion
1 teaspoon seeded and finely
  minced small fresh hot chilies

Mix all the ingredients together
well. Good with cold meats and
cold boiled potatoes, as a sandwich
spread, with celery and other raw
vegetables.

DILL AND
HORSERADISH SAUCE
England

Makes 1/2 cup
1/2 cup mayonnaise, page 142
3 tablespoons prepared horseradish,
  or fresh grated to taste
1/2 tablespoon minced fresh dill
  weed
1/2 teaspoon sugar

Mix all the ingredients together
and let sit overnight before using.
This is exceptionally good with
beef or white fish. In my estimation
it will absolutely destroy salmon,
but then there are very few things
I like with salmon other than salmon.

SOY MUSTARD
Japanese/Hawaiian Cuisine

Makes 1/3 cup
1/3 cup soy sauce
1 tablespoon grated fresh ginger
2 tablespoons dry mustard
2 tablespoons sugar
6 teeth of garlic
1/4 teaspoon coarsely ground
  black pepper

Put all the ingredients except the
black pepper in the jar of a
blender and whir until all is liquified.
Strain. Add the pepper and stir.
This is excellent with *sushi, sashimi,*
noodles, *dim sim,* cold meats, etc.

EASY DEVIL SAUCE
Sterling, my older son

Makes 1/2 cup
1/4 cup soy sauce
2 tablespoons catsup
1 tablespoon dry mustard
1/2 tablespoon sugar
4 teeth of garlic, finely minced
1/8 teaspoon cayenne
1/2 tablespoon olive oil

Mix all the ingredients together
exceedingly well. This is very good
with beef, hot or cold.

CHUTNEY SAUCE
Dana, my daughter

Makes 1 cup
1/2 cup mayonnaise, page 142
1/2 cup mango chutney
1/4 teaspoon cayenne
1/2 teaspoon finely grated fresh
 ginger

Put all the ingredients in the jar of a blender and whir to a smooth purée. Refrigerate for a few hours before using. Use with cold ham, cold meat pies, or pasties. Try using it with minced ham or chicken and onion and lettuce in pita bread or a flour tortilla.

MOLHO DE PIMENTA E LIMAO
Brazil
Sauce of Chilies and Lemon

Makes about 1-1/2 cups
6 *hot* pickled chilies, minced
1/2 cup minced onion
1 tablespoon minced garlic
1/2 cup minced green onions,
 including tops
1 tablespoon minced fresh cilantro
1/2 cup fresh lemon juice
1 teaspoon sugar

Combine all the ingredients in a bowl and stir. Let sit at least 1 hour before serving. Serve with pork, chicken, or beef. This is especially good with grilled foods.

CAPSICUM-GINGER GLAZE
Family Recipe

Makes about 1 cup
1/4 cup frozen orange juice
 concentrate
1 medium yellow onion, chopped
4 teeth of garlic, chopped
2 tablespoons grated fresh ginger
3 small fresh hot chilies, seeds
 and stems removed
1/4 teaspoon ground cinnamon
1/4 teaspoon freshly ground black
 pepper
1/4 cup Rhine wine
1/4 cup light-flavored vegetable oil

Whir all of the ingredients in a blender. Pour into a saucepan over high heat and, whisking all the while, bring to a rapid simmer. Reduce heat slightly and continue whisking for about 5 minutes. Strain. If you want it hotter, add cayenne during this cooking period. This is an excellent marinade or glaze for a number of meat or poultry dishes.

BERBERE
Ethiopia
Hot, Hot, HOT Seasoning Paste

Makes about 2 cups
4 tomatoes, coarsely chopped
1 tablespoon grated fresh ginger
1/2 teaspoon each ground
 coriander, cardamom, fenugreek,
 nutmeg, and cinnamon
1/8 teaspoon ground cloves
1 onion, minced
8 to 10 teeth of garlic, minced
1 tablespoon salt
1/4 cup dry red wine
2 cups paprika
3 tablespoons cayenne
1 teaspoon coarsely ground black
 pepper
1/4 cup vegetable oil
2 to 3 tablespoons sugar
2 tablespoons minced fresh cilantro

Put all of the ingredients into a saucepan and, stirring continuously, cook over a medium heat for 10 to 15 minutes or until a thick sauce results. Transfer to a jar or small crock for storage. This seasoning paste will keep for several weeks if refrigerated. Serve with Sik Sik Wat, page 60.

SALSA CRUDA
Mexico
Uncooked Sauce

On my last trip to Mexico I encountered *salsa cruda,* or fresh uncooked salsa. Once made aware of it, I realized that it is ubiquitous, being served from glass bowls set in larger bowls of cracked ice in posh restaurants that cater to the tourist trade, and being handed to you in a paper cup in truck stops and markets. Either way it's great, adding a light freshness to Mexican foods despite its volcanic quality.

Makes about 3 cups
5 large ripe tomatoes, chopped
6 small fresh hot chilies, chopped
4 teeth of garlic, minced
1 large onion, chopped small
4 green onions, including tops, chopped small
1/3 cup minced fresh cilantro
1/4 teaspoon coarsely ground black pepper
1 teaspoon sugar
Salt to taste

Put the tomatoes, chilies, and garlic into a blender and whir. Pour into a bowl and add all the remaining ingredients. Refrigerate before serving.

SALSA DIABLO
Family Recipe
Smooth Salsa

Makes about 2 pints
One 46-ounce can tomato juice
1 pound fresh very hot chilies, chopped*
4 large onions, chopped
6 teeth of garlic, chopped
1/3 cup minced fresh cilantro
1/4 cup sugar
1/3 cup distilled vinegar
1/2 teaspoon freshly ground black pepper
Salt to taste

Put all of the ingredients into a large pot and bring to a boil. Reduce the heat and simmer for 30 minutes. Let it cool somewhat. Put into the blender and whir to a smooth purée. You will probably have to do this in several batches. Be careful. This is *hot.* Do not touch your hands to your face until you have washed them very well. Pour the purée back into the pot and simmer over low heat, stirring frequently to prevent sticking, for another 30 minutes or until a smooth, thick sauce results. It will keep for about 2 weeks in the refrigerator or it may be frozen.

*If you want this salsa hotter, add cayenne to taste. If you don't want it so hot, remove the seeds from the chilies or use milder chilies. If you want it only mildly hot, use bell peppers instead of chilies and gradually add cayenne to achieve desired hotness.

HOT TERIYAKI SAUCE
Japan

Makes about 1-3/4 cups
1 cup soy sauce
1/4 cup smoky Oriental sesame oil
1/4 cup cream sherry
1/3 to 1/2 cup brown sugar
6 teeth of garlic, finely minced
1/2 tablespoon grated fresh ginger
1/2 teaspoon dry mustard
1/2 teaspoon crushed dried hot chilies
1/4 teaspoon coarsely ground black pepper

Put all of the ingredients into a glass jar with a tight-fitting lid and shake well. Refrigerate overnight. Every time you go into the refrigerator for something, give the jar a shake. The next day, strain through a fine mesh sieve. It is now ready to use as a marinade for fish, flesh, or fowl.

SALSA SON-OF-A-GUN
Family Recipe
Chunky Salsa

Salsa is a staple in our house. When schedules are so conflicting that the only way you know the other guy has been home in the past twenty-four hours is by the number of beers that aren't in the refrigerator, or when we're all just too busy to cook, we tend to put things, any ol' things, inside a tortilla or a piece of pita bread, pour salsa on it and stuff it into our mouths. Another family quick food is cottage cheese with salsa, or salsa poured over a quick omelet. My kids toss a chuck roast or chicken into a pan, pour salsa over it, and bung it into the oven. Good, healthy, and quick. We use salsa as a base for dips, or as a dip, for the beginnings of a salad dressing or marinade, and to zest up leftover (oops, excuse me, planned-over) meats. We use a lot of salsa, and at somewhere around a buck a throw, unless you have access to generic, that can become a good-sized chunk out of the grocery budget. So we make it. You can can it or freeze it, or keep it in the fridge for a couple of weeks.

Makes about 4 quarts
8 pounds ripe tomatoes, chopped small
1 pound fresh very hot chilies, chopped*
12 to 15 teeth of garlic, chopped
8 to 10 large onions, chopped small
1 bunch of celery, chopped small
1/4 cup light-flavored vegetable oil
1 cup distilled vinegar
1/2 cup sugar
1/2 cup minced fresh cilantro
1/2 tablespoon freshly ground black pepper
Salt to taste

Put a cup of the chopped tomatoes into the blender and add as many chilies as will fit comfortably. Whir to make a purée. Continue until all the chilies have been puréed. Pour the purée into a large pot. Add all of the remaining ingredients including the rest of the tomatoes, and cook over high heat for 10 minutes, stirring frequently to avoid scorching. Reduce the heat to moderate and continue cooking, stirring occasionally, for about 45 minutes or until the salsa is somewhat thickened. Taste and add salt, more sugar or vinegar or crushed dried hot chilies to taste. Cook for at least 10 more minutes after making any additions. The salsa will keep in the refrigerator for up to 2 weeks or it may be frozen.

If you are going to can it, follow the instructions for tomato sauce in the U.S. Department of Agriculture Pamphlet on Home Food Processing, or the canning instructions in any standard cookbook.

*The essence of this salsa is the flavor of fresh chilies. This recipe makes a fairly hot salsa. It could be hotter. For those of you bucking for lifetime membership in the Galvanized Gullet, add additional crushed dried hot chilies, freshly bought. Those of you who would rather not have it so hot, buy milder chilies and remove the seeds. If you don't want it very hot at all, but do like the chili flavor, substitute a pound of bell peppers for the pound of chilies and add crushed dried hot chilies a little at a time until the desired hotness is obtained.

Good Husband and Huswife,
when summer is done,
Go look to thy larder
that waste be there none.

Let salt, spice and brine
do their work best,
Eat fresh what you may,
then pickle the rest.
—*Thomas Tusser*

PICKLES

CROWN AND TREATY PICKLED ONIONS
England

One of the times when the king and Parliament tried to negotiate a peace, the king and his entourage rode down from his royalist stronghold in Oxford and the Parliamentarian representatives rode out from Westminster to meet at an inn in Uxbridge. A treaty was signed but it didn't stick. The only thing that stuck was the name, for the inn has been called the Crown and Treaty ever since. The Crown and Treaty and a few other good bargeman's pubs scattered along the banks of the Grand Union Canal are about all Uxbridge has to offer, except these wonderful pickled onions that originated at the Crown and Treaty.

Makes about 2 quarts
2 pounds small boiling onions (each should be about 1 inch in diameter)
12 small dried red chilies
1/2 cup salt
1/4 cup sugar
1 tablespoon mixed pickling spices
4 teeth of garlic, crushed
1 tablespoon salt, or to taste
Cider vinegar

To peel the onions quickly, drop into rapidly boiling water and leave for about 1 minute. Drain, rinse in cold water, and peel with a small sharp knife. Put the onions and the chilies in a bowl with the 1/2 cup of the salt and enough water to cover. Stir and let sit overnight.

The next day, drain the onions and chilies and rinse in fresh water. Put the onions and chilies into a saucepan and add the remaining ingredients. Add enough cold water to just cover the onions. Bring to a boil, then reduce the heat to a simmer. Cook for no more than 10 minutes. They are done when a skewer stuck into them will only penetrate the outside eighth of an inch before it shows resistance. Nothing is worse than soggy pickled onions.

Drain the onions and chilies, reserving the liquid. Rinse and pack into sterilized jars or a small crock. Pour the liquid over, then add enough vinegar to just cover. If using jars, screw down the lids and store in a cool place. If using a crock, cover and place in the refrigerator. They will be ready to eat in about 3 days, but will keep in a cool place for months.

Pickled onions, chutney, and mustard pickle are traditionally part of a "ploughman's lunch," which is nothing more than a chunk of good bread and a piece of English farmhouse cheese. That and a pint of good brown ale are enough to keep you ploughing on till dinner time.

PICKLED CHILIES
Cajun Cuisine

For each pint:
Small fresh chilies, hot or mild
6 teeth of garlic
1/3 cup light-flavored vegetable oil
1 fresh dill top, or 1/2 teaspoon dried dill
1/2 teaspoon sugar
Distilled vinegar

With a sharp knife, make a slit in the side of each chili. Fill a sterilized pint jar with a ring-and-dome lid with the chilies. Add the garlic, oil, dill, and sugar. Fill the jar with vinegar, put on the ring and lid, screw down, and shake. Leave in a cool place. The chilies will be ready to use in about 3 weeks. These pickles do not stay crisp. If you are of the macho type who loves to crunch on hot chilies, these will be fine for that game in 2 weeks. We mostly use them to cut up into things like burritos and *quesadillas* and for this we like them nice and soft. They get that way in a month or two.

ROYAL STANDARD OF ENGLAND HOT MUSTARD PICKLE
England

The Royal Standard of England is reputed to be the oldest pub in the country. Now mind, lots of pubs claim to be the oldest pub in England. However, no matter where I travel in the U.K. people will ask, "Have you been to the Royal Standard of England? It's the oldest pub in the country, you know."

"No, I didn't know that." I always tactfully lie. If you want to keep getting information from people, you have to make them think that you are very pleased with what they have already given you. Oldest pub in England or not, The Royal Standard is a good pub just outside the town of Beaconsfield, off the M 40. The building is beautiful, the beer good, they have barley wine on tap (which isn't a wine at all but a brew that makes Guinness look like greasy kid stuff), an outside beer garden, and an excellent lunchtime buffet.

Makes about 1-1/2 quarts

1 small cauliflower or half a larger one
2 medium green tomatoes, chopped
2 large onions, chopped
2 cucumbers, shredded
1 cup salt
1/4 cup unbleached all-purpose flour
1/2 cup sugar, or more to taste
1/2 cup dry English mustard
1/2 cup butter
2 cups vinegar, preferably malt
1 tablespoon ground turmeric
1 tablespoon capers, drained
1 teaspoon celery seeds
Salt to taste

Separate the cauliflower into the smallest possible flowerets. Cut any that are larger than your thumbnail. Put into a bowl with the other vegetables and pour over the salt. Toss all about in the salt and then cover with cold water. Let sit in a cool place for at least 2 hours but do not refrigerate. When ready to make the pickle, drain the vegetables and wash in cold running water. Put them into a large pot, cover with fresh water, and put over high heat. As soon as it comes to a boil, remove from the heat and drain. Rinse in cold running water and drain again.

Mix the flour, sugar, and mustard together in a saucepan and add the butter. Put over a moderate heat and cook until the butter is melted and a paste is formed, stirring all the while. Slowly begin adding the vinegar, whisking, until a thick sauce is formed. Add all of the remaining ingredients, lower heat to a simmer, and cook for another 5 minutes, stirring occasionally. Remove from the heat and add to the drained vegetables. Toss to coat evenly. Pack into jars or crocks and refrigerate.

In England this is traditionally served with cold meats, pasties and meat pies.

KIM CHEE
Korea
Hot Pickled Cabbage

Makes about 2 quarts

1 medium head Chinese (Napa) cabbage, cored and thinly sliced
2 large onions, cut into thin rings
1/2 cup salt
10 teeth of garlic, coarsely chopped
2 tablespoons slivered fresh ginger
1/2 tablespoon crushed dried hot chilies
1 teaspoon sugar

Put the cabbage, onion rings, and salt in a bowl, knead with your hands, and leave to sit overnight. Next day, rinse off excess salt under cold running water. Drain and rinse again. Drain. Add all the remaining ingredients and knead. Pack into glass jars or small ceramic pots. Add enough water to just reach the top of ingredients. Leave to sit at least 1 week in a cool, unrefrigerated place. Serve as you would pickles or chutney, to accompany cold meats or as a fiery snack.

CHUTNEY

QUICK AND EASY
CHEATIN' CHUTNEY
Family Recipe
Sweet Hot Chutney to
Accompany Indian Food

Makes about 3 cups
1 cup orange marmalade
1 cup *hot* mixed vegetable pickle, chopped very fine
1 cup raisins
1 teaspoon crushed dried hot chilies
1 cup dark brown sugar
1 cup cider vinegar
1/2 teaspoon ground cinnamon
1 tablespoon grated fresh ginger
4 teeth of garlic, minced

Put everything in a saucepan and bring to a boil, stirring constantly to prevent sticking. Reduce heat to a simmer and cook until much of the liquid has been reduced and the chutney is thick and jamlike, about 45 minutes to 1 hour. Stir frequently.

JAMAICA INN CHUTNEY
England

The Jamaica Inn of Daphne du Maurier fame sits alone on the isolated wastes of Bodmin Moor in Cornwall. It was here in this lonely hospice that the wan (aren't they always wan?) heroine of the novel by the same name met with terror night after cold, gray wind-torn night. Less than a mile away down a narrow rutted dirt road lies Dozmary Pool, reputed to be the lake into which Sir Bedivere lobbed Excaliber after Arthur died.

Inside the inn today you are greeted with a giant log fire, crackling merrily, ready to chase away the chill of Bodmin Moor. Like most good country inns today, the Jamaica Inn serves a reputable buffet lunch. Your mackerel, Cornish pasty, steak and kidney pie, or ploughman's lunch will be accompanied with this sweet and sour, hot and zesty chutney.

Makes about 2 quarts
3 pounds apples, chopped small, skins on
3 pounds onions, chopped
3 cups raisins
3 cups dark brown sugar
2 cups malt vinegar
2 tablespoons mixed pickling spices
1 tablespoon grated fresh ginger
1/2 to 1 teaspoon crushed dried hot chilies
1/2 teaspoon ground cinnamon

Put all of the ingredients into a large pot and bring to a boil. Reduce heat and simmer, stirring occasionally, for about 2 hours or until thick and glossy. Let the chutney cool in the pot it was cooked in. Pack into a crock, cover, and store in the refrigerator.

This is traditionally served with cold meats. It is particularly good with cold sliced ham or cold meat pies.

FIRE EXTINGUISHERS

If you are a hot-food fancier then you know that heat has many levels. There is the zip of garlic and onion, whose tastes linger for hours though the harshness dissipates rapidly. There is the sweet burr of ginger, and the growing glow of mustards. There's that incredible explosion in your sinuses caused by horseradish, making its appearance like a nova, and then almost as quickly fading to nothing.

Capsicums on the other hand, the chilies, definitely have staying power. So much so that sometimes it is necessary to cry uncle, wave the white flag, put out the fire. How to do that? The following recipes help. Generations of consuming fiery foods have taught the peoples of the cultures that consume them certain tricks. Trick number one is that, in most cases, water does not help. Beer is much better and something sweet is better yet. You will notice that in cultures where the capsicum runs rampant, desserts are either exceedingly sweet— sweet beyond most of our tolerances—or they are simply fruit, which is one of the finest fire extinguishers available.

When serving a dinner that is based on one of the cuisines designed to bring a significant conflagration to your palate, I almost always serve a platter of chilled fruit to end the meal.

Indian, Southeast Asian, and African hot cuisines offer a variety of sweet chutneys and condiments to accompany the meal. In small restaurants and market stalls, Mexicans accompany hot foods with a form of guacamole without chilies, a mild *salsa cruda,* and the ubiquitous lime. I find fresh limes with food no matter where I go in Mexico. If the establishment is fancy enough they are in bowls or baskets on your table, not so fancy and they are scattered down the center of the table and you reach boardinghouse style. I discovered on my last trip that sucking on a quarter of a fresh lime and pouring down some good Mexican beer is a wonderful fire extinguisher.

LEYLA'S ICED YOGURT AND CUCUMBER
Turkey

The first fire extinguisher I ever learned about must be attributed to Leyla, like so much of my culinary knowledge.

Serves 6 to 8
2 large cucumbers, peeled and grated
1 cup (8 ounces) plain yogurt
2 cups crushed or shaved ice

Mix all the ingredients together well and serve immediately. The ice should be fine enough that it is merely small crystals of coolness that sparkle on tongue and palate as you spoon it into your capsicum-seared mouth.

YOGURT ICE
Middle East

Despite their religious and military disagreements, Richard Coeur de Lion and Saladin held each other in high regard. It is said that once, when Richard lay quite ill and in a delirium, Saladin kept a fleet of runners busy supplying the ailing king with ices to reduce his fever. The image that usually comes to mind when one is told this legend is something akin to our sherbet; however, this chilled delight of fruit and yogurt is probably more accurate.

Serves 4 to 6
3 cups chopped fresh or canned fruit
2 cups (16 ounces) plain yogurt
1/2 cup sugar

Put the fruit into a blender and purée. Mix with the yogurt and sugar and put into freezer. Stir every 15 to 20 minutes to ensure that it sets smooth and creamy and the fruit is evenly distributed. Do not freeze solid.

A nice touch when using oranges, lemons, pineapples, small melons, etc., is to carefully scoop the fruit out of their skins and, when serving, pile the ice back into the skin.

MAST VA KHIAR
Iran
Yogurt and Herbs

Serves 6 to 8
1 large cucumber, shredded
1/4 cup minced red bell pepper or fresh pimiento
2 green onions, including tops, minced
1 tablespoon minced fresh dill, or 1 teaspoon dried
1 tablespoon minced fresh cilantro
1 teaspoon sugar
1 tablespoon fresh lime juice
1 cup (8 ounces) plain yogurt
Sprigs of dill or cilantro for garnish (optional)

Mix all the ingredients except the garnish together exceedingly well and put into the freezer. Stir every 10 minutes for 45 minutes to 1 hour. You do not want it frozen solid, just so it is beginning to get crystals in it. Mound into a serving dish and garnish if desired with sprigs of dill or cilantro. Serve immediately.

MINTED YOGURT
Family Recipe

Serves 6 to 8
1/2 cup chopped fresh mint leaves
1 teaspoon sugar
1 tablespoon fresh lime juice
1 cup (8 ounces) plain yogurt
Sprigs of mint for garnish (optional)

Put all of the ingredients except the garnish into a blender and whir until all of the leaves are incorporated. Pour into a serving dish and chill for at least 1 hour before serving. You may garnish it with sprigs of mint.

THE ULTIMATE FIRE EXTINGUISHER
Family Recipe

Serves 12 or more
1 large watermelon
1 large cantaloupe
1/2 honeydew
1/2 casaba
1 box strawberries
2 large seedless oranges
4 limes
2 cups seedless grapes
3 or 4 fresh mint sprigs for garnish
2 recipes Minted Yogurt, preceding

Jagged-cut the watermelon in such a manner as to make it into a long oval serving dish. You should only remove about one-fourth to one-fifth of the total bulk when making the "lid."

Jagged-cut the cantaloupe in half to make 2 dishes. Remove a small slice from the bottom of the watermelon and each half of cantaloupe, just enough so that they will sit firmly on their bottoms.

With a melon baller or a sharp teaspoon remove the meat from all of the melons. Wash the strawberries but leave the stems on. Leave the peel on the oranges and slice into thin rings. Cut each lime into 6 wedges. Toss all of the fruit together gently and put into the hollowed-out watermelon shell. Thread some of the fruit alternately onto short bamboo skewers and arrange around the edge of the melon shell. Arrange the mint here and there.

Put the minted yogurt into the now-empty cantaloupe shells and, when serving, place a cantaloupe shell at either end of the watermelon. Provide extra skewers. Your guests may use the preskewered fruit and dip it into the minted yogurt, or gather up fruit of their preference to dip. This is a marvelous fire extinguisher and a grand dinner party or buffet centerpiece.

AGUA DE FRUTA
Mexico

In Mexico at small restaurants and market stalls they sell fruit waters—not fruit juices but fruit waters—made simply by mincing fresh fruit and letting it sit in ice water for a few hours before serving. I would say that the result was more a suggestion than an actual flavor, and the colors are likewise subtle. Walking through the marketplaces you will see five-gallon jars filled with chunks of ice and pastel liquid, the outsides of the jars running rivulets of frost. The stand with the jar of fruit water makes a welcome haven on a hot Mexican afternoon.

Makes 1 gallon
6 cups minced (not puréed)
    fresh fruit
1 gallon cold water
Several large chunks of ice

Put the fruit into a large glass jar or pitcher. Add the water and stir. Let sit at room temperature for 2 hours. When ready to serve, add the chunks of ice. Do not expect this to be like fruit juice. There is not that intensity of flavor, nor is it particularly sweet. It is cool and refreshing, tasting lightly of the fruit from which it is made, and it's a wonderful fire extinguisher.

Appropriate fruits are watermelon, pineapple, strawberries, Persian melons, peaches, cantaloupe, or any tropical fruit you can afford 6 cups of.

PUT-OUT-THE-FIRE SALSA CRUDA
Mexico

Makes about 2 cups
4 large tomatoes, minced
2 large bell peppers, chopped small
1 large cucumber, chopped small
6 green onions, including tops, minced
1/4 cup minced fresh parsley
2 tablespoons minced fresh cilantro
1 medium sweet onion, minced
1/4 cup fresh lemon juice
1 teaspoon sugar
Salt to taste

Mix all the ingredients together and refrigerate for at least 2 hours before using.

GEWURZTRAMINER SHERBET
Strictly California

I told you in the foreword that one of the few people I have ever met who had a hot food tolerance that was equal to mine was a wine maker. Joel and I met one hot, hot summer afternoon at the Buena Vista winery where he and other close friends at the winery shared a picnic I had brought. The *boudin* put the others under the table, but Joel scarfed up chunk after fiery chunk saying only, "Yes, it's a little warm." That afternoon he eagerly joined ranks with the Galvanized Gullet and gave me this superb fire extinguisher recipe.

I always liked to envision guests at Joel's house asking, "This meal is delicious. Did you make it yourself?" And of course he could answer, "Of course, all of it," since he had made the wine as well.

Serves 4 to 6
1/2 cup sugar
1 bottle fine Gewürztraminer (Buena Vista or Hacienda are my favorites—both wineries are on the original Harazthy estate)
2 egg whites
1 cup (1/2 pint) heavy cream

Stir the sugar and wine together until the sugar has dissolved. Put into the freezer and leave until slushy but not frozen solid. Stir every 20 minutes or so to ensure that it sets evenly. When it has reached a thickish but not solid consistency, beat the egg whites until quite stiff but not dry. In a separate bowl, beat the cream until stiff. Gently fold the egg whites and cream together, then very gently fold this mixture into the partially frozen wine. Pile into individual sherbet glasses or leave in one serving dish and refreeze until set but not solid. This is a most elegant and delightful refresher.

ORANGE-GINGER FREEZE
Family Recipe

Serves 4

1 cup (8 ounces) yogurt
1 cup orange marmalade
1/2 tablespoon finely grated fresh
  ginger
3 egg whites

Put the yogurt, marmalade, and ginger in the blender and whir to a smooth purée. Set in freezer and leave until it is not solid but a thick mush. Stir every 10 to 15 minutes so that it sets evenly and does not become ice. When it reaches the consistency of a slushy, beat the egg whites until stiff and gently fold into the orange-yogurt mixture. If it has become too liquid, return to the freezer until it resets but is not solid. Serve immediately.

COTTAGE CHEESE REFRESHER
Family Recipe

Serves 6 to 8

2 cups (16 ounces) small-curd
  cottage cheese
2 celery stalks, very finely minced
1/4 cup finely minced fresh parsley
1/4 cup finely minced fresh mint
2 tablespoons finely minced fresh
  cilantro
1 medium bell pepper, seeded and
  finely minced
1 fresh pimiento, seeded and finely
  minced (optional)
1 teaspoon sugar
A hint of salt

Mix all the ingredients together and refrigerate at least 2 hours before serving.

BEER

Learning the complexities and subtle variations of the world's fine brews can be a sport equally as rewarding as that of learning to enjoy the products of the vintner's art. Wine is truly a delight and the perfect accompaniment to many meals, but not all. I can't imagine serving wine with most Mexican, Japanese (you see, I detest *sake*), Indian, Chinese, Thai, or Hawaiian food. Likewise, beer is an excellent companion to many American foods.

Often people who know of my love of good beers will ask which is the best. That's like asking what is the best food, poem, painting, dance, or song. Beer, like anything else, fortunately, comes in a variety of styles suited to a variety of needs and uses. Normally, my preference is for the fuller-flavored, top-fermented British brews, or the complexities of a good hoppy Mexican or Belgian beer, or our own San Franciscan steam. But not always. If I have just finished mowing the lawn on a California September afternoon, or cleaning the unventilated attic, I can't think of anything less appealing than a nice dark, flat, tepid pint of Oxfordshire's Old Hooky. What I want is a very cold glass of lager; pale, light-flavored and effervescent. However, when solving the world's problems on a chill evening in my favorite Oxford pub, The Turf Tavern, or participating in a song fest at The Blue Anchor in Cornwall, a glass of cold lager would be most inappropriate. Then I want a pint of delicious, full-flavored Tanglefoot or Spingo, and I want it served at a temperature that lets the rich flavor develop to its fullest.

Originally all beers were "top fermented." When fermentation takes place at higher temperatures, the yeast stays on the top of the fermentation vessel. The result is a fuller-flavored brew. Any time fermentation takes place at higher temperatures there is a greater complexity of flavors. Red wines are fermented at higher temperatures than white wines, and the result is not a better, but a bigger, wine.

The drawback of top fermentation is that it's harder to maintain quality control. Sometimes it is unbelievably delicious and, at other times, it may have all the charm of a pair of old gym socks.

England has a strong tradition of top-fermented brews. The major styles are bitter, mild, and pale ale. Forty percent of all beer consumed in England is bitter, only 20 percent is lager style, and the remainder is divided between mild, pale ale, bottled strong ale, and stout.

A word of warning to any of my fellow Americans who may be planning a trip to Merry ol' England and wish to spend an evening or so enjoying the delights of the English pub: please, do not embarrass yourself by asking for "a glass of bitters." Bitters are an added flavoring in some mixed drinks. You are going to have a hard time gagging down a pint pot of bitters. However, you will probably enjoy trying a pint or half pint of "bitter," which is a generic term for one style of English beer. Being quite heavily hopped, it usually has a more or less bitter flavor which gives it its name. It is full-bodied, malty and low in carbonation and is usually between 3 and 5.5 percent alcohol by volume. Be aware of this as well: you may be used to beer that is 3.5, and you are used to a pint being 16 ounces. In England a pint is 20 ounces, so watch it.

Mild is a distinctive draught beer, very rich in both flavor and color though not having the characteristic bitter bite of a "bitter." Many milds have a rich, smooth, velvety taste and texture, and they are making a comeback. They run from 2.5 to 3.5 percent.

An American myth that I would like to shatter is that English beer is served warm. It is *not* served warm. It is served at cellar temperature, which is usually pleasantly cool but not chilled. This allows the full complexity of flavors to come through.

Whereas almost all British brews are top fermented, only a few Continental brews are: the Trappiste brews produced in a few Belgian abbeys and the Netherlands; Kölsch, produced in the region around Cologne; and Dusseldorfer, found in Dusseldorf, Münster, and a few north Rhineland towns.

Almost all other beers made today are lagers or bottom-fermented brews. The word *lager* means "stored," or "iced," and the method is relatively recent given the long history of brewing. After all, many archeologists and geographers believe that grains were first domesticated for brewing, not baking.

Brewing was a touch-and-go business for centuries, the product often being cloudy or sour. This was attributed to "beer witches." After several millennia of sour beer, folks started noticing that beer that was either brewed in the winter or stored in cool caves didn't go sour as often and was frequently clear and pleasant looking. Sometime around the beginning of the fifteenth century, a few of our more brilliant ancestors started thinking that, just possibly, it wasn't witches or the devil but weather that determined the quality of beer. They started experimenting with making beer in caves and, sure enough, more of the beer was good more of the time.

Some few truly enlightened brewers even went to the extent of cutting ice from rivers and lakes in the winter, storing it in caves or packing it in straw, and then using it to cool the beer in the summer. When fermentation takes place at lower temperatures, the yeast eventually settles to the bottom of the cask, thus eliminating the necessity of skimming the beer before it's sold.

Until the invention of mechanical refrigeration, lagering or bottom-fermentation continued to be carried on almost exclusively in regions that had a ready supply of ice. At that time, however, lagering became the dominant style of brewing throughout the world. People were anxious to have beers that, although somewhat diminished in their complexity of flavors, were more consistent in their quality.

People often ask if I prefer lager or pilsener. All pilseners are lagers since they are a bottom-fermented beer. However, the term *pilsener* refers to those beers brewed in the style developed in the town of Pilsen in Bohemia.

Another misunderstood term is *bock*. The famed beer from Einbeck was widely acclaimed and, therefore, widely exported. In the days before either pasteurization or refrigeration, the alcohol content was

fortified so that it could survive its travels. Thus it was not only known for its fine flavor but for its strength. Like all good things, Einbeck beer was soon widely imitated. In Bavaria, where the accent is quite different, it became known as Oanbock and this gradually became simply *bock bier*.

Wherever a bock-style beer is produced it tends to be somewhat stronger than other beers of the region.

In the United States, it was traditional for breweries to totally drain their vats once a year in order to give them a thorough cleaning. This was usually done in the early spring. The last beer drawn from the vats was darker than the normal brew, having over the year collected sediment. It was bottled as bock. A few breweries today produce a bock beer which, though darker and somewhat richer in flavor than their normal product, is not any stronger. You can usually find it on the market around April.

The strongest commercially produced beer in the world is *doppelbock*, or double bock, brewed in northern Bavaria. It has an alcohol content of 13.2 percent by volume. Like all pilseners, all bocks are lagers, being bottom-fermented.

San Francisco is the home of America's only indigenous brewing style. Steam beer, of delicious fact and wondrous legend, grew out of the needs of a frontier society. Gold miners, adventurers, and frontiersmen had a great thirst. However, the California climate was not particularly favorable to the production of beer. Breweries in the east had access to ice to cool their lagering tanks, but brewers in California did not. Steam beer is basically a delightful compromise between top and bottom fermentation, producing a rich and full-bodied brew similar in character to the English bitters, but with a thick, creamy head produced by natural fermentation. Although the beer is highly effervescent it is not gaseous like many American lagers.

For those of you not fortunate enough to have access to this superior brew, the steam in the name does not mean that it's served warm. However, like all full-flavored beers, it should be served cool, not iced, thus allowing the full complexity of the flavor to come through.

There are several theories as to the origin of the name. It is possible that, in their heyday, the breweries were operated by steam power, a widely used form of energy at the time. My favorite theory is that old Pete Steam invented the process. However, as much as I love folk legends, I must admit to the probability that the name came from the head of steam that was released when a keg was tapped, since it was naturally fermented in the keg, like champagne.

There were dozens of steam beer breweries in the San Francisco Bay Area and my father sampled the wares of most of them. However, the Anchor Brewing Company is the only one to survive that American phenomenon, Prohibition. Even Anchor was on the endangered species list and, in 1965, it looked like Bay Area beer drinkers would once again be plunged into a steamless existence. Saints often crop up in strange places, and who would have thought that the son of a washing machine manufacturer would be the vehicle by which a San Francisco tradition would be saved from extinction.

Fritz Maytag bought the company and the press had a field day. "FROM SUDS TO SUDS" and "MAYTAG SAVES STEAM FROM A REAL SUDSING" were splashed across the headlines of San Francisco newspapers. The little company soon climbed out of the red and well into the black, much to the surprise of the business world.

I asked Fritz if he thought it was the financial shot in the arm and his background of business management that had reversed the company's downwards spiral. He answered that it surely hadn't hurt, but more than that, he thought, the time was right.

"We have been going through a taste renaissance in this country," he said. "In the fifties, if you didn't live in New York or San Francisco, you couldn't find a wine and cheese bar. Now they are popping up in almost every community. The time was right. People were ready to expand their tastes. We're not the only ones, you know. There are more and more 'home-beer breweries' opening every day."

And Fritz is right. You can now buy with ease products that were not readily available as little as five years ago. The number of fine beer imports expands constantly, the variety of cheeses is staggering, and the choice of wines, even in a supermarket, boggles the mind.

I can now walk into any standard chain market and purchase items that I used to have to spend a day running from specialty shop to specialty shop to get. Ten years ago, unless you really knew where to go and had the money to back it up, the wine choices were burgundy, rosé, and sauternes. Today, in any reputable grocery store, I have a choice if I want, let's say, a red, not only between Zinfandel, Merlot, Cabernet, Petite Sirah, and Pinot Noir, but also between Buena Vista, Hacienda, Stony Ridge, Stevenot, Fetzer, and Joseph Phelps, to say nothing of several imports.

My father had to satisfy his love of good beers with Tuborg, Ritterbrau, Asahi, Dos Equis, Guinness and, of course, Anchor Steam. Today I don't dare take up the room to list even a portion of the fine imports available. Fritz Maytag was right. The public was ready to look more favorably on a brew that went beyond the dimensions of standard American brewing.

And Anchor Steam Beer, like California's premium wines, is taking its place among the great brews of the world. I think it is a delightful bit of cross-cultural exchange that last year, when I walked into my favorite pub in Cornwall, The Blue Anchor, a tiny establishment that still brews its own excellent beer, the brewer was wearing a T-shirt that said, "ANCHOR STEAM BEER, made in San Francisco since 1896."

INDEX

INDEX

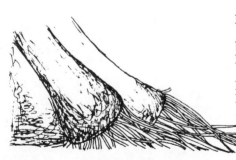

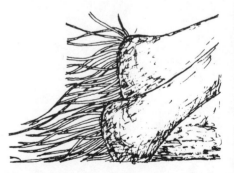

INDEX

INDEX

INDEX

INDEX

Geraldine Duncann's family roots go far back into California's past. "When my white ancestors came to California before the Gold Rush, my Paiute Indian ancestors were there to greet them," she explains. Her culinary roots extend back to the multicultural kitchen at the family cattle ranch in the San Joaquin Valley. Early in her life she was exposed to such exotic foods as oysters steamed in beer, a method that Jack London had taught her father. After leaving home, her knowledge of North African, Ceylonese, Oriental, and Polynesian foods was gleaned from her associations with some excellent cooks from other countries.

Duncann's formal training was in art, at the California College of Arts and Crafts in Oakland. She has kept her interest in art, and is the illustrator of this book. But her main interest soon became focused on the study of food. She has taught classes on the origins of cuisines at the University of California Extension in Berkeley, in New Orleans and abroad in Oxford and Dijon. In her extensive travels throughout the world, Duncann is an indefatigable collector of recipes, cooking lore, and interesting people:

"The best apple pie I have ever eaten was made by a ninety-year-old political activist who got the recipe from Henry Miller. The best Chinese food I have ever tasted was cooked by Frank Herbert." From the bottom of the Grand Canyon to the Swiss Alps, from Oaxaca to the Louisiana bayous, she has had the good fortune to make close friends, many of whom delight in sharing their culinary knowledge with her.

Duncann's international rovings in search of unusual food have led to a career as a food and travel writer. Her columns have appeared in the *San Francisco Examiner,* the *Los Angeles Herald Examiner* and in other newspapers through The Food Package syndicate. Her articles have been published in *The International Review of Food and Wine, Motorland,* and a number of in-flight magazines, and she is currently the food editor for *Old West,* a historical journal. Six of her recipes were included in the 1985 edition of *The Best of Food and Wine,* published by *The International Review of Food and Wine.*

When not writing or cooking, Geraldine Duncann pursues her many other interests, which range from California's wines and mines to the spinning and weaving of the Orkney Islands; from the ancient stone circles of forgotten Celtic cultures to the contents of the Museum of Modern Art; from scuba diving and sailing to set and costume design to singing American and British folk music. When not traveling, she lives in Lafayette, California, an East Bay suburb of San Francisco.

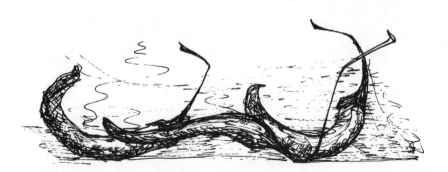